Stop Mugging Grandma

Stop
Mugging
Grandma

THE 'GENERATION WARS' AND
WHY BOOMER-BLAMING
WON'T SOLVE *ANYTHING*

JENNIE BRISTOW

YALE UNIVERSITY PRESS
NEW HAVEN AND LONDON

For information about this and other Yale University Press publications, please contact:
U.S. Office: sales.press@yale.edu   yalebooks.com
Europe Office: sales@yaleup.co.uk   yalebooks.co.uk

Set in Adobe Garamond Pro by IDSUK (DataConnection) Ltd
Printed in Great Britain by TJ International Ltd, Padstow, Cornwall

Library of Congress Control Number: 2019937942

ISBN 978-0-300-23683-5

A catalogue record for this book is available from the British Library.

10 9 8 7 6 5 4 3 2 1

Contents

Preface

I have been writing about generations for most of my adult life. First as an undergraduate in the mid-1990s, penning cross articles for *Times Higher Education* about the main issues (as I saw them) affecting students; then as a freelance journalist, writing a column for the *Daily Telegraph* under the strapline 'My Generation' on the kind of youth issues that perplexed the paper's rather more senior readership. As a writer for the left-wing magazine *LM* (*Living Marxism*) and its edgy progeny *spiked*, I spent a lot of time interrogating politicians' rhetorical nonsense about young people, education and culture. Then my children came along and I began to write about parenting instead.

That was an eye-opener, in many respects. When you have children, suddenly you stop obsessing on your own generation and start thinking about theirs – the kind of world they will be growing up into, the kind of people they will turn out to be. It also brings a sense of wonderment about your own parents – how did they do it, why didn't you notice at the time? But I was also struck by wider cultural and political changes: in particular, the way in which the relationship *between* the generations was becoming framed as some weird kind of problem.

I wrote *Standing Up to Supernanny*,[1] a broadside against self-declared 'parenting experts' telling people how to raise their kids. The assumption that, left to its own devices, the older generation (which, shockingly, now meant me!) would get everything wrong, seemed to indicate something very strange about the way in which relationships between older and younger members of our society were perceived. As parents, we are charged with the responsibility for raising these precious new beings, and socialising them into our world – yet at the same time, we are encouraged to hold back from doing what we feel is right, and to consult a website or TV programme instead. Political leaders at this time were busily breeding policies spelling out the various ways in which parents should be trained to bring up their children using approaches that were self-consciously different to those of their own parents. Everybody, it seemed, knew what was best for baby – apart from the people who knew baby best.

Meanwhile, relations between adults and children outside the family were perceived with outright suspicion. This was symbolised in Britain by a scheme introduced in the mid-2000s that subjected adults working or volunteering with children to a system of official vetting, where they needed to undergo a criminal-records check before being allowed unsupervised contact with the kids in a youth football team, Brownie pack, church group or any of the myriad informal organisations that adults set up to provide fun activities and social opportunities for children in their local communities. After researching the impact of this over-zealous scheme, Frank Furedi and I published a report – *Licensed to Hug* – revealing its damaging impact on people's contribution to community life.[2] Volunteers felt distrusted, disoriented and bewildered by the presumption that because they wanted to organise activities with children, they must be dodgy characters. And they were angry about the time and expense wasted on this officious scheme, which rested on the ridiculous presumption that 'child protection' meant ticking a box to protect children from the very adults who want to help them.

Developments such as the Vetting and Barring Scheme, which create an official distance between the generations, seemed to represent something quite new and problematic. I wanted to dig deeper, and began a PhD researching the sociological history of intergenerational contact and conflict. According to sections of the political elite, we were apparently in the throes of a fully fledged 'generation war', provoked by a greedy, immoral Baby Boomer generation that had robbed younger generations of their rightful future. Yet there was something odd going on. The more shrill this claim became on the pages of newspapers and in the echo chambers of policymakers, the less it seemed to reflect the way that people thought of themselves and their responsibilities to younger generations.

My research traced the emergence and development of claims about the 'Baby Boomer problem' from the mid-1980s to 2011, examining the various ways in which British newspapers discussed this generation and the historical context of these debates. The study found, in a nutshell, that feverish claims about the evil Boomers were really discussions about wider social and cultural issues: it was not a generation war, so much as a displacement activity for politicians and commentators running scared from the debates they really should have been having. I published the study as an academic book, *Baby Boomers and Generational Conflict*,[3] and briefly thought of moving on to something else. By this point, so much had been said about the Baby Boomers – how much further could it possibly go?

Quite a lot further, as it turned out. In 2014, when I completed my doctoral thesis, the 'generation wars' supplied catchy headlines and debate topics. More recently, the conceit that there is a conflict of interest between the generations has moved steadily up the policy agenda; and the language of 'generational conflict' has framed attempts to come to terms with the big political shocks of the past couple of years – Brexit in Britain, Trump in the USA, and a wave of electoral upheavals around Europe. The bitterness of the rhetoric, and the simplistic caricatures of 'older people' that have been reported as matters of fact, has been truly disturbing. It seems that when it comes to the generation wars, truth is indeed the first casualty.

The Baby Boomers are not the only generation to find themselves caught in the crossfire. I have subsequently analysed debates about the younger, 'Millennial' generation, and the work of organisations established to promote the cause of 'intergenerational fairness'. Like the Boomers, the Millennials are a diverse group of people, with many different fortunes, experiences and ideas. But for those determined to fight the generation wars, they have become mere cannon fodder, reduced to pathetic cut-outs whose voice is routinely appropriated, but rarely listened to.

So that's why I have written this book. I hope you enjoy it, however old or young you are. And while any errors are my own, I have many people to thank.

Taiba Batool, Eve Leckey and the team at Yale University Press, for their enthusiasm for *Stop Mugging Grandma* and for nurturing it to publication.

Frank Furedi, Ann Furedi and Ellie Lee, for their enduring friendship and intellectual inspiration. Joanna Williams, Charlotte Faircloth, Phil Mullan and Hilary Salt, for their thoughtful comments on earlier drafts and the contribution made by their work to some of the arguments developed here. Jan Macvarish, Verity Pooke and other friends and colleagues around the Centre for Parenting Culture Studies, for helping to make sense of this new academic field. Friends, colleagues and students from Canterbury Christ Church University, especially Sarah Cant and Anwesa Chatterjee, for their interest in this book and their collaboration on the next one.

Stalwarts of the parents' forum caravan conferences, for their stimulating discussions over the years: Beverley, Sally, Jane, Alison, Toby, David, John, Tony, Tara, John, Rosie, Tom, Josephine, Johny, Alka, Elisabetta, Cheryl, Nancy, Sue. Other friends, from near and far, both for the support and the distraction. And in memory of Helen, whose warmth and brilliance is always missed.

Mick Hume, editor extraordinaire, for training me to write when I was a young journalist and encouraging me to write this book as a rather older academic. David Jobbins and Paul Goodman, for taking the chance that a stroppy twenty-something might have something to say, and giving me the column inches in which to say it. Friends at *spiked* and the Academy of Ideas, for keeping the debate going – about this, and every other issue.

Tony, for the love, conversation and moral support. Emma and Annia, for everything they are and will be. The Grandmas and Grandads – my own grandparents, long deceased – and my parents who, along with my sister, nephews, in-laws and wider family, bring such depth and affection to our lives. Thank you.

CHAPTER 1

The generation wars

Imagine an actual generation war. Twenty-somethings would be raiding care homes, demanding they were sold off as one-bedroom apartments to first-time buyers. Affluent 60-somethings would be holed up in their five-bedroom houses, armed and alert to the sounds of an invasion by their children. Schools and universities would be the targets of a ground war, and golf courses marked as sites for strategic drone attacks. As the bodies of old and young piled up by the roadside, the middle-aged would tear themselves apart, frantically switching clothing brands and iPhone cases to fall in with whichever side appeared to be winning.

Mad, isn't it? And happily, it isn't happening – at least, not like that. Our streets are not battle zones, with wrinklies wielding walkers and kids hurling avocados. Care home residents are more worried about their grandchildren neglecting to visit than the possibility of an Occupy protest on their lawn; the 60-something owners of five-bedroom houses often have a grown-up child or two stashed away in what would have been the spare rooms. Studies consistently show that younger and older generations like each other, care for each other, and share many of the same values and aspirations. Even the motifs of generational conflict that we associate with the Sixties – the student barricades on the streets by the Sorbonne in Paris in 1968, the shooting of unarmed college students by the Ohio National Guard at Kent State University in 1970 – seem to be dramas of another age.

But throughout the Western world, there are some powerful voices agitating for a new generation war – a bitter and ugly confrontation that would pitch anyone under 35 against their parents, grandparents, teachers, colleagues and political representatives. Unlike the Sixties, today's generational warriors are not college kids, folk singers, radicals and hippies. They are members of the cultural and political establishment, virtue-signalling their concern for young people from the tarnished towers of government and national media institutions.

From North America and Australia to Britain and Continental Europe, we are presented with images of aggrieved Millennials, for whom the good fortune of the Baby Boomer generation, with their gilded pensions and overpriced houses, has allegedly made growing up so hard to do. Policymakers seek ways to reduce 'generational inequity' by frantically rewriting social security entitlements, and campaigners claim that voting systems are rigged in favour of older people. In national elections and referenda, the interests of young versus old are presented as one of the big divisions of our time. From the German magazine *Der Spiegel*, the journalist David Böcking warns that the conflict between the generations is in fact *the* big division, and has issued a call to arms:

> People vs. banks, north vs. south, and rich vs. poor? While all of these conflicts may be real, one of the biggest issues of the euro crisis is rarely discussed: Older people are living at the expense of the young, and it's high time the next generation took to the streets to confront their parents.[1]

Stop Mugging Grandma is written as an antidote to six dangerous myths. Myth 1 is that we are facing a war between the generations, in which the interests of young people are pitted against the needs and desires of their elders. I argue that the over-heated debates about generational conflict that feature so prominently in headlines and political manifestos are really a way for politicians to avoid engaging with the deeper economic and social problems that people do care about. Stagnant wages, job insecurity, the overheated housing market and the crisis of the welfare state are all major concerns that affect people in their daily lives, and impact on the way they plan for the future. But having a go at older people is no remedy for the difficulties we face today. On the contrary – it makes things a whole lot worse, for old and young people alike. The argument that older people have somehow stolen their children's future promotes a fatalistic view of the world, which does far more than student debt and rocketing house prices to suck the fun out of being young.

Myth 2 is that one particular generation – the Baby Boomers – is to blame for all this. The scapegoating of Baby Boomers is no accident. It has come about partly because this is the generation currently reaching retirement, at a time when austerity politics has placed the need to reduce public spending on pensions and healthcare high up the political agenda – and the Boomers make a convenient target. The Baby Boomers of the political and media imagination are not yet old, frail and the object of sympathy; they are carefree, affluent hedonists, living it up on the golf course thanks to their gold-plated pensions, high-equity houses and lack of care and commitment to anybody else. And there are loads of them. So, it is argued, they can afford the cutbacks – and they deserve them. This is the spirit in which grandma-mugging, as a policy agenda, is born.

Myth 3 is that members of any generation are all the same as each other. The labels 'Baby Boomer', or 'Millennial', carry with them a set of meanings and stereotypes that mask big differences in experience and outlook. Boomers are retired and working, rich and poor, healthy and frail. They come from all social classes, a range of ethnic backgrounds, and together hold a spectrum of political or religious beliefs. Millennials are not all university students, earnestly 'woke' and hopelessly soft – they are as different from each other as young people have always been, and not as different from their elders as it is often imagined.

Myth 4 is that younger generations today are uniquely disadvantaged, destined to die younger and poorer than their parents after a life filled with misery and debt. No. There are many problems around today, and some are distinct to our moment. Confronting these problems is a task for all of us, not just the young. But most of the issues that young people worry about – unstable employment, low incomes, terrorism and war, anxieties about the future – have plagued working people throughout time, including the Baby Boomers. What has changed is the overriding sense of pessimism and generational doom with which we now discuss political and economic issues.

Myth 5 is that the voice of young people has been sidelined by the vociferous voting behaviour of an enormous, self-interested generation, which is exercising undue influence over politics and policy. This is peddled by those who want to appropriate the voice of younger generations in order to speak on their behalf. It is patronising and anti-democratic, feeding off a sentiment that old people make the 'wrong' decisions and that young people can be manipulated into ticking the 'right' box. This myth feeds off a potent disdain for the past and the people associated with it, and a belief that 'future generations' are the only people with a genuine stake in tomorrow's world.

Myth 6, the most pernicious of all, is that the Boomers are a greedy generation, who have brought about the problems of the present day by demanding more than their fair share of wealth, political influence, and welfare resources. The myth of Boomer greed is marshalled to justify grandma-mugging, based on the claim that not only is Grandma richer than her children and grandchildren – she is richer than she should be, and therefore forcing her to share her ill-gotten gains is not just politically expedient, but also morally right. But the implications of this myth go much wider than the raid on Grandma's pension. It is an attack on the right of *any* generation to expect more than the basic necessities, to aspire to more than what some bean-counter judges to be 'prudent' or 'fair'. In making Boomer greed the focus of their attacks, the Generals in the new generation wars are launching an all-out assault on aspiration.

4

The irony is that the biggest casualties of this shrivelled worldview will be the younger generations: the very people in whose name the generation wars are being waged. In the morality play of Boomer-blaming, the main role assigned to the Millennial character is that of Lead Victim: an earnest, well-educated, hard-working young person, who has been robbed of the ability to get a good job or buy a small house by the consequences of years of Boomer excess. But there is always another part reserved for the Unworthy Complainant: the whingeing, entitled, self-obsessed Snowflake, who has absorbed the cultural message that children are unique, precious individuals deserving of a life free from failure, hurt and struggle, and now expects society to deliver on these pie-in-the-sky promises. The ugly cult of Boomer-blaming has spawned an equally ugly backlash of Millennial-baiting, with all sides hurling the common insult, You Want Too Much. And young people, with their lives stretching before them, are finding their expectations of life systematically ground down.

As a child of Baby Boomers, a teacher of Millennials, and a parent of those new kids on the block currently going by the dubious label 'Generation Z', I have no interest in defending the interests of one generation against another. My argument is that generations do not have competing interests, and that it is very dangerous to pretend that they do. The aim of this book is to cut through this phoney generation war, to understand why these poisonous myths have taken such a hold in our society. Generations are not scientific units of measurement – they are stories by which we make sense of our lives. In putting another side to these stories, I focus on what generations gain from each other, rather than speculating about how some might be losing out.

Boomer-blaming: The new acceptable prejudice

The current generation war is presented as a clear conflict between two opposing sides. On one side are the Baby Boomers, born in the 20 years or so following the Second World War; on the other are the Millennials, born in the final two decades of the twentieth century. Although, as I discuss in the next chapter, precise dates and definitions of generations vary, the labels 'Baby Boomer' and 'Millennials' have a pretty high recognition factor: we know who they are. Or at least, we think we do.

The Baby Boomers of the media and policymaking imagination are a very particular type. They are 'the luckiest people in history – the richest, most secure and most powerful generation the world has ever seen';[2] they 'enjoyed a life of free love, free school meals, free universities, defined benefit pensions, mainly full employment and a 40-year-long housing boom'.[3] They are 'the most selfish generation that history has ever known',[4] a generation that 'shaped the culture and values of the late twentieth century'[5] in the image of a 'self-indulgent individualism'[6] and an immature 'cult of "me"'.[7] They are an enormous, powerful generation, who have used their great size as a way to 'monopolise employment and housing and reduce social mobility for the next generation',[8] and use their voting power to lobby for their own interests ensuring 'that when bad times come, the young are hit first'.[9] They are 'the most self-centered, self-seeking, self-interested, self-absorbed, self-indulgent, self-aggrandizing generation in American history', claims Paul Begala in *Esquire* magazine, in an article headlined 'The Worst Generation: Or, how I learned to stop worrying and hate the Boomers.'[10]

Begala's article was first published in 2000, and reprinted in 2017 – by which time everyone was loving to hate the Boomers. Numerous books have been devoted to explaining just how bad the Boomers are, and what must be done to stop them . . . well, Booming. In Britain, the year 2010 alone brought titles such as *The Pinch: How the baby boomers took their children's future – and why they should give it back*, by David Willetts; *What Did the Baby Boomers Ever Do for Us? Why the children of the sixties lived the dream and failed the future*, by Francis Beckett; *Jilted Generation: How Britain has bankrupted its youth*, by Ed Howker and Shiv Malik; and *It's All Their Fault: A manifesto*, by Neil Boorman.[11]

In the United States, Canada and Australia, the titles pull even fewer punches. *A Generation of Sociopaths: How the baby boomers betrayed America*, by Bruce Cannon Gibney; *Generation Debt: Why now is a terrible time to be young*, by Anya Kamenetz (alternatively subtitled *How our future was sold out for student loans, bad jobs, no benefits, and tax cuts for rich geezers – and how to fight back*); *Barbarians: How baby boomers, immigration, and Islam screwed my generation*, by Lauren Southern; and *Please Just F* Off It's Our Turn Now: Holding baby boomers to account*, by Ryan Heath.[12]

How the baby boomers took their children's future. How the baby boomers betrayed America. It's All Their Fault. Please Just F* Off. This kind of inflammatory rhetoric is often considered unacceptable when used with regard to other groups in society. The 'twitch-hunts' that routinely emerge when a politician, commentator or celebrity says something that smacks of prejudice against women, gay people, transgender people, disabled people or particular ethnic or religious groups, shows that in many respects we are highly sensitive to attempts to whip up prejudice against groups of people. But the Baby Boomers, it seems, are fair game.

Why is this? The simplest answer, of course, is that the Boomer-blamers are right, and that all the problems we face today are the fault of this greedy, selfish, voracious, all-powerful 'generation of sociopaths'. This is certainly Gibney's view: when quizzed on the relationship between correlation (the Boomers just happened to be around at a lucky time) and causation (it's all their fault), he responded:

> Almost all the benefits [of policy changes] have flowed towards the boomers. The boomers have been in control the entire time, so unless the past 30 years have been some accident that just happened to enrich the most politically powerful group at the expense of marginal political groups – I don't know that Occam's Razor has dulled over the past three decades.[13]

But while Occam's Razor may be an appropriate guiding principle for scientific inquiry, in social life the simplest answer is rarely the correct one. The search for simple answers to questions about why people feel aggrieved, discombobulated, disadvantaged or dispossessed has led to some extremely ugly moments in history. This has made us rather sensitive to the practice of 'Othering' – reducing social groups to a less worthy category of person, which can justify discriminatory treatment. Gibney, however, is explicit that this is what he wants to do. 'Part of my goal throughout has obviously been to establish Boomers as a highly culpable Other, one whose deposition might lead to some real good,' he declaims.[14]

Gibney's diagnosis of the Boomers as 'the Other' is laid out in his book, with chapters slamming the values, culture, politics, entitlements and everything else associated with them. In these respects, he argues, 'Boomers really are different, as they often and proudly remind [us]. They do not share other generations' values and do not behave in ways that accord with America's better conceptions of itself. They are Other, even, in their own ways, enemies of state and society.' Although his book clearly sets out to inflame and provoke, Gibney is confident that his representation of the Boomers as a class apart is not all that far removed from the tenor of more mainstream Boomer-blaming. 'I don't think it's going to take very much to persuade younger people that the boomers have a certain Other quality,' he states complacently.[15]

Most of those leading the charge of Boomer-blaming are less explicit than Gibney in their rhetoric and conclusions. But they share the assumption that the Boomer generation is a problem, and that this problem stems from this generation's social position, behaviour and character attributes – all of which lends the discussion a highly symbolic, almost racialised, hue. The insistence that the Boomers are somehow fundamentally different to their ancestors and descendants is proposed as the basis for sanction, even outright discrimination. As Heath puts it, in *Please Just F* Off It's Our Turn Now*:

> Am I being nasty? If so, the important point is that generations differ from each other. The key question is how we

measure or discuss common or destructive behaviours within and between these groups. While we can and should treat people as individuals, so we must accept and respond to documented behaviour that helps or hinders the public good.[16]

As we will see, the attempt to mobilise the imperative of 'the public good' to justify attacks on Baby Boomers doesn't really go down too well with the public, who tend to have a more positive and balanced view of the ways in which generations support each other. But this has not stopped the nasty narrative of Boomer-blaming from gaining ground.

Myth-making and trouble-stirring

The feverish debates about generational conflict reflect very little about the lives of people in any generation. They rely on cut-outs, two-dimensional representations of the most extreme stereotypes, set up as targets for politicians and commentators to take pot-shots at. Numerous academics, campaigners and commentators have pointed out that in many ways the Boomer stereotype is as inaccurate as it is unfair. Portraying Boomers as a greedy, selfish, wholly fortunate generation concedes nothing to the more sensible idea that all Baby Boomers might not be the same – that, within the millions of people born across the Western world over a period of about 20 years, there might be some who are truly flabbergasted by the notion that they had it all, and now should 'give it back'.

For example, a report produced in 2015 by the UK's 'Ready for Ageing Alliance', a group of national charities focused on issues related to old age, sought to 'bust the widely touted myth that there is a uniform group of older people in the UK – so called baby boomers – who have benefitted at the expense of younger age groups.'[17] The Ready for Ageing Alliance argued that the term 'baby boomer' (defined in its report as those between the ages of 55 and 70) has 'become an overused and potentially dangerous shorthand to inaccurately describe everybody in a single age group.' In fact,

Boomers are 'a diverse group of people in virtually every aspect of their lives', and 'in reality, one of the few things this group shares is chronological age'. Its report presented, and succinctly trashed, a number of widely held prejudices about this generation, simply by marshalling a few cold facts about life for Boomers in the UK.[18]

Against the claim that 'the Baby Boomers got a free university education', the Alliance points to the reality that 'just over 13% of those aged 65–69 have a degree' – whereas just under 50 per cent of today's youth cohort engage in higher education. It is claimed that the Boomers 'are so well off they can afford to retire early', and that they 'can look forward to security in retirement thanks to their generous pensions'; in fact, 'more than seven out of ten people in their 50s and early 60s are in work', and 'nearly 2 million people aged 55–64 do not have any private pension savings'. The Boomers are charged with having 'bought cheap housing' and 'sitting on a fortune': but 'not all baby boomers are homeowners and those who bought their homes had to pay high interest rates'. Boomers are portrayed as 'especially selfish and self-interested people' who 'spend their life taking cruises and playing golf', yet 'there are 3.3 million volunteers aged 45 to 64 in England' and 'people in their 50s and early 60s are no more likely to be planning a cruise than younger people.' And so on.

In a similar vein, the Australian writer Jocelyn Auer, author of *Baby Boomers: Busting the myths*, seeks to expose claims that are 'wrong, deceitful or deceptive'. The 'appealing simplicity' of the powerful, political myth-making around Baby Boomers, she argues, 'overrides and hides what was, and is, the reality of different lives and the complexity of those differences' – a reality that she gives voice to in challenging the refrain of 'burdensome boomers', the claim that this generation is 'selfish and greedy', and the way that policy narratives around work and retirement often blame the Boomers for their good fortune, even while making their lives harder.[19]

'Defining baby boomers in terms of what they have in common allows us to slip easily into the assumption that they are virtually all the same,' writes Auer. A clear distinction can be drawn 'between older and younger boomers because of different employment experiences throughout their lifetimes, due in large part to economic ups and downs including the crisis of the 1980s–90s'. This is equally true, of course, for the USA and the UK. To imagine that the Baby Boomers who came of age during the postwar economic boom had the same experience as those whose formative experiences lay in the 1970s requires a level of historical ignorance unworthy of anyone with a memory – or access to Google. Auer also draws attention to the 'persistent and substantial differences between women and men, rich and poor, employed and unemployed: differences in income, spending patterns, family and living arrangements, relationship to place, health and wellbeing, spiritual belief, political position, and social values' – all of which reveals the stereotype of the Australian Boomer to be 'a furphy – a tall story'.[20]

For anybody who knows actual people belonging to the Baby Boomer generation, it should be obvious that they have not all enjoyed the same good fortune and opportunity. How could they? If this generation is to be defined simply as everybody born between 1946 and 1965, of course there will be enormous variations in experience. When challenged, most Boomer-blamers will grudgingly concede this point. But as the old saying goes, why let the facts get in the way of a good story? And although the lucky-greedy-Boomer myth has masqueraded quite successfully as objective economic analysis, careful social policy planning, and a youth-friendly campaign for 'intergenerational justice', it remains, fundamentally, a story – a dystopian fairytale that sections of the political and cultural elite are telling us about our past, present and future.

Symbolic warfare, with dangerous consequences

In the coming chapters, I reveal how the story of Boomer greed has been written, and by whom. It is not, as is often pretended, a tale that has sprung spontaneously from the keyboards of aggrieved

Millennials – indeed, it remains a story that most people of all generations see as quite alien to their lives, and the problems they face. Boomer-blaming is a narrative that has been constructed by political elites of Western societies to suit their policy agendas. Part of it is motivated by attempts to reduce spending on pensions and healthcare, in a context of sluggish economic growth and rising levels of public debt. As such, Boomer-blaming reflects one-sided and overblown anxieties about ageing populations: it has nothing to do with generations, and has come to focus on the Boomers mainly because they will soon be old. The mischievous myth-making that has positioned the Boomers as affluent, greedy and irresponsible – as the undeserving rich, who deserve to have their belts tightened – neatly serves the cost-cutting cause.

But there is more to this story than political cynicism and economic belt-tightening. At its heart is a deeply symbolic conflict, to do with how we view the recent past, what we expect from the near future, and the value we attach to relations between the generations. Myths, like stereotypes, are not figments of some-body's deranged imagination: they have some basis in reality, and are peddled to serve some cause. The basis of the Boomer myth lies in their association with the social and cultural upheavals of the Sixties, and the way this period of history has come to be re-imagined by the fearful, conservative mindset that dominates public debate today.

The argument that the Boomers have used up more than their 'fair share' of welfare resources and have benefited disproportion-ately from the spoils of the postwar economic boom may be empirically incorrect, but it has a commonsense logic that defies attempts to argue the case by marshalling the facts. This is because the basis of the Boomer myth is not, as the Blamers claim, that generation's actual size, strength, behaviour or affluence. It is its location in history: the living, breathing embodiment of a more optimistic time. Claims that this massive generation has used up all the economic resources merge seamlessly with criticism of the happy-go-lucky attitude attributed to the 'Sixties generation', which is charged with depleting the world of happiness, creativity and hope. 'For too long the world has been run by this extraordinary generation – a generation that was simply born lucky,' charges the journalist Sarah Vine:

> Not only were they economically blessed – affordable housing, low energy costs, free university education, fluid economies – they also had some of the most hedonistic and uncomplicated fun since the Romans: all the sex (by the time that we came of age, HIV had put a stop to all that), the best music (I'm sorry, Coldplay is no match for Jimi Hendrix), all the easy idealism of privilege. They drove expensive, gas guzzling cars without a care for the cost or the environmental impact (most babyboomers think a CO_2 emission is something that you get from drinking too much bubbly).[21]

The reason everyone seems to be loving to hate the Boomers today is that they are seen to symbolise a different outlook on life; a time when people expected that life could be more fulfilling and liberated. In these times of economic austerity and cultural pessimism, we are constantly reminded that the music has stopped and that it's time to do penance for the fun we had. This fuels a sense of grievance amongst people who never had a licence to have much fun in the first place – the grim Generation Xers, the over-protected Millennials, the youngsters currently best known as 'Generation Z', with whom history presumably ends. Such generational labels and stereotypes, ridiculous as they might seem, have come to assume a strange significance in attempts to make sense of ourselves and those around us.

I explore what it means to talk about generations: and why this means taking a step back from the facile prejudices that dominate media and policy debates. The idea of generations developed to describe moments in history and the people who lived through them. But increasingly, they are used to define, even determine, the experiences and expectations of whole groups of quite diverse individuals; to reduce people's biographies to the accident of their birth year, a sharp-toothed demographic trap that exaggerates the differences between the generations at the expense of understanding the relationship. Most of what passes for debates about generational difference and conflict today is better understood as something very different: a discourse of *generationalism*, in which social and political problems are described and explained using the language and symbolism of generations.[22] This distorts both our understanding of social and political problems, and our appreciation of what is special, precious and problematic about generations.

Obsessional generationalism has come to frame discussions about political power and participation, with some alarming implications for democracy. From Brexit in Britain to the election of Donald Trump as the President of the USA, the Baby Boomers are getting it in the neck for mobilising their allegedly vast numbers and outdated prejudices to vote young people out of their allegedly rightful political future. 'After Brexit, there was this demonisation of older people – in some cases [people said] "take away their votes",' said Jane Vass, head of public policy at Age UK, speaking at the International Longevity Centre's 2017 'Future of Ageing' conference. Kate Jopling, former head of public affairs at Help the Aged, argued:

> There was a casual use of demonising and divisive language – the bandying around of stereotypes about who older people are, about their economic circumstances, their motivations and even their ability to form rational judgments. Baby boomers used to be talked about as the generation that were going to change everything, now it is almost a term of abuse.[23]

Yet as I discuss in later chapters, the generational split in voting and values is far less clear-cut than has been presented. When sections of the political elite complain about the voice of young people being ignored, it is because – in that moment – the youth vote chimes with their own agendas. In this regard, political generation talk should be seen as an undemocratic act of manipulation, which uses the gloss of 'young' or 'future' generations to argue that some sections of the electorate are more worthy of a voice than others.

People are living longer, healthier lives – yet instead of this being seen as a cause for celebration, 'ageing' is presented as a problem. Pensioners who, thanks to advances in medical treatment, have survived cancer and are living with chronic illnesses for longer than expected, are presented as 'bed blockers' using up scarce health and social care resources. The ongoing pensions crisis afflicting Western societies is often blamed on the number of retired people and the size of their pensions. Younger people are presented as the victims of this scenario, in having to 'pay the bills' for the elderly – and this is used as an argument for driving down expectations about the living standards that people can expect to have in retirement, and bullying young people into saving more.

Such arguments both incite resentment against the old, and trap young people into expecting less. As Michael Hiltzik points out in the *Los Angeles Times*, 'treating Social Security and Medicare spending on the one hand and spending on kids on the other as though they're opposite sides of a zero-sum game is just an act of ideological legerdemain aimed at undermining those programs' – which, in the end, will hurt young people the most:

> Let's not forget, too, that the people who will really suffer from gutting Social Security won't be today's seniors, who will escape the worst of the cutbacks – they'll be today's young people, for whom Social Security would become much less supportive when they retire.[24]

The important question is not how many people there are, but how people can best be employed and their talents made use of. We are not harnessing the economic or social potential either of older or younger people, and nor do we have a sensible approach to social policymaking. The problem here is not pensions, but employment and wages. As a society, we are writing off older (more expensive) working people prematurely, and then blaming them for being a burden on the public purse, while refusing to confront the implications of an insecure, low-wage, over-credentialed labour market. I discuss the anxieties that afflict 'Generation Debt' in their journey through education and employment, and show that elite attempts to lay responsibility for these problems at the door of their parents and grandparents provide a convenient distraction from engaging with their cause.

The same goes for the much-discussed youth housing crisis. Spiralling prices and a shortage of housing stock are frequently blamed for young people's inability to leave the parental home, start their own families, and become economically, as well as emotionally, independent. The reliance of the British economy on inflated house prices is clearly unhealthy, and the disparity between young people's wages and the cost of rent or mortgages is not easily surmountable. But this situation has not come about because the Boomers are 'sitting on housing stock' – they are just living in their homes. Those Boomers who have benefited from an increase in the worth of their assets tend to be relying on this to supplement pensions (which are also, in the main, less generous than we are led to believe), or to subsidise their adult children's living standards, by allowing them to live at home for years or by lending them money for property – the so-called 'bank of mum and dad'.

Lurking beneath the housing crisis is a more important, and unsettling, question about the difficulties young people now face in making an independent life and home for themselves – and it's just too simplistic to explain this in terms of housing costs alone. I suggest that wider cultural changes have come to frame the responsibilities of adulthood in ambivalent, even negative, terms – not least because generationalist arguments incite young people to blame their parents for the problems they face, rather than to see themselves as authors of their own lives.

And what about the Millennials – the young adults in their twenties and thirties, in whose name the new generation wars are being waged? The cult of Boomer-blaming has attracted something of a backlash against 'entitled Millennials', sneering at an over-sensitive 'Snowflake Generation' that just doesn't understand how rubbish real life is. This spiteful name-calling avoids tackling the reasons why young people, having been constantly told that older generations have stolen their futures, might come to see the world in this way and kick back against it – albeit often in a rather childish fashion. Young people did not launch this generation war, and blaming the young for being fed up is no better than blaming the old for having had it all. Those politicians and commentators who complain to each other about spoilt, whingeing youth are often complicit when it comes to indulging them. Indeed, when it comes to the bombastic rhetoric of Boomer-blaming – they started it.

CHAPTER 2

Boomer-blaming

An elite bloodsport

A striking feature of the weird, symbolic generation wars currently being played out, with the so-called Baby Boomers clearly positioned on the villainous side and 'the younger generation' victimised on the other, is that the rhetoric and symbolism is shared by politicians and commentators who would otherwise claim to have nothing in common. They see themselves as right-wing and left-wing, young and old, in different countries facing different concerns: yet when it comes to blaming the Boomers, they all sing along to the same playlist.

The dominant selection of tracks in the Boomer-Blaming Collection is made up of the **austerity ballads**. These take their inspiration from the sluggish state of Western economies in the early twenty-first century: stagnant wages, limited opportunities for social mobility, growing levels of public and personal debt, over-stretched welfare states. Worthy and paternalistic in tone, conventional in composition, and plodding in rhythm, these tracks tend to be composed by members of the political elite: often breast-beating Baby Boomers themselves. Austerity ballads are released by organisations such as the Intergenerational Commission in the UK, the Concord Coalition in the USA, and the Australian government's Treasury, which produces a five-yearly 'Intergenerational Report'[1] to highlight the apparently divergent fortunes of different age groups. They play to the sentiment that 'we're all in it together', united in a common aim to prevent the tragedy befalling younger generations as a result of old folk living for too long, and too expensively.

Punk posturing is designed to upset and offend. These are the headline-seekers, the vitriol-spitters, the shameless rampers-up of rhetoric. A quick search on Google for 'Baby Boomer greed' throws up some recent gems. 'How Baby Boomers Became the Most Selfish Generation' (*UK Business Insider*), 'I Became a Greedy Baby Boomer, and I'm Sorry' (*Huffington Post*), 'Millennials Blame Baby Boomers for Betraying Generation' (*Daily Mail*), 'Here's What Baby Boomers Say When You Accuse Them of Wrecking the Economy' (*Washington Post*), 'Why Are the Baby Boomers Desperate to Make Millennials Hate Ourselves?' (*Guardian*), 'How the Baby Boomers Destroyed Everything' (*Boston Globe*). Google searches 'related to baby boomer greed' apparently include: baby boomers ruined Britain; baby boomers selfish UK; baby boomers worst parents; baby boomers selfish grandparents; baby boomers most entitled generation; baby boomers the most selfish generation; baby boomers luckiest generation; baby boomers bad parents.[4]

Tempting as it is to blame the sensationalist media for whipping up a quick two-minute hate, punk posturing shouts from the rooftops what the austerity ballads warble. The headlines reflect the arguments laid out in books accusing the Boomers of being 'a generation of sociopaths', of 'taking their children's future' and creating a 'jilted generation' of bankrupted, dispossessed youth.

Millennial angst is a shriller, shallower kind of track. Lead vocalists are self-proclaimed 'young people', who favour one-note melodies and straight-from-the-heart tales of woe. 'What would you do if you grew up and realized that everything America has always promised its children no longer holds true for you?' demands Anya Kamenetz in the opening sentence to *Generation Debt: Why now is a terrible time to be young*. She continues:

I am twenty-four years old and I was born into a broke generation. I look around and I see people who have borrowed more to go to college than they can repay, who can't find a good job, can't save, can't afford basic necessities like health insurance, can't make solid plans. Their credit card bills mount every month, while their lives stall out on the first uphill slope. Born into a century of unimaginable prosperity, in the richest country in the world, those of us between the ages of eighteen and thirty-five have somehow been cheated out of our inheritance.[3]

Commentators have been quick to attack this kind of self-absorbed plaint. 'Millennials would be wise to be a little more reflective whenever they snipe about how unfair life is,' writes Stephen Koukoulas in the *Guardian*, reviewing the chequered fortunes of previous generations in their youth and correctly pointing out that, '[y]oung people today are facing significant financial challenges, but this is not a new story'.[4] 'Millennials, Generation Y: many of you are now in your 30s and it's time to grow up and stop whining,' huffs Alex Proud in the *Telegraph*.[5] In the bickering commentary that fills the pages of newspapers and periodicals, for every expression of Millennial angst, a lengthening list of unflattering adjectives is hurled back in response – narcissistic, entitled, lazy, pathetic, whingers.

But while Millennial angst is irritating in its solipsism, these are the most understandable tracks in the Boomer-blaming playlist. Having a bad job or no job; struggling to form an independent, intimate relationship; falling into a deep spiral of personal debt to pursue a university education that seems to promise little and deliver even less . . . of course young people would want to make sense of these things. It is hardly 'entitled' to expect that, as a citizen of an advanced, wealthy society, you might be able to get a half-decent job and a place to live; for a twenty-something to be preoccupied with their own future is neither new nor particularly narcissistic, it's just a feature of being young. The bigger question is why Millennial angst now takes the form that it does – a grimly pessimistic sense of grievance, levelled at a particular generation.

Taken together, austerity ballads, punk posturing and Millennial angst create a febrile mood music, in which all the dramas and difficulties of our present moment are cast in generational terms. They pretend to be authentic expressions of young people's pain and wisdom, projecting the sentiment that greedy Baby Boomers are blocking what we all know, deep down, is the right and responsible thing to do for the future. In reality, this is a soundtrack scripted by political and cultural elites. Generation warriors come from divergent political persuasions, fixate on a number of different issues, and range wildly in age – but they are united in their mission to create a conflict between the generations, by persuading us that mugging Grandma is a necessary and righteous cause. They present this cause in the language of 'intergenerational justice', 'intergenerational equity', 'intergenerational fairness'; they rail against 'intergenerational theft' and talk about 'restoring the contract between the generations'. Yet it all amounts to the same thing: a grubby attempt to whip up animosity against older people, to justify their own agendas.

Constructing the campaigns

Campaigns for intergenerational equity have long been regarded with suspicion by social policy scholars, who see another agenda going on. A recent edition of a mainstream undergraduate text book notes that concerns regarding the 'demographic time bomb' and intergenerational conflict over welfare resources 'have been inflated to justify welfare state reform'.[6] Over two decades ago Alan Walker, Professor of Social Policy at the University of Sheffield, contended that the 'intergenerational equity' debate 'should be regarded as a 'socio-political construct', which some countries have manufactured as 'an economic-demographic imperative' to facilitate the restructuring of their welfare states. The primary concern of policymakers promoting this argument was 'with the perceived burden of pensions on public expenditure rather than any manifest concern about distributional justice between age cohorts', and as such has 'little or nothing to do with "intergenerational" conflict'.[7]

Everything that we are told about generational conflict is the wrong way round. We are told that there is a real danger of a war between the generations, brought about because young people feel they are unfairly treated, and that the only way to keep the peace is to develop policies designed to improve 'intergenerational equity', which will shift resources more in the direction of younger generations. In reality, politicians are looking for ways to cut back on welfare entitlements – particularly pensions – and have come up with the concept of intergenerational equity as a way to make these cuts more palatable. There is no conflict between old and young waiting to explode: at least there wasn't, before politicians started saying that there should be one, and media reporters jumped eagerly on message. And even the claim that resources should be redistributed from old to young is only a cover for cutting public spending on older people – no more resources are going to come the way of the kids.

But – it's not a conspiracy. Recognising that claims about intergenerational conflict, inequity and injustice are socio-political constructs that mask another agenda does not mean assuming that everyone spouting the cause of fairness between the generations is cynically promoting a furphy. The passion with which writers and organisations devoted to the pursuit of intergenerational equity conduct their campaigns shows that they believe in their arguments; they really do think that the only way to balance the books is to press for lower expectations about the kind of old age we can hope for, and to promote the presumed interests of the young over those of their seniors. It is this dogged conviction that makes their cause so dangerous – for they are prepared to take some drastic measures to drive home the point.

Attempts to make the case for policies promoting intergenerational equity go back some time, first developing in the United States in the 1980s. In 1984, Republican Senator Dave Durenberger founded Americans for Generational Equity (AGE) 'to promote the concept of generational equity among America's political, intellectual, and financial leaders' by calling into question 'the prudence, sustainability, and fairness to future generations of federal old age benefit programs'. As Faye Lomax Cook of Northwestern University explains, although AGE is now defunct as an organisation, it had considerable influence on the emergence of the issue of intergenerational equity and in reshaping its political discourse.[8]

The model of campaigning established by AGE – an organisation set up by a section of the political elite to gain influence among other political, intellectual and financial leaders – has remained the model for the pursuit of the intergenerational equity cause. Everywhere, the cause presents itself as something that goes beyond party-political differences, uniting left and right in the pursuit of a common moral and pragmatic good. In this vein, the Concord Coalition was founded in 1992 by a self-consciously non-partisan gang of opinion formers: the late former Senators Warren Rudman (Republican) and Paul Tsongas (Democrat), with former Secretary of Commerce Peter G. Peterson.[9] The Concord Coalition describes its mission as 'putting the national debt on a sustainable course and protecting future generations', identifying as important drivers for the high levels of national debt 'the aging of the population and rising health care costs', leading to debt growth that 'will damage the economy, undermine our standard of living, and leave our children and future generations worse off'.[10]

Back in 1999, Sara Rix, then Senior Policy Advisor at the American Association of Retired People (AARP), wrote that '[o]ver the past decade or so, efforts have been made to foster what might be regarded as a "politics of the young", as witnessed by the creation of several organisations of largely younger persons seeking to draw attention to what they have seen as an excess of resources going to both the baby boomers and older people'.[11] And so in the USA, a healthy wariness of such organisations has gone some way to blunting their teeth. 'Many professionals dedicated to defending and promoting the interests of America's children see the generational equity debate as a dangerous effort to divide the young and the old and to undercut public support for important government programs such as Social Security,' writes Faye Lomax Cook. 'Consequently, they have made a concerted effort to quell the divisive rhetoric of generational equity.'[12] In particular, Cook notes their efforts in founding Generations United, whose mission is 'to improve the lives of children, youth, and older people through intergenerational collaboration, public policies, and programs for the enduring benefit of all'. This organisation argues that resources are 'more wisely used when they connect the generations rather than separate them', points to the problem of discrimination against older people, and insists that '[g]randparents and other adults who step forward to raise children are keeping families together and providing an economic service to our country'.[13] The British charity United for All Ages was established in 2010, with a similar agenda.[14]

The vision of Generations United – of 'a world that values and engages all generations' – comes much closer to the way that most people think about society's responsibility to old and young than do the shrill demands for intergenerational equity emanating from elite organisations. 'Studies have found, at best, mixed results demonstrating that different age-groups are self-interested when it comes to welfare arrangements and begrudge provision for other cohorts,' states Kate Hamblin of the Oxford Institute of Population Ageing. 'Generally, it has been found that younger people are in favour of support for older generations and vice versa.'[15] 'Is there conflict between age groups in their support for programs for older people?' asks Cook. 'Studies show the answer to this question is no.'[16] And as I indicate below, certain attempts to play the 'intergenerational equity' card to introduce unpopular policies have become quickly exposed for the Grandma-mugging they represent.

Sadly, this has not stopped the intergenerational equity cause from gaining ground – quite literally. All influential policy ideas – even (often, especially) bad ones – diffuse to other societies, particularly when those societies have similar political and economic conditions and welfare state structures.[17] So it is not really surprising that this imperative should have made it across the pond to the United Kingdom, and across the Pacific to Australia. Nor is it surprising that, once the global financial crisis struck and governments scrambled for ways to service growing levels of public debt from weak and sluggish economies, they turned up the volume of Boomer-blaming.

Austerity ballads: Creating a generational drama out of an economic crisis

The composer-in-chief of generational austerity ballads in the UK is David Willetts (born 1956), the former Conservative minister for Universities and Science. More cerebral than most politicians – a characteristic that earned him the nickname 'Two Brains' – Willetts is author of the startling book *The Pinch: How the baby boomers took their children's future – and why they should give it back*. The book draws on a strange blend of demography, evolutionary biology, game theory and Conservative philosophy to argue its central point: that 'the boomers have been guilty of a monumental failure to protect the interests of future generations', and that politics must act to address this problem.[18]

Willetts stepped down from Parliament in 2015 and up into the House of Lords. He became Executive Chair of the Resolution Foundation, 'a non-partisan and award-winning think-tank that works to improve the living standards of those in Britain on low to middle incomes',[19] and chaired the Intergenerational Commission, established in 2016 to 'set out changes that will strengthen and renew the social contract between the generations'.[20] The Intergenerational Commissioners are big names, as well – they included the Chief Executive of the respected polling organisation Ipsos MORI, the Director General of the Confederation of British Industry, the Director of the Institute for Fiscal Studies, and the General Secretary of the Trades Union Congress, among others.

Torsten Bell, Director of the Resolution Foundation, was previously Director of Policy for the Labour Party. So this is a cross-party policy shindig, with A-list guests.

The Intergenerational Commission has been energetic, churning out report after report bemoaning the grim state of Britain's economy and, in particular, the problem of unfairness between the generations. Its inaugural report, *Stagnation Generation: The case for renewing the intergenerational contract*, set out to 'establish a framework for thinking about intergenerational issues and highlight the scope for policy to make a difference'.[21] Since then, reports on democratic engagement ('the growing turnout gap between the generations'),[22] the implications of demographic trends for living standards, pensions, wages, asset accumulation, housing, trends in household consumption, inheritances, and welfare transfers, have drawn up a rudimentary map that signposts all the ills of British politics and the economy as landmarks in the crisis of generations.

In this vein, the problem of democratic disengagement in British politics since the 1990s is recast as a 'generational turnout gap', which resulted in the Baby Boomers having a 'ballot box advantage' of 'more than four million votes' over the Millennials in the 2015 General Election.[23] Wage stagnation is presented as the concerning finding that 'millennials who have entered work so far have made no earnings progress on generation X before them',[24] and the effect of wages being dragged down by 'pension deficit payments' resulting from increased longevity and expensive (defined benefit) pension schemes.[25] The housing crisis is examined in terms of 'the housing outcomes achieved by different generations over the life course and . . . the extent to which intergenerational inequalities exist when it comes to security, to affordability and to quality',[26] and the Commission's projections of future retirement incomes are informed by the widespread fear that 'young people today will "never be able to retire" '.[27] Concerns about private asset accumulation are expressed in terms of generational unfairness: 'Millennials are currently half as likely to own their own home at age 30 as the baby boomers (born 1946–65) were, and all cohorts born after 1955 are accumulating less wealth than their predecessors at the same age had.'[28] Underlying all these problems, argues the Commission, is a 'turning point' in demographic trends, brought about by a combination of continued improvements in longevity and a large cohort of Baby Boomers now reaching retirement age, meaning that 'the demographic dividend we've enjoyed in recent decades is starting to reverse'.[29]

A similar downbeat narrative is offered by the Australian government. In 2015, the Australian Treasury released its fourth Intergenerational Report. Since the publication of these reports began in 2002, they have 'been used to herald a looming demographic disaster – variations on a budget emergency, primarily attributed to the rising numbers of older Australians and their draining effect on the budget', wrote Ian Yates, Chief Executive of the advocacy organisation COTA Australia, responding critically to the 2015 report. Yates provided a pithy summary of the Treasurer's argument:

Pensioners eat up way too much of the government budget; all older people need to work much longer; seniors are a terrible drain on the health system; if we didn't have so many older people, especially pensioners, all would be OK.

Yates went on to speculate that older people would be looking to the report to see if the Treasurer 'continues to berate them for their very existence'. 'Since he has already told us we are all going to "fall off our chairs" when we see the graphs in the report, I am concerned that yet another Intergenerational Report will scapegoat older Australians,' he predicted glumly.[30]

Yates's prediction turned out to be a safe bet. Whatever the specific proposals in each five-yearly Intergenerational Report, their very basis is the scapegoating of older people as the cause of Australia's economic and fiscal problems, and the motivation is for policy changes designed to make the pensioner population more affordable. The focus of these reports is the impact of population ageing on 'economic growth, workforce and public finances over the following 40 years', and uses data designed to highlight that the impact will be negative. The Treasurer's 'fall off your chair' graphs are developed projections that adopt a 'point-in-time' format – 'that is, using the assumption that current government policies will continue over the next 40 years, without change'[31] – as though policy ever stands still for 40 years, and as if nothing else is going to change either. Indeed, when the 2015 Report states that '[w]ith an ageing population, economic growth is projected to be slightly slower over the next 40 years than over the past 40 years,'[32] we see just how static and narrow a vision is offered by the intergenerational equity cause.

There is something about the portentous certainty of intergenerational equity campaigners, the relentless marshalling of statistics and graphs drawn from population data, that make their findings seem obvious and unarguable. They are certainly a gift to headline writers, who need to do very little to sex up the dry data as the latest chapter in the generation wars. 'Baby Boomers to Get Far More Welfare Support than Generation X and Millennials,' shouted the *Independent* in response to the Intergenerational Commission's report on welfare transfers. 'Wealth taxes are the only way to avoid harsh future welfare cuts, study says – as the post-war generation prepares to drain the public finances.'[33] 'Millennials Spend Three Times More of Income on Housing than Grandparents,' stated the *Guardian* in response to the Commission's *Home Affront* report.[34] Even what looks like good news for Millennials is presented as a bad thing. 'Millennials Set to Reap Huge Rewards of Inheritance Boom,' reported the *Guardian*, before offering the dreary caveat, 'younger generation will profit from high value homes owned by baby boomer parents – but not till they are 60', resulting in 'higher wealth inequality' and arriving 'too late for most people currently excluded from the property ladder'.[35]

The trouble is that such grim analysis is, fundamentally, wrong. While demographic trends can highlight problems and provide insights into how they have developed in the past, these data neither give the full story about the present nor a reliable prediction of the future.

The dangers of demographic determinism

The theory underlying the austerity ballads is a fairly simple one. Until the mid-twentieth century, there were more people of working age than there were of retirement age – and, once people retired, they tended to drop dead quite quickly. This meant that we had lots of people paying taxes, and pensioners could be relied upon to hobble along for only a few years before doing the decent thing and shuffling off this mortal coil. When people developed serious illnesses, such as cancer, they tended to die from them – now, they are increasingly likely to live with them for many years, drawing on considerable healthcare resources and being unable to work full time, if at all. And we have a relatively large cohort of people retiring in their mid-sixties and living until their nineties or beyond, all expecting to be supported by a shrunken, mule-like cohort of younger people, whose wages are gobbled up in taxes to pay for the lifestyles of their idle elders.

Is this true? Only up to a point. The incredible improvements in longevity that Western societies enjoyed over the second half of the century did take many policymakers by surprise – it is fair to say that when William Beveridge, credited as the principal architect of the postwar British welfare state, promised that the battered population emerging from the rubble of the war would enjoy protection 'from cradle to grave', he probably didn't foresee the grave receding quite so far into old age. Nye Bevan, founding father of the National Health Service, pledged that all British citizens would receive free diagnosis and treatment without consulting a crystal ball that would warn him of the number of new illnesses that would come to be diagnosed; the extent to which treatments would turn fatal illnesses into chronic illnesses, requiring ongoing medical intervention; and the way that improvements in living standards would enable people to carry on visiting their doctors long past the sell-by date that society had previously granted them.

In the glass-half-empty vision projected by the austerity ballads, the vision held by welfare state pioneers is criticised for its failure to anticipate the 'problem' of advances in health and longevity. But this can easily be flipped around. What policymakers failed to anticipate was the good news story of the twentieth century: the extent to which living standards and life expectancy would outstrip the expectations of our forebears in the 1930s and 1940s. The same goes for the US systems of Social Security and Medicare, which campaigners for intergenerational equity have been attacking since the 1980s. Claims about the burden of longevity brush past the happier reality of healthier ageing – in other words, people are living longer, but not as dependent 'old people'; many are healthy, active and playing a significant role in keeping society going. Some pensioners are still working, and paying into social funds; others are providing childcare to enable their grown-up children to carry on with their careers.

Even claims about the so-called 'demographic deficit' – the idea that, as a matter of natural fact, we have more older people than younger people – need to be questioned. Both in the UK and the USA, the Millennial cohort is now larger than the Boomers: not really surprising, given that the Millennials are their children (hence their alias, the 'Boomer Echo'). A greater proportion of women are engaged in paid work for longer than was the case with the Boomer generation – a fact that not only illuminates the need for somebody to provide childcare (often, the much-maligned Boomer Grandmas), but should also counter arguments that there are 'too few' people working. Given the obsession with old-age dependency it is curious that relatively little attention has been paid to the implications of increased *youth* dependency, with young people effectively barred from the labour market until they are at least 18, and increasing proportions being cajoled into staying in higher education until their early 20s.[36] This has knock-on effects both on public spending and on the incomes and career progression of younger people. But policymakers have become so fixated on the misplaced notion that more education means more wealth that this contradiction has been steadily ignored.

There are serious problems with the funding of pensions and healthcare, and these are underpinned by even more serious problems with stagnant wages and sluggish economic growth. But these are problems of politics and the economy, not of generations. There is no magic policy that would restore decent wages and therefore enable public services to be better funded, pensions to be secured, and houses to be afforded. Far easier, it seems, to attempt to claw back some cash and entitlements from older people, and to bash young people over the head with the expectation of even less in their own old age. In this respect, the austerity ballads are talking about generations *because* they don't want to address these bigger, deeper questions.

What's even worse is that in banging on about demographic time bombs and generational inequalities, the austerity ballads are not talking about generations either. This is a concept they have borrowed and distorted to frame their arguments, with little regard for what a generation actually is, and the many ways in which this concept has come to be defined over time. Understanding generations means understanding something much deeper than a cohort: it is about history, and relationships, and how people make sense of their world. As such, it is about far more than numbers, circumstances and experiences – it is also about agency, and the way people act upon their lives and the world around them. The greatest injustice of the austerity ballads lies in the way they strip this agency away.

Punk posturing: Sticking it to the Boomers

Punk posturing aims its fire at the alleged bad attitudes and behaviour of this large, greedy, selfish generation. This helps the generational equity cause no end. Because while nobody really wants to look like they are attacking defenceless little old ladies to shave a few pounds or dollars from their social security budget, it all becomes more palatable when presented as the Boomers' own fault.

In Britain, the punk posturing duo Ed Howker and Shiv Malik had a hit with their book *Jilted Generation*. Both are journalists who, when their book was published in 2010, were 29 years old and lived in London. They are co-founders of the Intergenerational Foundation (IF) – a spikier, less well-established organisation than the Intergenerational Commission, but one with very similar goals and no small amount of influence. Established to 'draw policy-makers' attention' to the problem of generational injustice, IF's rhetoric draws on the same tropes as all the others: non-partisan, simply stating the facts:

> We're non-party-political and vehemently independent. We simply provide the evidence needed to say enough is enough. We think it's only fair that younger generations should have the same standard of living as generations who have gone before. That means creating a new, fairer contract between the generations that provides for tomorrow as well as today.[37]

The Intergenerational Foundation was established shortly after the publication of *Jilted Generation* – a book that begins with a dire warning. Having noted that the UK Treasury drew attention in 2002 to the 'profound effects' that population ageing was likely to have on Britain, Howker and Malik conclude their Introduction:

> Slowly, sombrely, inevitably, the storm is gathering pace. Those 'profound effects' are waiting to be felt in full force. The gener-ation who will bail Britain out can't quite get started. The gener-ation waiting to retire are nervously looking on, wondering why. Meanwhile, the debts are getting bigger, jobs are getting scarcer, lives are getting tougher. If circumstances get worse, people will begin looking for simple shapes. They will start to seek out a narrative, any narrative. And then people will find someone to blame.[38]

The most curious feature of *Jilted Generation* is the way it presents its arguments for intergenerational equity as a response to 'simple' narratives about elder-blaming at the same time as providing the script for those same arguments. In a book dedicated, ingenuously, 'To our parents, thank you', Howker and Malik lay out the malign, distorting and dominating effect of the Baby Boomer generation on housing, jobs, inheritance and politics – while continuing to deny that they are seeking 'to lay the blame for specific and some-times catastrophic errors at the feet of an entire generation',[39] or that the book is 'just about one dissatisfied group in society, a whinge by one generation about another'.[40] In the preface to a new edition of *Jilted Generation*, published in 2013, they muse:

> There were . . . a couple of things we missed. One was just how enthusiastically the media would stoke the idea of 'gener-ational conflict' – of a war between the young and old. By comparing . . . the experiences of different cohorts of British society and counting the changes in housing and labour markets, in public debt and private living standards, perhaps we encouraged the soubriquet 'Generational Jihadis'. We certainly argued that much of what has happened to the jilted generation is 'unfair'. True though this is, the greater point is that the young must be assisted as a matter of economic neces-sity. It was never our intention to put the elderly on trial, only the political and economic decisions made in their name.[41]

It is embarrassing to have to point out that, as journalists for national newspapers and periodicals, Howker and Malik *are* the media – and can scarcely be excused for not recognising that a book explicitly about generational conflict would play some role in 'stoking the idea'. Especially when their own organisation, the Intergenerational Foundation, has issued press releases headlined 'Young Held Back by Burden of Pensions' (2016); 'The Packhorse Generation's Plight' (2014); '65 Year Olds Have Seven Times More Voting Power than 18 Year Olds' (2012); and – in capital letters – '25 MILLION UNOCCUPIED BEDROOMS' (2011), reporting on IF's first ever piece of 'research', which found that:

> The under-occupation of housing has jumped by around 45% since 2003 and is continuing to grow at an alarming pace. This is mainly because older people are living longer and staying in the family home rather than downsizing to more appropriate accommodation.[42]

From Australia, punk posturing turned out to be a great career move for Ryan Heath. 'It's time to bump those Baby Bleaters and their ceaseless cries for more milk, and their figureheads who have all the originality and sophistication of bratty two-year-olds,' postulated Heath (born 1980) in *Please Just F* Off It's Our Turn Now*. The type of public culture 'currently applauded in Australia' is, he claimed, 'an old person's paradise', 'familiar and slow', still in thrall to the 1960s and the people who were young at the time. The motive for his own book 'is countering the mediocrity that is too prevalent in Australia after three decades of Boomer promises'; the book's conclusion, he claims, 'is as hopeful as the demand is clear – please, please, please just fuck off – it's our turn now'.[43]

Ironically, Heath himself f*d off from his native Australia before the Boomers even got the chance to heed his command. He studied politics and journalism at university in Sydney, heading the students' union there and making his name as a writer on 'youth issues' for the *Sydney Morning Herald*. But by the age of 23, he had moved to London, 'by luck getting a job with the Blair Government at their Cabinet Office', and he went on to become a spokesperson and speechwriter for the European Commission in Brussels.[44] For all the bluster of the title, Heath's argument is really just a plea to let the kids play too.

Like the austerity ballads, the softer end of punk posturing aims at nothing more radical than finding a plan to live within the limits and means of the current political and economic system. Howker and Malik want to make it clear that 'we believe in capitalism, we believe that the mechanisms of the market are appropriate; that the creation of wealth is not just desirable but vital – it's the underpinning of any decision that we take as individuals or as a society'. But what they want is capitalism without the uncomfortable capitalistic bits: 'We need security. We need stability and opportunity.'[45] In a chapter titled 'I [heart] capitalism, it's not 1968', Heath informs us that his generation has come to accept that 'capitalism is the only game in town', and that '[w]e expect more from capitalism than anyone else – so we are going to force it to work less corruptly, more ethically and to deliver more choices to us than anyone else has been able to so far'. If there's one word to describe the youth of today, claims Heath, it's 'responsible'.[46]

The beat of punk posturing becomes more aggressive with venture capitalist Bruce Cannon Gibney (born 1976), author of *A Generation of Sociopaths: How the baby boomers betrayed America.* The problem bothering Gibney is the rise of economic inequality within the United States, and the way policies have contributed to that. But his target is a specific one: 'America's present dilemma resulted substantially and directly from choices made by the Baby Boomers.' He spells out how this has happened:

> Their collective, pathological self-interest derailed a long train of progress, while exacerbating and ignoring existential threats like climate change. The Boomers' sociopathic need for instant gratification pushed them to equally sociopathic policies, causing them to fritter away an enormous inheritance, and when that was exhausted, to mortgage the future. When the consequences became troubling, Boomer leadership engaged in concealment and deception in a desperate attempt to hold the system together just long enough for their generational constituencies to pass from the scene. The story of the Boomers is, in other words, the story of a generation of sociopaths running amok.[47]

'A generation of sociopaths' is certainly a headline-grabbing title, and it would be tempting to see it as a merely rhetorical flourish.

But Gibney is dead serious. According to the fifth edition of the psychologists' bible, the *Diagnostic and Statistical Manual of Mental Disorders* (DSM-V), sociopaths are 'selfish, imprudent, remorseless, and relentless'; according to Gibney, '*as a generation*, the Boomers present as distinctly sociopathic, displaying antisocial tendencies to a greater extent than their parents and their children'.[48]

Gibney's book was published in 2017, in the febrile aftermath of the election of Donald Trump as US President – a time when 'sociopath' has become just one of a number of slurs that critics love to level at The Donald. 'As I watch my fellow boomers, Paul Ryan, Donald Trump and Mike Pence grin and fistbump at the idea of killing their fellow Americans with their newly passed health bill, I suspect that no one, not even their children, can redeem these people,' remarked the Pulitzer prizewinning novelist Jane Smiley in her review of Gibney's book.[49] Gibney told the Canadian news magazine *Maclean's* that 'Trump, in a way, is the boomer id': he is 'reckless, entitled, anti-empirical, and hostile. He does not appear to have empathy', all qualities that make him emblematic of that sociopathic generation, the Boomers.[50] But Gibney's contempt for Boomers is not reserved for Trump. It extends to 'generational representatives' of all parties, including;

> Bill Clinton, Newt Gingrich, George W. Bush . . . and Dennis Hastert – a stew of philanderers, draft dodgers, tax avoiders, incompetents, hypocrites, holders of high office censured for ethical violations, a sociopathic sundae whose squalid cherry was provided in 2016 by Hastert's admission of child molestation, itself a grotesque metaphor for Boomer policies.[51]

And, of course, the people who voted for them:

> *Someone* had to elect these tornadoes of vice and it was, of course, Boomers who were content, often enthusiastic, to vote for people who looked like them and showered them with

improvident goodies, whose failures were often overlooked and forgiven because they seemed so familiar.[52]

Austerity ballads draw on the naturalised explanations and predictions offered by a shallow and partial reading of demographic trends. In that worldview, numbers account for everything, and the idea that people have any control over their own, or a collective, future is given short shrift. Punk posturing adds a *frisson* of loathing, in depicting the Boomers as the wrong kind of people, who have used the power of their vast numbers to lead society into a selfish, sociopathic nightmare. An image is created of the Boomers as a peculiarly omnipotent, malevolent force against which younger generations are powerless. Both rely on a heightened sense of crisis, in which the only hope is that the younger generation will save us from the excesses of our elders. And both situate the cause of this crisis in the past, back when the Boomers were young themselves.

CHAPTER 3

Dramatising the crisis

When we think and talk about the Baby Boomers, we are thinking and talking about people. Whatever caricatures come to mind – long-haired hippies, corpulent golfers, busy grandparents, pickled rock stars, disgruntled old white men – the Boomer is not an abstract concept, but a living, breathing individual. Love 'em or loathe 'em, they are part of our world. The Boomer-blaming play-list, however, is not interested in the lives, hopes, dreams and struggles of individual Boomers, even in caricatured form. The 'Boomer' of the cultural imagination is a cipher for long-running anxieties about the past, present and future. In attempting to explain why the Boomers are such a problem today, Blamers go back as far as their limited historical imaginations will take them – to that moment known, simply, as 'the Sixties'. Boomers have become fall guys for the Sixties, and everything that is seen to have gone wrong since.

The question of why the Sixties looms so large in the political and cultural imagination today is discussed throughout this book. In part, it is because the upheavals of the Sixties were, by any account, a Big Deal. 'Mention of "the Sixties" rouses strong emotions even in those who were already old when the Sixties began and those who were not even born when the Sixties ended,' writes the historian Arthur Marwick in his powerful study of 'social and cultural transformation in Britain, France, Italy and the

United States, 1958–74'. As he points out, the feelings evoked by the period cover a whole spectrum:

> For some it is a golden age, for others a time when the old secure framework of morality, authority and discipline disintegrated. In the eyes of the far left, it is the era when revolution was at hand, only to be betrayed by the feebleness of the faithful and the trickery of the enemy; to the radical right, an era of subversion and moral turpitude.[1]

When Marwick's book was published, back in 1999, he argued that in consequence of the powerful emotions evoked by the Sixties, '[w]hat happened between the late Fifties and the early Seventies has been subject to political polemic, nostalgic mythologising and downright misrepresentation.'[2] Twenty years further on, it seems that the symbolism of this period looms larger as our memory of the facts recedes. Nowhere is this clearer than in the mythologising and misrepresentation of the Baby Boomers.

Vitriol is levelled at the Baby Boomers from both the political right and the political left. While they focus on different, specific Boomer evils, the legacy of the Sixties provides a common target. Lauren Southern's *Barbarians: How baby boomers, immigration, and Islam screwed my generation*, is an Angry Young Woman's attack on the cultural left and the rise of post-structuralist relativism on campus. She moves swiftly from a complaint based on her own experience of being taught English literature by 'tenured hippies' to generalisations about 'the worst generation in history'; the 'mass influx of spoilt brats' who entered American universities and 'drove free inquiry and reason out in the name of chaos, hypocrisy, illiteracy, and madness'.[3] Francis Beckett, a British 'Old Labour romantic'[4] and self-confessed Baby Boomer, bemoans the rise of individualism and the decline of the welfare state. 'While the philosophy of the sixties seemed progressive at the time, it was really symbolised by the television picture from 1968 of a flower child in a flowing skirt, dancing in a circle and singing, "Down with the police, down with income tax",' he writes. 'It was the direct intellectual precursor of the Thatcherite view that there is no such thing as society. The children of the sixties were the parents of Thatcherism.' As a consequence of their self-indulgent individualism, claims Beckett, the Baby Boomers 'set about destroying the old certainties', including squandering their inheritance (the postwar welfare state), and then turned on their children. '[T]here seems to be a special venom in the loathing they show to their young,' he continues:

> It is as though the sixties generation decided that the freedom from worry which they had enjoyed was too good for their children, so they kicked away their children's legs, and now they sneer at them for being lame.[5]

Beckett's book *What Did the Baby Boomers Ever Do for Us?* is subtitled *Why the children of the sixties lived the dream and failed the future.* For all its talk about revolution, he complains, 'the generation of 1968 was not at all like the generation of 1918' – when 'at last the generation that fought the First World War came to power, in 1945 under Major Clement Attlee, they changed the world' through building the postwar welfare state; but the generation of 1968 focused on tearing things down in the name of freedom and individual self-expression. The charge of 'destruction' runs across the Boomer-blaming playlist. 'The more power Boomers accumulated, the more self-serving and destructive their policies became,' writes Gibney. 'For purely selfish reasons, the Boomers unravelled the social fabric woven by previous generations.'[6] 'We pulled down one culture with its rules and imagined that another would spontaneously take its place,' proclaims the economist Will Hutton. 'How could we have been so destructive?'[7]

Across the political spectrum, the legacy of the Sixties is depicted in a strikingly uniform way: as a historical blip with profoundly negative consequences, a self-indulgent 'party' for the Boomer generation, for which younger generations now have to pay the price. 'What if it's actually the older generation, the baby boomers, who have been throwing the party and leaving behind a mess for the next generation to sort out?' demands David Willetts.[8] 'The truth is the baby-boomers' party went on too long,' complains the historian Dominic Sandbrook. 'They ignored the warnings of their parents and were enjoying themselves so much they could barely hear the cries of their children.'[9]

Of course we should continue to debate the meaning and legacy of the Sixties. As Marwick points out, whether you think of the period as a happy golden age or the decline of civilisation, it is impossible to deny that the consequences of this social and cultural transformation were significant and long-lasting: 'there has been nothing quite like it; nothing would ever be quite the same again'.[10] But the shallow motifs offered by the Boomer-blaming playlist avoid this challenge. Rather than seeking to understand and critique the Sixties, Boomer-blaming takes the problems we face today and plonks them back half a century, with scant regard for the wider context.

The representation of the Sixties as a destructive, thoughtless 'party', an unfortunate blip in the responsible sobriety of the twentieth century, is particularly bizarre and one-sided. What about the two catastrophic world wars that had dominated the first half of the century; the cynical hedonism of the 'Roaring Twenties'; the parasitism of colonialism and racial segregation? While the Sixties had its excesses of consumerism and self-indulgence, it also mobilised people to fight for freedom and equality, against war and prejudice. But this is conveniently forgotten in the attempts to depict the people who grew up and came of age in this period as Svengali-like villains, on a mission to destroy their children's future.

Of all the charges levelled against the Sixties generation, the most intriguing is that of 'individualism'. This term – which is usually deployed as a fancier version of the charge of 'selfishness' – is a favourite for Boomer-blamers across the political spectrum. Conservative complainants accuse the Boomers of destroying the social contract through the promotion of individualism over responsibility to future generations; 'old left' worriers view the decline of the welfare state as a consequence of a generation that placed individual self-interest over the common good; 'jilted' Millennials see the promotion of a short-termist individualism as eroding responsible citizenship; Gibney fixates on individualism as the root cause and effect of the Boomers' sociopathy. Of all the Boomers' crimes against history, it seems that the promotion of 'individualism' is the worthiest of a lynching.

But while 'individualism' trips off the tongue like an epithet, there are some glaring contradictions in the way this term is deployed. '[I]f, as the [DSM-V] definition the author cites extensively, sociopaths are inherently egocentric, individualistic and unfeeling toward the needs of others, then how could they meaningfully comprise a functional, ruling power bloc?,' muses John Semley in his critical review of *A Generation of Sociopaths*. 'It would, to nip one of Gibney's jokes, be like asking anarchists to form a police constabulary.'[11]

'Just because they're all individuals doesn't mean that they're frenzied individualists too. We begrudge them neither their wealth nor their freedom,' insist Howker and Malik. But, they continue, 'we also now know that they could have done better if more of them had remembered that they aren't just individuals but citizens too'.[12] This leaves us none the wiser. The individual is the basis of citizenship – that's why we have one vote each, rather than relying on a benevolent dictatorship to do the right thing. And Boomer-blamers are far more scathing about the way this generation has exercised its citizenship, by allegedly devising generationally self-interested policies, than it is about the handful of drop-outs who took to LSD to supply their dreams of a better world.

In their glib attacks on 'individualism', Boomer-blamers achieve a number of rhetorical sleights of hand. They conflate the spirit of freedom and self-expression associated with the Sixties – the reaction against stifling conventions around sex and sexuality, the spirit that brought us the decriminalisation of homosexuality and the legalisation of abortion – with the strike-breaking, welfare-state reforming policies of the Eighties. They set the pursuit of self-interest against the needs of an imagined 'collective', as though until 1968, voting was all about being nice to other people. Above all, in imagining a mass of 'individualists', they erase the status of *individuals* within the Boomer generation. All we see is a cohort hell-bent on getting its own, uniform way over the young, at whatever cost.

The concept of generation is mobilised here as a static, determining force, which needs to be corrected in favour of other generations. The over-inflation of this imagined generational agency denies any sense of individual agency amongst members of the Boomer generation, let alone those that followed. The Boomers are dehumanised as a demographic lump, propelled by their historical moment into screwing up the world for everybody else. The only solution, as some of the Blamers see it, is to wipe the slate clean and start again.

Year Zero fantasies

'If and when the chance comes again, I hope wiser, younger people do not throw it away, as we did,' hopes Beckett.[13] But Gibney does not want to wait on the 'if': dismantling the 'generational sociopathic domination' of the current period requires, he argues, nothing less than a ' "cultural reorientation" '.[14] 'It has been forty years since the Boomers began accumulating real power and about twenty-five since they gained command of the nation's highest office and many of its legislatures, and they are still upending the social order in fairly radical ways,' he states. 'Like all sociopathic revolutions, the Boomer revolution wishes to be permanent.' The task is too urgent to wait for the Boomers to shuffle off their mortal coil: a more proactive strategy is required. 'What might work,' he suggests, 'is an Other, the common enemy the philosopher Carl Schmitt believed societies needed to push them into decisive action.'[15]

Gibney recognises that some people might feel awkward about endorsing the ideas of Schmitt, who, 'being a German of a certain era, reached some ugly conclusions about Otherhood'. Actually, Schmitt was a Nazi – not in the facile twenty-first century sense of being somebody you don't like with dubious ideas, but a card-carrying member of the German Nazi Party, who joined in 1933 and quickly rose to an influential position in the legal profession, where his anti-Semitism was well known.[16] He wasn't just 'a German of a certain era', as Gibney quips, and he didn't 'reach some ugly conclusions' so much as develop some ugly arguments. Gibney counsels that we should look beyond this awkwardness, however, for 'he was not without a point': 'A Schmittian menace does motivate society, sometimes to good ends, if the Us is genuinely commendable and the Other, not so much.'[17] By Othering the Boomers, he explains, generationalism can lead to a powerful sense of collectivism – the Bad Boomers against the Good Everybody Else:

> The goals of this cultural reorientation are straightforward. The first is to provide a foundation for unity against the Boomer agenda, and to do it quickly. If that unity requires a degree of anger about what has happened to the country and at those responsible, so be it. The Boomers deserve America's displeasure and they ought to repay what they can. The second is to remember that the anti-anti-social agenda is, at heart, a *pro*social agenda, one that strengthens the ideals of a commonwealth.[18]

Even Gibney, in his closing remarks, seems to grasp that there is something odd about mobilising division in the name of unity. 'The Boomer Other is only a framing device, hopefully useful, but not an end in itself,' he concedes. 'Remembering the prosocial goal helpfully limits how far we proceed against the Boomers, because for all their considerable faults, they are part of society, too.'[19] But if Gibney is calling for exile rather than extermination, that is bad enough. The Boomers are not just 'part of society' – they are part of *us*. As our parents, grandparents, teachers, friends, neighbours, lovers, political representatives, and very much more, members of the Baby Boomer generation form part of the intimate fabric of our lives. To imagine they exist in a separate zone, some kind of psychic retirement ghetto, you would have to live in a very small, dark fantasy world.

The darkness lurking within fantasies of generational conflict was revealed in a stark fashion by Steve Bannon, former chief strategist to President Trump and Executive Chairman of *Breitbart News*, before he plunged out of favour. Bannon was rather taken with the generational theory popularised by Neil Howe and William Strauss in their 1998 'American prophecy', *The Fourth Turning: What the cycles of history tell us about America's next rendezvous with destiny*,[20] using this as the basis for his 2010 documentary film *Generation Zero* and subsequent media interviews.[21] Headlines such as 'Steve Bannon's Obsession with a Dark Theory of History Should Be Worrisome' (*Business Insider*), 'Steve Bannon Believes the Apocalypse Is Coming and War Is Inevitable' (*Huffington Post*), and 'Steve Bannon Wants to Start World War III' (*The Nation*), indicate a certain horrified scepticism about this particular take on generational conflict. But Neil Howe is delighted by the impact of his ideas: as he reveals in an article for the *Washington Post*, modestly titled 'Where Did Steve Bannon Get His Worldview? From My Book.'[22]

The generational model offered by Howe and Strauss is a premodern one, which looks to natural or otherwise pre-ordained rhythms to give an explanation for the role played by generations in determining the course of history. 'We reject the deep premise of modern Western historians that social time is either linear (continuous progress or decline) or chaotic (too complex to reveal any direction),' Howe explains, continuing:

> Instead we adopt the insight of nearly all traditional societies: that social time is a recurring cycle in which events become meaningful only to the extent that they are what philosopher Mircea Eliade calls 'reenactments'. In cyclical space, once you

strip away the extraneous accidents and technology, you are left with only a limited number of social moods, which tend to recur in a fixed order.[23]

Within each 'recurring cycle' of social time, Howe and Strauss identify four 'turnings', each of which last 'about 20 years – the length of a generation'. They compare these turnings to seasons, 'starting with spring and ending with winter'; and in every turning, a new generation is born as an older generation enters its next phase of life. Every generation will live through some kind of civic crisis, which comes about 'every 80 or 90 years, or roughly the length of a long human life'; and the point at which the crisis comes will, they argue, shape the kind of generation that exists. Howe and Strauss provide a painstaking pen-portrait of the four 'types' of generation, along with their experiences, expectations and character attributes, in their original prophecy: *Generations: The history of America's future, 1584 to 2069*, published in 1991.[24]

By relentlessly cobbling together expressions of the zeitgeist from a number of historical periods, Howe and Strauss manage to construct a beguiling narrative of generational stereotypes over the centuries. This has made them acutely sensitive to the attributes associated with the generations more recently coming of age, and accounts for Howe's enduring influence on recent debates about the features and fortunes of the Millennial generation (William Strauss died in 2007). But while stereotypes can tell us something about generations past and present, they are very far from the full story. And when a cyclical worldview is used as the basis for predictions of the future, it all becomes rather disturbing.

Howe and Strauss view the cycles of generations as an inexorable process of crisis and cleansing. America entered a new Fourth Turning in 2008, explains Howe, and things are likely to get worse before they get better: 'Further adverse events, possibly another financial crisis or a major armed conflict, will galvanize public opinion and mobilize leaders to take more decisive action.' But then, around 2030, 'the Fourth Turning crisis era will climax and draw to a close' and a new First Turning will begin. 'Young families will rejoice, fertility will rebound, economic equality will rise, a new middle class will emerge, public investment will grow into a new 21st-century infrastructure, and ordered prosperity will recommence,' he prophesies. And Millennials, as we move into the 'next Awakening', will take the reins, finally able to 'showcase their optimism, smarts, credentials and confidence'.[25]

This narrative of destruction and rebirth, of sin and redemption, has a distinctly biblical quality. 'Get ready for the creative destruction of public institutions, something every society periodically requires to clear out what is obsolete, ossified and dysfunctional – and to tilt the playing field of wealth and power away from the old and back to the young,' he counsels. 'Forests need periodic fires; rivers need periodic floods. Societies, too. That's the price we must pay for a new golden age.'[26] And indeed, Ecclesiastes plays a starring role both in Strauss and Howe's *The Fourth Turning*, and in Bannon's *Generation Zero* documentary. But the inspiration for the 'generation zero' fantasy comes less from a religious attempt to come to terms with death than from a very modern disenchantment with life.

The 'generation zero' fantasy rejects modern, Western views of history, in preference for a pre-modern view that sees history as a natural, cyclical process in which everything comes around again. This is true, at least for the Strauss-Howe theory of generations, which came around the first time in the interwar period, in the work of the Spanish philosopher José Ortega y Gasset. As Andrew Dobson notes in his account of Ortega's work, Ortega's theory of generations was for a long time 'generally recognised as being the most extreme (some would say outlandish)' of all generational theories, largely because 'its imposition of biological rhythms on socio-historical phenomena is absolute and universal, whereas less ambitious theories have held that generations of thought are produced within the historical process as a whole'.[27]

So why has this outlandish, cyclical view of history come back into vogue in the twenty-first century? It's not because generations have somehow become easier to define and predict – if anything, the obsessive generation chatter that goes on in policy and media circles has made it more difficult to work out what is meant by the concept of generation, let alone where one generation starts and another begins. The answer lies in generation chatter itself, which seeks to impose a naturalistic view of history onto ideas about generations, and to box people into rigid generational identities.

Generationalist identities and the politics of division

'Often, and increasingly, social and political life is narrated using the concept of generation,' observes Jonathan White of the London School of Economics.[28] White argues that the political claim that generations have competing interests can be put to a number of problematic ends. One is that it can be used as a rationale for restructuring the welfare state: for example, by cutting resources for older people on the grounds that young people have to foot the bill. This is the motivation that drives policymaking around the 'intergenerational equity' cause, as discussed in the previous chapter.

Generationalism – 'the systematic appeal to the concept of generation in narrating the social and political'[29] – can also serve the end of avoiding discussion about inequalities between social classes, or other social divisions. As discussed in later chapters, it has become increasingly fashionable for commentators to speculate on how age has become the 'new political divide' in elections or referenda – a conceit that tends to brush over more stark and established divisions that voting preferences represent, such as those between the middle and working classes, or affluent urban areas compared to struggling, provincial regions.

White also argues that generationalism can be deployed to bring groups of people together – it can be used as 'a new language of collectivism, a way to speak to those presumed no longer reachable with a class vocabulary'.[30] While the old left-right class politics attempted to mobilise working-class people against the ruling class, generationalism uses the language of 'haves vs have-nots' to mobilise younger generations against older generations. Economic conflicts between rich and poor have long been a feature of capitalist societies, which the Left attempted to capture as part of a vision for a future society organised around the principles of greater wealth equality. Generationalist thinking, by contrast, reformulates these as generational conflicts between old and young, looking backwards to an imagined past in which older people had it so good, and concocting strategies to redistribute the pain of the present.

Shortly after the UK's 2017 General Election, a video clip produced by Momentum, the self-styled 'hard' left organisation set up to propel Labour Party leader Jeremy Corbyn into power, parodied older voters ridiculing the Labour leader and his welfarist policies.[31] Titled 'Pulling up the Ladder' (a favourite metaphor of the intergenerational justice lobby), the video portrays guests at a dinner party dismissing young people's gripes about university tuition fees, the struggle to get on the housing ladder, and the quest for desirable jobs. Captions flashed up to drive home the hypocrisy: 'Didn't pay anything for university', 'Bought her first home for £20,000 in 1981; now it's worth £1.5 million'; 'Got his job at a media agency through his father ... who started the agency with money from his father.' According to Momentum, the video was seen by nearly half a million Facebook users in under five hours.[32]

Maya Goodfellow, writing in the *Guardian*, lauded the video for its message of 'intergenerational unfairness and the importance of collectivism': ideas that, she argued, 'if continuously talked about, have the power to appeal to all sections of society'.[33] Columnist Deborah Orr countered that the video was 'full of simplistic prejudices' and, far from promoting a message of collectivism, was a 'divisive attack on baby boomers'.[34] Orr was right – but in the warped logic of generationalism, divisive attacks come to be viewed positively, as a means of promoting a kind of collective identity based on a sentiment of historical grievance.

Neil Howe muses that when *The Fourth Turning* was published in 1998, he and his co-author 'were surprised by the book's popularity among certain crusaders on both the left and the right'. Democrats were their 'biggest partisan fans', who saw in their description of the emerging Millennial generation 'the sort of community-minded optimists who would pull America toward progressive ideals'. But they also had 'conservative fans, who were drawn to another lesson: that the new era would probably see the successful joining of left-wing economics with right-wing social values'.[35] Part of the reason for this, he suggests, is that generational thinking lies 'beyond ideology'.

In fact, generationalism has come to operate as a symbolic vessel, into which all political persuasions can pour their anxieties, and from which a whole range of claims about the future can be drawn. It is, as White suggests, 'an emergent master-narrative on which actors of quite different persuasions converge as they seek to reshape prevalent conceptions of obligation, collective action and community'.[36] In this regard, those who believe that playing the generation card can drive support for any established ideological or political cause – whether from left or right – are deluded.

Generationalism has come to find its most comfortable home within identity politics, that shrill sentiment of victimisation and grievance that has become an increasingly powerful cultural force. Identity politics developed from the countercultural movements of the Sixties, and until recent years has been most prominent in intellectual circles and on university campuses.[37] It is most crudely caricatured by the 'social justice warrior' who pounces on any perceived slight to an individual's gender, sexuality, ethnic background, religion or disability, to demand censure for the offender and validation for the aggrieved party: for example, through 'no-platforming' controversial speakers, or by demanding that statues of historical figures associated with colonialism or slavery be removed. But the influence of identity politics has spread way beyond the college campus, and is no longer associated only with the cultural left.

In *Kill All Normies*, a fascinating study of the 'online culture wars', Angela Nagle traces the relationship between the 'once obscure call-out culture of the left emanating from Tumblr-style campus-based identity politics', and the emergence of the 'white nationalist alt-right' as an increasingly vocal force in the identity wars. The alt-right initially styled itself as reaction against the politically correct excesses of the intersectional left: as Nagle notes, the 'hysterical liberal call-out', through which 'everything from eating noodles to reading Shakespeare was declared "problematic", and even the most mundane acts "misogynist" and "white suprema-cist"', produced a 'breeding ground for an online backlash of irreverent mockery and anti-PC' from charismatic alt-right figures such as Milo Yiannopoulos and Lauren Southern.[38] In this way, explains Maren Thom, 'Nagle shows how both sides of the new culture wars are the product of the same postmodern zeitgeist':

> Just as the counterculture of the Sixties was pitted against the authoritarianism of the socially conservative, so the alt-right is pitted against the authoritarianism of the liberal establish-ment, whose members are determined to control and regulate artistic expression, proscribe who and what should be repre-sented in cultural outputs and what can and can't be said in everyday conversation.[39]

The consolidation of identity politics as a mainstream form of political discourse was fully revealed during the Clinton-Trump Presidential campaign of 2016, 'with Hillary using terms like "check your privilege" and "intersectionality"'[40], and condemning 'a new Internet age right-wing movement as part of Trump's "basket of deplorables"'.[41] But as Nagle observes, after years of 'crying wolf', nobody knew what to do when 'the real wolf eventu-ally arrived, in the form of the openly white nationalist alt-right who hid among an online army of ironic in-jokey trolls'.[42] The 'identitarian movement' is one such wolf. A white nationalist movement that began in France and has gained traction in North

America, identitarians define themselves in the language of oppression and victimisation associated with the identity politics of the cultural left, pitting themselves against the 'liberal establishment' and openly calling for racial conflict.

In one chilling example, *Generation Identity: A declaration of war against the '68ers*,[43] presents itself as the voice of 'European youth', mobilising against the Baby Boomer establishment ('the '68ers') to put an end to what they see as the collapse of European civilisation brought about by mass immigration. 'We young Europeans grew up on a continent that doesn't belong to us anymore,' whines Austrian Millennial Markus Willinger. 'We have only known a culture in collapse, our peoples at the ends of their lives. We had to withstand the attempts of our parents and grandparents to uproot us and make us into "individuals" without any identity. They want us to rejoice that Europe is failing, to accept and submit to its defeat. But we won't. We rebel.' Willinger concludes his preface to the book:

> Our generation is rising up to dethrone the '68ers. This book is no simple manifesto. It is a declaration of war. A declaration of war against everything that makes Europe sick and drives it to ruin, against the false ideology of the '68ers. This is us declaring war on you.[44]

The ease with which the far-right identitarian movement is able to adopt the generationalist frame, pitting the voice of dispossessed youth against what is perceived to be the corruption brought about by the 'liberal establishment' Baby Boomers, reveals how easily fantasies of generational identity can be weaponised – and to what ends. Willinger's 'declaration of war against the '68ers' is very different to, for example, Ryan Heath's pathetic entreaty to 'please f*** off, it's our turn now', both in terms of the explicit violence of the message, and the kind of world that it wants to see. But contained within all generationalist accounts is a common assumption: that young people have a legitimate grievance against their elders, and this grievance should be validated *because they are young people* – however misguided, dangerous or downright vile such ideas might be.

What unites the identity politics of the alt-right and the cultural left – making them, as Thom puts it, 'different cheeks on the same postmodern arse'[45] – is that both have turned against the quest for a deeper moral, political or ideological cause. The universalist principles that once formed the core of movements for equality, democracy and tolerance – the principles that, for much of the twentieth century, united many people in the struggle against oppression – have been cast aside in favour of a particularistic, intractable cultural conflict in which people lob missiles of outrage without much concern for where it all might lead, and who might get caught in the crossfire. 'The emptiness of their gestures and their performance of transgression reveal their combined failure of political thinking,' writes Thom. The symbolic, and actual, violence that results from these degraded identity wars – burning books and toppling statues, demanding that 'transgressors' be sacked from their jobs, attacking mosques and synagogues – shows the moral vacuity of an outlook that prizes the expression of grievance above all else.

Of all the features of Boomer-blaming, the way that it dovetails with divisive identity politics is the most pernicious. The politics of generational identity has very little to do with actual generations; rather, it is an off-the-peg narrative that can be used to give a fake hue of authenticity and collectivism to other ideas or agendas. But in the emotionally charged culture wars, which are raging not only online but everywhere else, the self-righteous mobilisation of generational grievance can have vicious consequences.

'Healing' divisions or inflaming resentment?

In their dystopian economic tract *The Coming Generational Storm*, first published in 2004, finance experts Laurence J. Kotlikoff and Scott Burns accused America of committing decades of 'fiscal child abuse'.[46] Their 2012 sequel *The Clash of Generations* developed the metaphor in gory technicolour. Noting that 'a recent report shows that nearly 3 million children were abused or neglected in a single year', Kotlikoff and Burns write:

> We respond to stories of this kind of abuse with justified shock and outrage. But what about abuse that isn't so obvious? What about abuse that is so subtle it simply isn't noticed, abuse so common it is like part of the air we breathe? That abuse exists not so much in one family or another, but in our society as a whole. It is not physical abuse. It is economic abuse. It is built into government policies, right in front of our noses, and we say little about it. We don't learn of it through media reporting, we cannot see it, and we don't understand it because, well, it lacks blood. How many fingers do you need to count the times you have heard fellow subway riders or office workers discussing the implications of the growing fiscal gap? None.[47]

The idea that fiscal policy is bloodless and boring, and that nobody cares about 'the coming generational storm' because they haven't been made to sit up and pay attention, is perhaps why politicians and pundits reach for the most hyperbolic language they can. 'Intergenerational theft' has become a well-worn rallying cry. Republican opponents of President Obama's 2009 fiscal stimulus plan renamed it 'The Generational Theft Act of 2009' and accused the Democrats of trying to spend and borrow their way to economic recovery, at the expense of younger generations.[48] The hedge fund manager and philanthropist Stan Druckenmiller spent 2013 touring college campuses warning about generational theft because, as *Business Insider* put it, Druckenmiller 'Wants Every Young Person in America to See these Charts about how They're Getting Screwed'.[49] In Australia, a scheme promoted to improve young people's access to housing was decried as an act of 'intergenerational theft';[50] in Britain, journalists have issued dire warnings about 'the inter-generational theft of Brexit and climate change'.[51]

Others prefer to present their arguments as neutral-sounding 'findings', and their responses as constructive strategies to 'heal divisions'. In 2014, the influential US Pew Research Center published an essay and related book titled *The Next America*, based on analysis of demographic trends and public opinion surveys.[52] The data make for fascinating reading, and contain a number of important insights: unfortunately, these were blunted by Pew's demographically blinkered dramatisation. The essay begins by stating that America is in the midst of two 'demographic transformations':

> Our population is becoming majority non-white at the same time a record share is going gray. Each of these shifts would by itself be the defining demographic story of its era. The fact that both are unfolding simultaneously has generated big generation gaps that will put stress on our politics, families, pocketbooks, entitlement programs and social cohesion.[53]

As with the Australian government's Intergenerational Reports and the UK Intergenerational Commission's research briefings, an alarmist rhetoric is accompanied by graphs and projections designed to illustrate just how profound the effects of such demographic change are likely to be.

Pew received a fair amount of flak for appearing to 'foment a "generational war" over Social Security and Medicare', prompting a response by Paul Taylor, the essay's author and the organisation's former executive vice president. 'Is this an effort to start a Battle of the Ages? I certainly hope not,' reassured Taylor.[54] 'To the contrary, one of the goals of the essay and book is to highlight the trove of demographic and attitudinal research my colleagues and I have conducted which show that young and old in America aren't spoiling for a generational war – not over entitlements, nor any other realm of their increasingly interdependent lives.'

Although Taylor insisted that the problem, at its core, is intergenerational inequity, he acknowledged that members of the public are not convinced. The majority of people say that they do not see much conflict between young and old; today's young adults say they 'get along better with their parents than older adults did when they were young', and generations depend heavily on each other: 'more than 50 million Americans, a record, are living under the same roof in multi-generational family households, their fortunes braided together by the bonds of love and the stress of economic insecurity.'[55] Yet in the twisted logic of the generation wars, the public's very reluctance to engage in a conflict over resources between the generations becomes an argument for why they should be signing up to the policies of intergenerational equity:

> If Americans can bring to the public square the same genius for generational interdependence they bring to their family lives, the politics of entitlement reform will be less toxic and the policy choices less daunting. That's a big if. It's also the most promising way to frame the conversation.[56]

In the UK, the Conservative Party's 2017 election manifesto contained a chapter devoted to 'A restored contract between the generations', in which it presented fairness between the generations as the rationale for continuing austerity measures. 'Conservatives believe in balancing the books and paying down debts – because it is wrong to pass to future generations a bill you cannot or will not pay yourself,' intoned the manifesto.[57] It took pains to emphasise 'solidarity' between the generations as a core Conservative principle, but made clear that decisions, and divisions, would be made:

> As our society ages, the costs of caring for older generations – pensions, pensioner benefits, health and social care – rise; and these are borne by working people through their taxes. As the relative number of younger people is falling, those costs increase, not just in total, but also for individuals. So if we are to give older people the dignity we owe them and younger people the opportunities they deserve, we face difficult decisions.[58]

One such 'difficult decision' included a reform to the funding of care for the elderly, with a proposal to take into account the value of the family home 'along with other assets and income, whether care is provided at home, or in a residential or nursing care home'. This proposal was quickly dubbed the 'dementia tax', and greeted with outrage by voters across the land. Indeed, the ill-judged dementia tax was widely reported as a turning point in the Conservative Party's election campaign, which began as a coronation for Prime Minister Theresa May, and ended with her fighting for her political life. But the generation warriors continue, undaunted. 'So far our attempts to address this challenge have been clumsy, and responses hysterical,' admitted Intergenerational Commission chair David Willetts in March 2018, citing the dementia tax debacle as an example. 'But we cannot avoid this issue.'[59]

The Intergenerational Commission itself takes pains to deny that it is inciting conflict between the generations. 'Too often the debate is framed as an intergenerational war, which doesn't reflect how people feel about the issue or live their lives as families,' claims its website; all the Commission wants to do is to 'strengthen and renew the social contract between the generations'.[60] The fact that people outside the Commission refuse to believe that this contract is broken in the first place is perceived only as an obstacle in public perception that needs to be overcome. If people aren't thinking in terms of generational conflict, goes the argument, we need to change the way they are thinking.

The problem of public opinion

A revealing insight into the working of this mind-bending logic is provided in the Intergenerational Commission's 2017 report *The Millennial Bug: Public attitudes on the living standards of different generations*, commissioned from Ipsos MORI.[61] The report begins by noting the important role played by the Intergenerational Commission in highlighting the problem: that 'the principle of generation-on-generation progress that has come to define 20th

Century Britain shows signs of being disrupted', and that in a range of areas, 'including their earnings levels, housing situation and the extent to which they are building up resources for later life, the living standards of younger adults appear under threat.'[62] But to what extent, wonder the report's authors, is this diagnosis of the problem shared by people themselves?

In this report, we see the topsy-turvy way in which claims and policies designed to tackle generational inequality have been developed. Once upon a time, it was considered that politicians and policymakers were elected by the people with a brief to tackle the problems that voters felt were important. Housing, healthcare, economic growth, and poverty have consistently featured as areas of social life that concern the public, and history is replete with examples of the different solutions that policymakers have tried to develop, as they attempt to marry the often contradictory demands of what is right, what is possible, and what is popular. But when it comes to policies designed to promote intergenerational equity, the cart is very much seen to be leading the horse.

'For those interested in pursuing policies to address these challenges a key question is the extent to which they are reflected in public perceptions,' states *The Millennial Bug*. The short answer is: they aren't. Researchers surveyed over 2,000 British adults and held a workshop involving members of different generations – and found, overwhelmingly, that there is little appetite for Boomer-blaming among the public, and even less for redistributing resources from old to young.

This is not because people think that everything in the garden is rosy. Far from it: the report's headline finding was that there is 'widespread pessimism' about young people's lives compared to those of their parents. Only 23 per cent of those surveyed believed that young people will have a better life than previous generations, and 48 per cent 'believe that millennials will have a worse life than their parents'. Even the pessimism has got worse. 'This pessimism – present in other developed economies but more apparent in Britain than most – represents something of a change from the pre-crisis view when the balance of opinion on the outlook for the young was clearly positive,' notes the report. Young people were reported to be particularly miserable: one third of millennials 'would prefer to have grown up at the time when their parents were children, while only 15 per cent of baby boomers and members of generation X would rather grow up today'.[63]

The question of *why* people are so pessimistic, and find it scarcely possible to believe that things could get better, is explored in later chapters. The explanation lies in a complicated cocktail of structural economic problems, cultural anxieties, political atrophy masquerading as random unpredictability, and the hangover of *fin-de-siècle* gloom. But even amidst all this misery, the report finds little sympathy for the idea that older generations are to blame. 'Housing and jobs market failures' are seen to been the key causes, with 'relatively little blame placed on the actions of generations themselves'; and the researchers identified 'high levels of intergenerational solidarity, with sympathy from older generations regarding the challenges young people face and little resentment among the young towards older people's more favourable circumstances'.[64]

The most important areas for government action identified by *The Millennial Bug* report relate to 'underlying structural economic issues' – the reasons why people think Millennials are having a tough time in the first place. One-third of those surveyed said that the government should focus on making jobs more stable and secure, supporting growth in the economy as a whole, and increasing the number of houses available to rent or buy. By contrast, state the researchers, 'policies that imply intergenerational redistribution – including shifting the balance of taxation from young to old or reducing welfare benefits to pensioners – are viewed as least important'.[65]

You might think the Intergenerational Commission would be disheartened by such a vote of unpopularity. But while generation warriors often seem surprised by the lack of popular buy-in for their cause, it merely affirms their conviction that more must be done to press the message home. 'We need to change the conversation, acknowledging that repairing the intergenerational contract matters to everyone,' wrote the Commission's Laura Gardiner in the run-up to the 2017 General Election.[66] In other words – it's not only what we do about generations that has become a matter for public policy intervention, but how we *think* about them.

The narrative of Boomer-blaming draws on the authority of demography to make its arguments and create its graphs – but any half-decent demographer knows that the picture is far more rounded and complex than the crude assertions popularised by policies claiming to promote 'intergenerational equity'. Similarly, historians with an understanding of the many factors involved in social and cultural change find themselves horrified by the selective approach to the Sixties – and near-total amnesia about the Fifties and Seventies – that is required to paint the grotesque caricature of the selfish, greedy, individualistic Boomer.

Unfortunately, this sensitivity barely impinges on the elite fantasy of the generation wars. If people don't identify with generationalism as a worldview, it is presumed that this is because they are unable to grasp reality, and that they should have their perceptions changed. For some, this means 'changing the conversation' so that public opposition to policies promoting intergenerational equity is recast as public support for 'intergenerational solidarity' – involving the very same set of policies that people are opposed to. For others, it means forcing the change in conversation through bringing on a crisis. And for those who really want to go to war, it means mobilising young people around an identity of self-righteous generational grievance. In these ways, the dogma of generationalism ends up attacking the very thing that makes generations meaningful: their relationships with each other.

CHAPTER 4

What's so special about
generations?

The fashion for talking about generations presumes that we know who they are, what they are, and why they are important. But we don't agree on any of those things. I tried it out on my students. They had heard of the Baby Boomers ('Sixties, hippies'), and the Millennials – though some were quite shocked to hear that that particular label applied to them. 'We're the 1990s babies,' said one, before launching into an explanation of how different they were to the 30-somethings currently acting as the voice of youth. They didn't remember the turn of the century, or the terrorist attacks of 9/11 – the formative events associated with Millennials. Generation X received not a glimmer of recognition, until I mentioned Kurt Cobain. Then they got it.

One clue to the phoney caricature of the new generation wars is that they rely heavily on cultural caricatures – as indicated in the most popular generation labels. The exact titles, birth years, or attributes might vary slightly according to who is doing the labelling, but in general, we can throw these labels around and know what, or who, we are talking about.

The **Generation of 1914**, also known as the Lost Generation or the First World War generation, came of age around the time of the Great War. This generation is known by its writers – Wilfred Owen, Siegfried Sassoon and Erich Maria Remarque in Europe; Ernest Hemingway, F. Scott Fitzgerald and E.E. Cummings in the

United States. Through their bleak expressions of moral and spiritual alienation, the Generation of 1914 found its place in history through articulating the sense of crisis and confusion that dominated the early twentieth century.

The **Greatest Generation** were born during the Depression years and came of age to fight in the Second World War. The youth of this time have a rather more glossy and heroic image, certainly in the Allied countries. Imagined mostly as brave fighters for Good against Evil, they ended the war and returned to build a peacetime based on prosperity and freedom.

The **Silent Generation** missed out both on fighting in the war and reaping the benefits of the peace. Coming of age in the Fifties, they have been represented as a conformist, apathetic generation; a new, 'other-directed' character type theorised by David Riesman's landmark study *The Lonely Crowd*, whose identity and behaviour is shaped by its relationships, rather than by a deeper sense of purpose. Women, who had made an active contribution to the war effort in munitions factories and military units, were chased back into the home to become the depressed housewives of Betty Friedan's *Feminine Mystique* and Richard Yates's *Revolutionary Road*.

The **Baby Boomers**, also known as the Sixties generation, were the products of two simultaneous 'booms' – a sharp rise in the birth rate as soldiers returned from the war and got busy making babies, and an economic boom that began in the 1950s and continued throughout the 1960s. Reared according to boundless love and a new, 'fun morality',[1] these babies initially symbolised peace, freedom and optimism. But instead of acknowledging their good fortune, the 'lucky generation' turned on the values, conventions and institutions of the postwar world, spawning a radical countercultural movement on university campuses and in wider middle-class society.

Generation X took its name from the 1991 novel by Canadian writer Douglas Coupland, whose 'tales of an accelerated culture' depict a group of twenty-something slackers drifting aimlessly through a series of 'McJobs' in California.[2] The story resonated with anxieties about the small, embittered generation born in the shadow of the Boomers, and growing up through the spiky Seventies and unforgiving Eighties, where the good economic times had turned to recession and crisis, and the institutions of the welfare state were already past their heyday.

Millennials were initially, unimaginatively, branded 'Generation Y', in recognition that they were a different breed to the Xers: more constructive, conservative and optimistic, but also more fragile. In place of Generation X's grimly self-destructive nihilism, the kids who came of age at the turn of the twenty-first century were anxious and stressed, entitled and desperate to please. Millennials were also the 'Boomer Echo', the diminished children of that vast and glitzy Sixties generation. Their coming of age was marked not only by the turn of the century, but by the terrorist attacks of 9/11 and the global financial crisis.

The newest generation are still awaiting an enduring label. For now, most commentators are going with **Generation Z** – the children of austerity, whose lives beat to the staccato of school test results and streaks on social media; the so-called 'digital natives', lost in communication and incomprehensible to those for whom a phone is a useful device rather than an extension of self.[3]

Taken literally, of course, these labels seem both stupidly schematic and frustratingly imprecise. All we have is a series of partial cameos drawn from moments in historical time, with extreme – even fictional – characters inflated to represent a whole swathe of human life. Following each lively, golden generation destined to change the world comes a stunted, misery-guts cohort of whom little can be hoped or demanded. In presenting generations as a cycle of hope and gloom, these categorisations gloss over different experiences, and different interpretations of the same experience – young men who rushed to join up to fight in the First World War; the uncertainty, fear and disillusionment that gripped many of the 'Greatest Generation' as the Second World War dragged on; women and ethnic minority groups, who lived within generations but were rarely part of their designated 'voice'; the

Boomers who missed out on the affluence and radicalism of the high Sixties; the Gen Xers who bought into the shinier promises of Thatcherism and finance and did very well out of it, thank you very much.

Stereotypes, by definition, do not reflect everybody in that generation; usually, they reflect the most extreme and tiny minority. The association of Baby Boomers with free-loving hippies happens despite the fact that, as Marwick points out, attempts to measure the actual number of hippies back in 1967 – even using 'very wide parameters' that included people who held executive or professional positions and maintained nine-to-five jobs – came up with a figure amounting to 'considerably less than 0.1 per cent of the total American population'.[4] The stereotype of the avotoast-munching Millennial reflects a very particular experience – someone who is white, middle-class, university educated, with a professional job, living in a dynamic urban area. This Millennial is far from 'representative' of the majority of young people, for whom depressed wages and living standards form a more widespread reality.

The promiscuity and one-sidedness of generation labelling is starkest in what the journalist Adam Lusher describes as '[t]he race to label the next generation of teenagers', a task most fervently pursued by those working in marketing and the media, who love to find a catchy label for a new market or audience. 'First there were the baby boomers, who begat Generation X, who were succeeded by the millennials, who were born in the early Eighties and in the Nineties,' writes Lusher. 'And now, largely begat by Generation X – or at least those sections of it that didn't grow up to be dinkies (dual income no kids), but may have been yuppies or slackers – has come . . . well, what exactly?'[5] Lusher reports that in 2015, the television channel MTV 'proudly announced that it had come up with the term "founders" to denote youngsters born after December 2000', a term that speaks far more to a desperate desire to put a positive spin on the nameless generation more commonly referred to as 'Generation Z' than to any serious analysis.

But while it is tempting to write the whole thing off as a cynical marketing-and-politicking exercise, generational stereotypes are not randomly made up. They are based on something – a distinctive form of behaviour, appearance or attitude – that has been identified in, or articulated by, a bunch of people associated with the same point in time. Generation labels capture something about how the zeitgeist is reflected in the kind of people coming to young adulthood. When it comes to making sense of generations, we are making sense of moments of history, and the people who are shaped by, and will shape, those moments.

Generations situate us in a time and place that makes sense to us in a way that the dry pages of a history book often cannot. Most of us are not architects of world-defining events; we do not win wars, lead governments or create works of staggering genius. But we are there when they happen, and we are part of these events in the same way they are a part of us. This gives us a connection with members of our own generation: that flash of recognition we have with those who were there too. And it connects us, too, with the generations older and younger than ourselves; the history that is being written as life is played out.

The trouble with slicing and dicing

Generation is a muddled concept, which means different things to different people in different contexts.[6] With all the current policy chatter, it has become harder than ever to work out exactly what people mean when they talk about generations – let alone 'younger generation', 'older generation' or 'intergenerational' relations, justice, equity, equality, fairness, solidarity or any of the many other buzzwords. Sometimes the talk is of age, not generation. Some accounts present the study of generations as a natural science, where biological rhythms determine the course of human history; others as a process of economic modelling, where the numbers count for everything.

The lack of precision involved in the concept of 'generation' has bothered sociologists for a long time. Back in 1970, Philip Abrams argued that efforts to apply the term 'generations' to the 'whole age categories of a society' tend to 'end up either as genealogy (the history of fathers and sons in particular families) or as waffle'.[7] Ten years before that, Bennet M. Berger noted that the question 'how long is a generation?' was confused further by the tendency to leap on every new phenomenon as an epoch-defining change. 'From a "Victorian age" spanning about 60 years, we seem to have reached a point where a change in zeitgeist may be expected at approximately ten-year intervals,' he mused.[8]

But in making sense of generations, a certain amount of waffle and wooliness is preferable to the rigidity of much of the current generation chatter, which reduces generations to birth cohorts, boxed in by their biology. For example, the Intergenerational Commission's analysis of inequalities between the generations relies on relentlessly comparing the fortunes of precisely defined birth cohorts:

- The Forgotten Generation, born 1896–1910
- The Greatest Generation, born 1911–1925
- The Silent Generation, born 1926–1945
- The Baby Boomers, born 1946–1965
- Generation X, born 1966–1980
- The Millennials, born 1981–2000
- The latest generation, born 2001–2015.[9]

Slicing up a population like this, according to its birth year, looks straightforward enough, and even kind of scientific. But is it really? 'Spanning 15 years, different social classes, cultures and continents, it is ridiculous to imagine that millennials have a unified identity,' wrote the journalist Kate Lyons, in her introduction to a special *Guardian* series on 'Generation Y' [aka 'Millennials']. Lyons defined this cohort as including people born 'between 1980 and the end of 1994 (with some more generous definitions taking in those born up to 2000)'. 'In the UK, there are 13.8 million millennials, and a 20-year-old in Ipswich is no doubt facing vastly different issues to a 35-year-old in Glasgow, and that's without even looking beyond the borders of the UK,' she acknowledged, citing the response of one *Guardian* reader to the invitation to 'describe the main issues facing Gen Y in his country': 'You want me to sum up the main issues facing an entire generation in an entire country? That sounds less scientific than a fucking horoscope, you mad bastards.'[10]

The 'madness' of generational generalisations is even more pronounced when it comes to the Baby Boomers, the generation that has been the most feverishly analysed for the longest time. As noted previously, it's a catchy label, capturing two very real events: a booming birth rate, and a booming economy. But the label misses as much as it catches. If we are looking at Britain, even the term 'Baby Boomer generation' is 'borrowed from America and quite wrongly applied to the postwar pattern of British birth rates'.[11] Unlike the pronounced rises in the birth rate experienced in the USA and Canada in the two decades following the Second World War, Britain had two much smaller spikes. '[E]ven the absolute peaks of the two Baby Booms constituted only an additional 25 per cent over the average for the postwar decades,' writes demography professor Jane Falkingham. 'In place of every four births, in these years there were five.'[12]

The impact of the economic boom was also more limited in Britain than it was across the pond. As the American satirist P.J. O'Rourke puts it, in his introduction to the UK edition of *The Baby Boom: How it got that way, and it wasn't my fault, and I'll never do it again*: 'Post-war experience in America was very different from post-war experience in a place where war, in fact, occurred. That is, we had the 'post-' and you had the war.'[13]

Even in the USA, the experience of a Boomer born in 1964 and coming of age during the 1970s is hugely different to that of the Boomer born in 1947 and growing into the Sixties glitz. And of course, Boomers born at exactly the same time in exactly the same place had different experiences. Wiping out differences of class, gender, ethnicity and opportunity through the blunt instrument of the birthday seems the very opposite of precise.

The counterposition of the large Boomer generation with the runty Generation X seems less convincing when the number of Boomers is calculated, as the Intergenerational Commission does, over a 19-year period, but Generation X over just 14 years. In one sense, the precise numbers don't change the overall picture. But as we will see in later chapters, generation warriors set a great deal of store by bean-counting. They obsessively calculate the 'demographic time bomb' stored up by a declining 'age-dependency ratio', where smaller numbers of younger workers are supporting the retirement needs of a larger, older cohort; or witter about how the Boomers are skewing the outcome of elections through mobilising their relatively vast numbers. In these cases, it really starts to matter where the claims-makers get their figures from.

Taken literally, definition by birthdate makes no sense. How could somebody born at midnight on December 1965 be a 'Baby Boomer', and the person born one minute later be a member of 'Generation X'? And why choose 1965 as the cut-off anyway? It's not as though this date has been inscribed on a tablet of stone, to indicate the line between one epoch and the next. These are dates that have been chosen by academics in order to define and study particular cohorts of people, rather than dates that are necessarily significant to begin with. The cohort approach has added a powerful dimension to the study of demographic change: conducted properly, it looks at the point at which people of around the same age embark on key life transitions, such as marriage and family formation, and attempts to explain these through an analysis of wider social trends. But it is widely acknowledged that the study of cohorts is quite different from the study of generations – and collapsing these concepts together weakens both.

The demographic determinism favoured by Boomer-blaming starts with a particular idea about the problems of society today and looks for causes and solutions in the form of biological rhythms, historical cycles, or numerical formulas. This boxes generations in, accentuating differences between cohorts and using dates that provide the best fit with pre-existing theories.

Strauss and Howe take this to extremes, concocting a naturalised view of history to determine when particular generations begin and end. They present four 'types' of generation: 'four basic types of peer personalities and life-cycles'. These are 'determined by age location relative to social movements' and 'normally recur in the following fixed order': Idealist (encounters a spiritual awakening entering rising adulthood and a secular crisis entering elderhood); Reactive (encounters a spiritual awakening entering youth and a secular crisis entering midlife); Civic (encounters a secular crisis entering rising adulthood and a spiritual awakening entering elderhood); and Adaptive (encounters a secular crisis entering youth and a spiritual awakening entering midlife).[14] A generational cycle, they say, is 'a set of consecutive generations beginning with an Idealist-type and ending with an Adaptive-type'. Strauss and Howe present their arguments in quasi-scientific terms, offering no less than a 'prophecy' about the shape of things to come as '[t]he cycle of history keeps turning, inexorably'.[15] But this is a history of the authors' own selection: their typology, as laid out in their 1991 tome *Generations*, uses different dates and labels to those deployed elsewhere, categorising generations in such a way that they fit the model. And even if it were possible to use generational cycles to predict 'the history of America's future, 1584 to 2069', why would you want to?

There is a good reason why nobody manages to define a generation in advance, and this is that it has not yet found its voice, and made its mark. However much wishful thinking goes into imagining what the next wave of young people will bring to the historical table, the kind of 'prophecy' offered by Strauss and Howe, or even the trend-spotting beloved of marketers, is impossible to pull off in reality. Generations are not patterns, or cycles, or numbers – they are concepts, which draw upon people with a range of different experiences, who live through a similar historical period but interpret their relationship with it in a variety of ways. Rather than slicing and dicing, we need to look at how generations relate to each other, and to the world around them.

Concepts of existence

At its core, talking about generations means talking about how we make sense of the world: the passing of time, the events that we experience, what we learn from our elders and what we pass on to our children. The historian Laura Nash has described generational thought in terms of 'concepts of existence', whose origins lie in Ancient Greece. She explains that our 'most secure standard for defining a generation rests on the Greek root of the word, *genos*, whose basic meaning is reflected in the verb *genesthai*, "to come into existence"' – and right up until the 1960s, 'procreation' was offered as the first dictionary definition of 'generation'.[16] But generation is not just about being born – it is about how we give meaning to the 'ever-shifting threshold in time'[17] revealed by the continuous process of birth, ageing and death.

In traditional societies, generations were understood mainly in the context of kinship relations, and were rather easier to get a handle on. The son of a lord, a peasant or an artisan would continue in this tradition, and become a father to children who would follow the same course. Change was slow and incremental; hereditary privilege was cast as a fact of life; concepts such as 'the individual' and 'freedom' were yet to be developed. There was a continuity of generations, because there was no way out. But in modern times, this continuity within the family had to contend with the wider disruptions of social change. To survive and succeed in the world, young people would forge a different path to the generations that had gone before. As the historian John Gillis explains, '[g]enerational tensions often characterise societies in the first stages of economic and political modernisation'.[18]

This clash between tradition and modernisation is famously dramatised by Ivan Turgenev's 1862 novel *Fathers and Sons*.[19] Set during the Great Reforms, the novel is an allegory of the broader social changes sweeping Russia and the wider world at the time: a violent clash between the conventions of the past and aspirations for the future, and the destabilising forces that bonded members of the younger generation together around a consciousness of their 'historical purpose'.[20] The two young men at the heart of the story are fascinated by science, progress, and the 'nihilism' of the new world, which pits them against the 'the old aristocratic sentimentality, with its attendant good manners and decadent gentility'.[21]

Yet the conflict erupts most bitterly, not between the eponymous 'father and son', Nikolai Petrovich Kirsanov and Arkady, but between the son's uncle, Paul Petrovich Kirsanov, and Arkady's university friend, Evgeny Bazarov. While this tension ultimately destroys both uncle and friend, the intimacy between the father and the son, and their enduring relationship of respect and interdependence, tempers it:

'Our successors – yes,' re-echoed Nikolai Petrovich despondently. Throughout the conversation he had been sitting simply on pins and needles; throughout it he had dared do no more than throw an occasional pained glance at Arkady. 'My brother, there came to me just now a curious reminiscence. It was of a quarrel which once I had with my mother. During the contest she raised a great outcry, and refused to listen to a single word I said; until at length I told her that for her to understand me was impossible, seeing that she and I came of different generations. Of course this angered her yet more, but I thought to myself, "What else could I do? The pill must have been a bitter one, but it was necessary that she should swallow it." And now *our* turn is come; now it is for us to be told by our heirs that we come of a different generation from theirs, and must kindly swallow the pill.'

'You are too magnanimous and retiring,' expostulated Paul Petrovitch. 'For my part, I feel sure that we are more in the right than these two youngsters, even though we may express ourselves in old-fashioned terms, and lack their daring self-sufficiency. Indeed, what a puffed-up crowd is the youth of today! Should you ask one of them whether he will take white wine or red, he will reply, in a bass voice, and with a face as though the whole universe were looking at him, "Red is my customary rule." '[22]

Fathers and Sons is widely acknowledged as 'the classic portrait of conflict between generations'.[23] But it is also a sensitive depiction of the intimate bonds between generations within families, and how these temper the conflicts between old and new that may rage in the wider world: an effect that continues to be observed in modern studies of intergenerational relationships. While Bazarov and Paul Petrovich end up destroying each other, Arkady and Nikolai Petrovich have a more open, constructive relationship, which accepts the need for the wisdom transmitted from fathers to sons, but also the need for the older generation to accept that the younger generation will mould this wisdom in its own way. Even during times of great upheaval, generational change is not a linear or violent process; it takes its own, more muddled, form.

Generations come about because of relations between individual and family, between biology and society, between culture, social structures and historical events; they are shaped by time and place, and given meaning through their experience. This 'concept of existence' has become one way in which we make sense of ourselves in a world of rapid change, grounding us in the continuity of the past and our responsibility for the future, but also expressing something profound about our present moment. It is not a narrow understanding of 'youth', because younger people are shaped in their relations with other generations. It is about knowledge – the relationship between past, present and future; the knowledge that endures and how it is re-made by those who encounter the wisdom of the past for the first time, shape it and make it their own.

This way of understanding 'social generations' was developed by the Hungarian sociologist Karl Mannheim, who was living in exile in Germany in the 1920s, a period in which generational tensions were at their peak.[24] For Mannheim, what mattered was the interaction between 'new participants in the cultural process', and the society in which these participants are born, develop and, in turn, transform. A group of people who have grown up with a particular idea about the way things are, and why, will see things differently to those who come across this knowledge afresh. This is not because they happen to be older or younger, or different kinds of people – it is because of their location in a historical moment, and the wider social events of their time. Understanding generations requires appreciating the features of both their biological existence – the fact that we are always absorbing new members into our society – and their social experience, which will always be distinct from that of their elders.

The continual emergence of new participants in society, who would make 'fresh contacts' with the existing wisdom and interpret it in their own way, gives knowledge its dynamism and creativity. In passing on the cultural heritage, society was able to remember what it knew to be important – but equally important was how the knowledge developed in this process also enabled us to forget. Historical memory worked through generations of people to combine the power of accumulated wisdom with the 'up-to-dateness' of youth, enabling an 'elasticity of mind' that is able to provide continuity and engage with change.

While there is clearly some friction involved in this process, it does not normally erupt into conflict – because the relationship between the generations is continuous, spontaneous and often informal. The fact that '[g]enerations are in a state of constant interaction' means that they develop a sensitivity to one another – 'not only does the teacher educate his pupil, but the pupil educates his teacher too'. Within the intimate relationships of the family, much of what young people know about the world is absorbed unconsciously: it is the way things are. But as the young person matures and 'personal experimentation with life begins', they gain the possibility of 'really questioning and reflecting on things'. This is when tensions between the generations potentially come to the fore. Young people, being closer to the problems of their time, 'are dramatically aware of a process of de-stabilization and take sides in it', while 'the older generation cling to the re-orientation that had been the drama of their youth'.[25]

This is why generations only make sense when we try to define them, not by the dates in which they happen to be born, but by the social events that characterised the time at which they came of age: the First World War, the Sixties, 9/11. When we think back on the formative experiences of our younger lives, it is often the events that we experienced just at the point where we began 'really questioning and reflecting on things' – wars, disasters, terrorism – that shaped our outlook and propelled us to question the wisdom handed down by our parents and teachers. And how we work up those experiences *as a generation* will shape the wider knowledge of these events; the sense, going forward, of 'the way things were'.

Dislocation and disorientation provide the basis for an emergent generational consciousness; a distinctive interpretation of the zeitgeist born out of the experience of coming of age in a time that is, in Hamlet's terms, out of joint. When the world as it appears in the present comes into stark conflict with the knowledge and values with which they have been raised, young people experience a rupture with the wisdom of their elders and a heightened sense of fellow-feeling for those around them. Broader schisms take a generational form – a gap opens up between the younger and older generations, not because anything has changed in the relationship between them, but because wider events have brought about a clash of realities, putting young people's sense of 'the way things are' dramatically at odds with 'the way things were'.

Reality clashes

In one important way, the labels that have been given to the generations of the twentieth century – starting with the Generation of 1914 – reflect shifts in consciousness brought about by wider social events. They reflect particular points in time, which have made their deepest mark on those beginning to question and reflect on their young, adult lives. This is why labels such as the 'Sixties Generation', 'Generation X' and 'Millennials' speak to moments in which young people would, as Mannheim put it, become 'dramatically aware of a process of de-stabilization and take sides in it'. It is also why the labels stick, and become reference points as we look back through history, as markers of a distinct social time and the people who made it their own.

For example, the rise of generational tensions during the First World War reflected a more general discombobulation. Those young men who had initially been eager to join up to the fight came back shattered and disillusioned, a visible reflection of the dislocation between the experiences and aspirations of the younger generation and those of the 'old guard' who had led them into battle. 'The feeling that all the sacrifice was in vain embraced the disenchanted public of the victor and the defeated nation alike,' writes Furedi – a feeling that 'directly contributed to a loss of belief in the legitimacy of the institutions and ideals associated with the pre-war regimes'.[26]

In his account of the Generation of 1914, the historian Robert Wohl writes of the common 'conscious[ness] of generational unity' that distinguished the interwar period from 'any era before or afterwards'. The intellectuals of the war generation saw themselves as '"wanderers between two worlds"', through a time of great crisis, bringing an urgent sense of destruction but, also, renewal. This accounts for the 'privileged place' occupied by the Generation of 1914 in our idea of the early twentieth century. 'They color our memories and creep into the best of our books,' Wohl writes:

They are the prisms through which we view the years between the two world wars. Films, novels, poems, autobiographies, songs, remembrances have pressed these images indelibly into the deepest layers of our minds. Who can forget Remarque's young soldiers lamenting that, live or die, their world was lost forever; Hemingway's Jake Barnes drowning with alcohol the memory of the man he once had been and would never be again; or Robert Graves saying goodbye to all that and abandoning a declining England for the pagan pleasures of Majorca?[27]

Labels such as the 'Generation of 1914' are, of course, one-sided. They relate not just to a generational experience, but a *particular experience* of the experience, which is developed in a distinctive and often partial way. The young men who made up the Generation of 1914 shared the experience of the trenches, cutting across the boundaries of nationality and social class – but they experienced different risks, problems and privileges. Disenchantment may have been the overriding theme of the times, but the bitter betrayal articulated in Owen's 'Dulce et Decorum Est', or Remarque's *All Quiet on the Western Front*, was not shared by all of their peers. The fellow-feeling shared by the Generation of 1914 had to compete with a range of powerful ideologies, political parties and social differences that drew people of the same age in quite different directions. Any attempt to understand generations has to account for these differences – and for why a particular 'voice of a generation' comes to speak louder than all the others.

Mannheim argued that each social generation contains separate 'generation units', which 'work up their experiences in different specific ways'. A generation can experience the same wider events, but develop a different relationship with them – and, crucially, express themselves in a distinctive fashion. What defines that generation is not the common experience of all of its members, but the way that a particular 'generation unit' has most clearly expressed and shaped the zeitgeist.

This is what gives generational labels their strangely symbolic quality – seeming, at the same time, to represent a whole group of people and nobody at all. As Wohl points out, despite the power of images evoked by the Generation of 1914, 'their status is uncertain. They hover strangely, like the shades of dead soldiers, in a no-man's land between literature and legend'.[28] The Generation of 1914 is almost a myth: one that is grounded in events of the time, but shaped by the cultural imagination to provide a particular narrative of the past and make sense of our present circumstances. But it goes beyond a mere idea: a particular experience of events was embodied in a significant group of young people coming of age at the time, shaping the way they came to know themselves and the world around them. And this, in turn, shaped the way that later generations came to know the Generation of 1914.

Vera Brittain's famous memoir *Testament of Youth*, published in 1933, aimed to express 'what the whole War and the post-war period . . . has meant to those men and women of my generation';[29] but Brittain is candid in her understanding that this, too, was an image and not a history. 'The task of creating a matrix for these records has not been easy, for it is almost impossible to see ourselves and our friends and lovers as we really were seven, fifteen or even twenty years ago,' she wrote:

> Many of our contemporaries of equal age, in spite of their differences of environment and inheritance, appear to resemble us more closely than we resemble ourselves two decades back in time, since the same prodigious happenings and the same profound changes of opinion which have moulded us have also moulded them. As Charles Morgan so truly says in *The Fountain*: 'In each instant of their lives men die to that instant. It is not time that passes away from them, but they who recede from the constancy, the immutability of time, so that when afterwards they look back upon themselves it is not themselves they see, not even – as it is customary to say – themselves as they formerly were, but strange ghosts made in their image, with whom they have no communication.'[30]

Viewed in this way, generations are the product of history, and they shape our knowledge of history. But they are not a *substitute* for history – and that is the problem with the current generation chatter. Generation warriors focus myopically on selected ideas and images associated with the Baby Boomers. They present these symbols as the cause of our current political and economic malaise while ignoring both the historical causes of these problems, and the historical context that shaped the Boomer generation and accounted for its influence. And who are they actually talking about? Not the millions of individual Baby Boomers, nor even the protagonists of the Sixties generation, but 'strange ghosts made in their image', summoned up to frighten us into attacking our own flesh and blood.

Family stories

The current tendency to fetishise generation labels – Baby Boomers, Generation X, Millennials – exaggerates the similarities between people born around the same time, and the differences between those who are older and younger. Apparently, it is impossible for those who came of age when mobile phones were a novelty – and merely phones – to comprehend the relationship between today's 'digital natives' and the new world of social media. The world is changing so fast that human beings, like technology, are obsolete from the moment we arrive on the scene.

Deep down, we know this is not true. In their critique of social generations as 'the new emerging orthodoxy in youth studies', Alan France and Steven Roberts raise a number of important questions about the current fascination with the 'social generation paradigm' as a way of analysing young people's relationship with the life course, not least to do with the ways this tends to flatten differences in experiences between young people, and distract scholarly and political attention from more significant social divisions.[31] The world is full of 'silver surfers' who have mastered the technology of smart phones and the language of emoticons, and presumptions about 'digital natives' have been roundly debunked by empirical research.[32] In the discussions that matter – politics, culture, social issues – we are just as likely to find ourselves at odds with people from our own generation as we are with those who happen to be younger or older. Generational differences do not lead to mutual incomprehension; yet increasingly, it is assumed that they do.

In explaining the apparent empathy gap between old and young, some have pointed the finger of blame at increasing age segregation: even 'age apartheid', as the charity United for All Ages puts it.[33] They have a point. Young people spend their formative years in education, where age segregation is brutally precise – it is easy to identify peer groups when children spend half their lives in school classes with children of exactly the same age. At the other end of life, towns boast 'retirement communities', into which residents are only accepted once they reach a certain age. The huge expansion of higher education in many Western societies means that increasing numbers of young adults spend their late teens and early twenties mostly hanging out with – and often living with – their peers.

But these developments are not entirely new, and there is no obvious reason why they should result in the dire consequences that United for All Ages warns about: a lack of connection between different generations, leading to mistrust, misunderstanding, ageism and exclusion. Where sentiments of detachment and defensiveness between the younger and older generations are expressed, these result from deeper cultural confusions, about the value we attach to the past and the meaning we attach to family.

Generations are about our relationship with history, but they are, equally, underpinned by our relationship with family. Modern societies pulled people away from the notion that generational continuity would frame their existence, that they would simply follow in their father's or mother's footsteps. Peer groups, and age segregation, emerged as a feature of everyday life. But relationships between generations in families remain a powerful way in which people make sense of their existence in the private realm.

Families embody the relationships of care and commitment that enable us to socialise young people, look after elderly people, and absorb the harsh realities of everyday life. In our intimate relationships of care and commitment, we become more than ourselves. As the late, great Tom Wolfe put it back in 1976, in his eviscerating critique of 'The Me Decade':

> Most people, historically, have *not* lived their lives as if thinking, 'I have only one life to live.' Instead they have lived as if they are living their ancestors' lives and their offspring's lives and perhaps their neighbors' lives as well. They have seen themselves as inseparable from the great tide of chromosomes of which they are created and which they pass on.[34]

Families mediate the wider relationship between past, present and future by passing on norms and values, and making sense of new events. Through family stories, myths and rituals, history is personalised and a connection drawn between 'the way we were' and 'the way we are now'.

Most families continue to have their own version of the stories that have enabled them to feel 'as if they are living their ancestors' lives and their offspring's lives and perhaps their neighbors' lives as well'. My own family favourite is the story of how my grandparents met: a story that, in its continuous telling and re-telling, has underlined the relationship between family and wider historical events, and the reality of generational continuity and change.

My grandfather, Donald (Don) Bristow, was called up into the Royal Air Force (RAF) on the outbreak of the Second World War, at the age of 19. In February 1941, he was the wireless operator and machine gunner on an RAF Blenheim Bomber, which was shot down in France; for the next four years he was held captive in a number of German prisoner-of-war camps. During his time in the camps, the young Don made assiduous copies of 'every letter and card I sent to family, friends and girl friends in order that when, some six months later, a reply was received, at least I could refer to the copy to pick up the thread of the newly received letter'.

Some years after Grandad's death in 1993, my uncle collated this correspondence, along with ten short essays Don had written in the camp. Reading all this now, it is clear that writing, for Don, was a way both to make sense of and alleviate what he described as 'the stagnation of life behind wire'. It was also a way of communicating with loved ones – and potential love interests. Don's life in the camps formed a significant backdrop to my childhood, largely because this was how he met my grandmother. Nan (née Betty Hathaway) had just turned 17 years old when she received this card at her home in Slough, Berkshire:

> *Stalag Luft 1, 18 October 1941.*
>
> *I hope you will excuse my writing to you 'out of the blue' but Jordie (brother Bill to you) was coerced into showing me one of your letters, and well . . . here I am. About me – my handle is Don and a description held by Scotland Yard is somewhat like this: – age 21; height 6ft; weight 150 pounds; hair, undetermined, vices, love of pleasure, virtues, precious few, last dwelling place. Guildford (not too far from Slough!). Naturally, I'm hoping that your description will come by return in the shape of several photographs; so till then, cheerio, and be as good as your boyfriends will let you.*

Don had become friendly with another captive, Bill, who was married to Betty's older sister Phyllis (Phyl). Don, a young man on the cusp of adulthood, was engaging in the prison-camp equivalent of online dating, and his pursuit of a photo of the youthful Betty across war-torn Europe is the stuff of romantic novels. Don eventually returned to England at the end of the war, met Betty for the first time, and they married in 1947. My father was born in December 1948, and his brother Paul not long after that: quintessential 'postwar babies', born to young war veterans in the first years of peacetime.

As a child, I was entranced by the fairytale quality of a match made by two young people over the time and space of war-ravaged

Europe, falling in love with each other's words and photographs until, miraculously, they met in the flesh and fell in love 'for real'. How easy it would have been for Nan to have decided on one of her other 'airman' admirers in preference to hanging around for her pen-pal, or for both to have found the reality not matching up with the fantasy. 'My mental picture of you is constantly changing,' wrote Don back in 1943 – how could it not, when it was based on nothing more than letters and a photograph?

For my sister and me, this was a story that underpinned both our family history and our wider understanding of history. The prison-camp romance brought our father into being: without that correspondence, we would not be here today. It also brought a reality to the history of the Second World War, which we learned at school and read in novels but which we also saw very much as our own. The past was not conceived as something separate or irrelevant to the present, but nor was it something that dictated the way we live now. As the younger generation in this living history, we knew that our lives, outlook and values would be different from some of those held by our grandparents, but that moving on from the past also required learning from it, and from those who had been there.

Grandad appreciated that point too. In an article written for the Press Association magazine in 1986, on his retirement from that organisation, Don reflected that '[f]or my generation at least, the other truly significant birthday was the 21st' – an event that had been ' "celebrated" in surroundings far removed from a centrally heated, close-carpeted office'. 'The view that October day 44 years ago was of a rain-swept compound surrounded by barbed wire punctuated with "goon" towers from which machine guns menaced the huts housing RAF prisoners of war – "kriegies" in camp jargon,' he wrote.[35]

Don noted that his letter to his parents made 'only a brief reference' to his birthday: 'I became entitled to vote on the 22nd but did not receive the key to this particular door. It was pretty dreary and the rain confined me to the room for most of the day.' But, he explained:

Letters to England were hardly informative since they were all rigorously examined by the Nazi censors. I could not and did not mention the 'celebration' which had taken place a week or so earlier, since it could have led to awkward questions. One of my particular mates – recently retired from a City firm of stockbrokers – is 17 days older than me. We decided to mark our coming of age jointly on a day midway between the two birthdays.

By dint of bribe and scrounge we managed to get hold of half a cauliflower, a rare relief from the low and dreary diet of caraway seed in everything. My taste bud memories tell me that the half cauliflower shared in a celebratory mood was as mouthwatering as any birthday cake!

The tale of the cauliflower has long since passed into the folklore of my family. Five years ago my 'kriegie' pal was a guest at a somewhat bibulous party to mark my 60th birthday. At an appropriate moment, my wife and sons temporarily stopped the drinking to present us with half a cauliflower suitably decorated with wire fencing! The old bores had been capped, and actually we don't talk about our 21st any more.[36]

Through the repetition of this story, the prison-camp cauliflower became a story owned not just by Grandad, but by my father and uncle as well. Once they had appropriated it, the 'old bores' may well have been capped – I don't remember Grandad talking much about his twenty-first birthday, but only because the story of the retirement-party cauliflower cake had superseded the original, and that is what we talked about instead. And now, of course, we tell our own children not just the story of the two cauliflower cakes, but the story of the story; the ghosts of a life as if we had lived it.

The families we live by

One of the most disturbing features of twenty-first-century generationalism is its frontal assault on the meaning of the past, as mediated through family relationships. As we will see in the following chapters, in blaming the Baby Boomers for the ills of the present day, generation warriors are imposing a selective and one-sided impression of history onto the people who lived through it. The Baby Boomers are not 'the Sixties', and attempting to hold them responsible for everything that happened back when they were kids is neither fair to them, nor helpful in understanding the predicament of younger generations today. Quite the opposite: it cuts young people adrift from an important source of meaning in their own lives.

There is something clearly unhealthy about encouraging young adults to blame their parents, or their grandparents, for all the problems in the world today. This is bound to breed resentment within everyday family relationships, particularly when it is mixed up with the relations of dependence and support that come with living as part of a family. But family is also an increasingly important source of cultural meaning. 'We not only live with families but depend on them to do the symbolic work that was once assigned to religious and communal institutions: representing ourselves to ourselves as we would like to think we are,' writes John Gillis, in his historical study of 'myth and ritual in family life'. Gillis explains:

> To put it another way, we all have two families, one we live *with* and another we live *by*. We would like the two to be the same, but they are not. Too often the families we live with exhibit the kind of self-interested, competitive, divisive behaviour that we have come to associate with the market economy and the public sphere. Often fragmented and impermanent, they are much less reliable than the imagined families we live by. The latter are never allowed to let us down. Constituted through myth, ritual, and image, they must be forever nurturing and protective, and we will go to any lengths to ensure they are so, even if it means mystifying the realities of family life.[37]

In trying to capture the significance of 'the families we live by', Gillis was not only talking about the idealised versions of the family that have been periodically constructed by conservative moralisers: the Victorian paterfamilias, the Fifties 'Golden Age' of Mom, Dad and 2.4 children. By the mid-1990s, when he was writing, the world was well aware that these were largely artificial constructions, and the 'dark side' of the families we live with – domestic violence, child abuse, loveless marriages, careless divorces – had already suffered decades of exposure. Rather, Gillis was exploring the ways that people derive a sense of meaning from family that they are increasingly unable to find in 'the cosmos or in the community'. Our attachment to family myths, rituals and images comes about, he argues, because 'we no longer have access to other locations onto which we might map our deepest moral values'. This creates an additional tension for the families we live with:

> Finding no other location for such values as cooperation, enduring loyalty, and moral consideration, modern Western culture has mapped these exclusively onto the families we live with, a cultural burden that members of these domestic groups find difficult, if not impossible, to sustain on an everyday basis.[38]

This wider crisis of meaning-making results in families being, simultaneously, the thing we most cherish and the thing we most rail against. It is true that this creates a burden for families, who constantly have to navigate the tensions, disappointments, flaws and injustices of their everyday being, while at the same time representing a sense of how things should be. But this symbolic work also provides individuals with a sense of who they are, in a world where other attachments and principles seem to be constantly shifting. Young people can absorb the values of the families they live by, or reject them, or a bit of both: but they can only do this because their families have tried to create the meaning in the first place.

The cult of Boomer-blaming attempts to destroy all that. Its relentless critique of the values, attitudes and behaviours attributed to the older generation attacks the intimate myths and stories that make up the families we live by, presenting them all as a self-serving con perpetrated by a generation of sociopaths. In place of the intricate web of meaning spun by generations in families over the years, this politicised narrative proffers a fragile, artificial sense of generational identity, which invites young people to obsess on 'the world we have lost'[39] at the expense of imagining the world they want to become.

CHAPTER 5

Generation fables and the 'end of history'

As generational thinking has become more prominent, it has become something that we need to handle with increasing care. Generationalism – using the language of generations to narrate the social and political – means that we are in danger of taking historical stories way too personally.

Wohl's account of the Generation of 1914 was both an attempt to make historical sense of the First World War generation, and also to engage with the 'formidable wave of generational thinking during the first few decades of the twentieth century' – when wider social and cultural dilemmas were being discussed through the idea of generations. This early generationalism resulted, Wohl suggests, from the convergence of a number of ideas that were already out there – the 'nineteenth-century tradition of the young generation as the vanguard of cultural and political change', the emergence of youth as a clearly defined, organised and 'demographically significant social group', and 'a growing sense of collective historical destiny'.[1] In the absence of a clear political project or moral framework, the Generation of 1914 was a way to understand the recent past, and to get a tentative handle on the kind of person that would shape the future.

A similar thing happened with the Baby Boomers. From the moment the first Boomers reached their teenage years, they were viewed uneasily both as a product of the turmoil of the Sixties, and as the embodiment of cultural and social change. That is why the 'generation unit' dominant in the story of the Baby Boomers was personified by 'New Left' radicals, student protestors, and protagonists of the counterculture, rather than the millions of others who voted Conservative or Republican, focused on their jobs and families, or remained active in the Trade Union movement and the established parties of the Left. The generationalism of the Sixties was as much about the failure of established institutions and ideologies to grasp what was happening as it was about the experience of the kids and the counterculture.

Moving on half a century, the generationalism of the early twenty-first century tells us as much about our present anxieties as it does about the Sixties as a historical period. Whereas the Sixties Boomer was, until fairly recently, a source of wistful fascination, often bringing with it a romanticised nostalgia for a time when people felt they could think and live outside the box, the Boomer-blaming of the present day mobilises the stereotype as an example of everything that is seen to be wrong with the past.

What are generations responsible for?

In his review of Tom Brokaw's book *The Greatest Generation*, Michael Lind scorns Brokaw's claim that the generation that fought the Second World War made breakthroughs in science and medicine, developed new art and literature, 'came to understand the need for Federal civil rights legislation', and 'gave America Medicare'. Lind retorts:

> Generations do not discover cures or write books. And why give credit for civil rights legislation and Medicare to an entire cohort, rather than to the liberals who backed these reforms – particularly when the reforms were opposed by conservative veterans of World War II?[2]

When weighing the balance of the Boomers' credit and culpability for the Sixties, we can ask similar questions. The narrative that gives the Boomer generation all the credit for the glamour and creativity of the Sixties also heaps disproportionate blame upon them for the problems that happened later. The Sixties was a moment in time, which had a wider ripple effect on the young people coming of age: the self-conscious rejection of traditional values, institutions and ideas; the sense that a commitment to social change could be expressed by dropping out of society. A serious attempt to assess the role played by the Boomer generation in all this is not straightforward.

Turbulent events informed a consciousness that things were changing – and as young people, the Boomers were part of that change as much as the change was a part of them. 'Individually, we may not have been the authors of today's flux, uncertainty and lack of social and cultural anchors, but we were at the scene of the crime,' mused Will Hutton sadly in 2010. In wrestling with the 'paradox' of the modern age – 'more freedom but more angst and uncertainty' – he writes:

> The cultural, economic and institutional cornerstones of British life have been shattered – and the way our love of fun was channelled is undoubtedly part of the story. The upside is that some of the old stifling prohibitions and prejudices have gone, hopefully for ever. But the downside is that we have become authors of our own lives without society offering us a compass to follow.[3]

The shattering of 'cultural, economic and institutional cornerstones' – not just of British life, but of societies throughout the Western world – is what makes the Sixties stand out as a significant historical period, after which 'nothing would ever be quite the same again'.[4] To the extent that members of the Baby Boomer generation internalised and expressed the spirit of the age, they were not merely 'at the scene of the crime', but active participants in it. On the other hand, the Boomers were products of much wider social and cultural forces, coming of age in a context where all of the big questions – truth, freedom, right and wrong, humanity's very survival – had been placed on the table by thinkers of a previous generation, still trying to make sense of the horror leading up to the Second World War and the new world that it ushered in.

It is hardly credible to blame the Boomers, in any capacity, for ripping up the certainties of their time, for the world after the Second World War was very far from a stable place. Victory over fascism had come at a hefty price, in terms of both the destruction of human life and infrastructure, and of Western societies' vision of themselves. The speed with which European countries had fallen to an authoritarian leader brought to a head existing doubts about the virtues of democracy and freedom; among the political elites, strategies of appeasement had been accepted as pragmatic by many, while others had flirted openly with the ideology of National Socialism. The Holocaust revealed the horrifying logic of racial assumptions and eugenic ideas that had been openly espoused in Britain and the United States before the war.

Conventions surrounding gender roles and sexual morality had been powerfully challenged by the active role played by women in the munitions factories and military support organisations, and the 'GI babies' born to girls who neither expected to see their fiancés again, nor wanted to wait until the end of an endless war before enjoying moments of intimacy. Wartime nurseries, established so that women could work in the factories, and mass evacuation programmes for young children, flew in the face of conventional ideas about motherhood. And that was only in the countries that won. Conquered nations had to deal with a new legacy of defeat and collaboration. The voice of the latter-day heroes of the French Resistance echoed loudly against the silent shame of the Vichy regime. Germany had to begin a new purge, attempting to cleanse its historical memory through a drawn-out process of 'de-nazification'.[5]

The world into which the Baby Boomers were born was one of destruction and disorientation. Even peacetime turned out not to be especially peaceful, as the United States squared up to its former ally, the Soviet Union – a giant Communist power that simultaneously mocked and terrified the capitalist economies of the West, by seeming to stand for everything the Free World was against. Born in 1949, David Raleigh grew up in 'Dr Strangelove's America', where '[t]he perceived Soviet menace helped to fashion my generation the way the threat of terrorism defines today's'. 'Characterised by a state of tension, competition, conflict, and even threat of nuclear annihilation, the Cold War, the confrontation between the United States and the Soviet Union from the end of the Second World War to roughly 1990, represented a clash of two universalist ideologies, two ways of understanding the world,' Raleigh writes, in his oral history of 'Soviet Baby Boomers'. 'The dispute produced a stratified, bipolar global power structure in which the two superpowers towered over all the rest.'[6]

Present-day depictions of the Swinging Sixties with its folk music and flower power conveniently gloss over this dark side of the Fifties, in which the threat of nuclear war hung over Western nations – and politicians made good use of this as a way of keeping their own populations in check. Raleigh recalls the 'frequent "duck and cover" air raid drills launched by a piercing siren blast' at his Chicago elementary school, where:

> Our humourless physical education teacher . . . supplemented the drills with mandated and improvised fitness regimes and nagging reminders that we should 'eat bread, not candy,' so that we might be as strong as the Russians. On top of this, raised Roman Catholic, I clocked in hundreds of hours on my knees, praying for the conversion of the atheist Communists. During the Cuban Missile Crisis in October 1962, I remember being glued to the television set, fearing an imminent nuclear attack.[7]

The fear, not just of another war but of total global destruction, formed the backdrop to the hippyish 'peace and love' mantra that came later – as well as contributing to the hedonistic injunction to 'live for today', as we could all be dead tomorrow. The repressive regimes of countries in the Soviet bloc, with their barbaric gulags, enforced conformity, and the fear of denunciation or reprisal that seeped into everyday life, were made much of by the elites of Britain and America, as a way of expressing the Western virtues of freedom and democracy. It worked as a strategy of cohering fear about the 'Red Menace', but backfired as citizens of the self-proclaimed Free World grew sensitive to the limits of freedom, political participation, and power that operated at home.

The resulting 'spirit of the Sixties' – a spirit that infected, and came to be personified by, the generation unit now called the 'Baby Boomers' – is essentially a story about history: clashes of ideology, economic and political systems, attempts to challenge established truths and find new forms of activism and idealism. Up until the turn of the century, this was how the story was told, often in a partial or biased fashion, but one which at least took account of the bigger picture. Generations featured as part of this story, but as a product of these wider shifts, not the sole protagonists in a fable of moral neglect and decline. So what has changed, today?

The Boomers haven't changed – apart from getting older. What has changed, since their infancy, is the way we talk about them. From the start, they have been watched, commented upon, and invested with hope and despond in equal measure – first as babies, the happy products of peacetime prosperity; then as long-haired radicals, whom some hoped would overthrow the system for a better world and others feared would destroy what little stability remained of the past; then as parents, struggling to make a living and raise their children in the sharp-toothed Eighties; then as political leaders and statespeople, bringing a much-needed 'generational change' to exhausted party politics. Only recently have the Boomers become folklore demons, and that is something that should worry other generations, too. Because when a generation can become defined according to the mood of the moment, who knows what they'll say about us?

Generation X and the 'end of history'

Writing in 2000, at the dawn of the new century, Howe and Strauss noted that '[u]ntil very recently, the public has been accustomed to nonstop media chatter about bad kids – from mass murderers, hate criminals, and binge drinkers to test failers, test cheaters, drug users, and just all-round spoiled brats.' If you were to believe the US news media in the 1990s, observed these generation theorists:

> [Y]ou'd suppose our schools are full of kids who can't read in the classroom, shoot one another in the hallways, spend their loose change on tongue rings, and couldn't care less who runs the country. According to a national survey, barely one adult in three thinks that today's kids, once grown, will make the world a better place.[8]

The picture of youth was no prettier in Britain. In the late 1990s, I was writing a weekly column for the *Daily Telegraph* newspaper, titled 'My Generation: A weekly look at the latest facts and fallacies about young people'. My brief was to identify some scare story from the week's headlines and dig a bit deeper, to find out what evidence and prejudices these claims were based on. From socially excluded 'NEETS' (young people not in education, employment, or workplace training) to schoolchildren doing too well in their exams ('grade inflation'); from teenage sex leading to pregnancy, chlamydia and Aids to intimations of 'commitment-phobia' and the rise of a 'singleton society'; from alcopop drinking, cigarette smoking and eating disorders, to body-piercing, voter apathy and children suffering from too little or too much self-esteem – there was always something to write about, and it was usually bad.

But my generation was, of course, a different generation to the Boomers. Where the Boomers had made their presence known, Generation X was marked by its absence. A sharp decline in the birth rate, widely attributed to the availability of the contraceptive pill and the legalisation of abortion, marked the end of the postwar baby boom, while Western economies entered a new period of recession and stagflation, marking the end of the postwar economic boom. Everywhere, it seemed, the world turned bleaker.

Writing that '[t]wo unfolding barometers of cultural optimism' in the twentieth century were 'the height of buildings and the height of girls' hem-lines', the journalist Christopher Booker wryly observed:

> In times of high excitement, like the Twenties and the Sixties, when people looked forward to the future with hope, the skyscrapers and the skirts went up. At times when men became fearful of the future, or began to look back nostalgically to the past, as in the early Thirties, the late Forties and the Seventies, they stopped building towers and the skirts came down again. Never, however, did skirts rise so high, nor was there such a universal frenzy for building tower blocks as in the Sixties: and never, in either case, was the reaction so complete as it has been in the Seventies.[9]

Generation X was the product of a peculiar moment in time. It came of age just at the point when the great battles of the twentieth century were drawing to a close. The Second World War had not been followed by a terminal Third, and the Cold War was stuttering to an end, with the Soviet Union busy opening up to the West. Talk of 'glasnost' and 'perestroika' consumed the international news pages of the 1980s, while the British news focused on Prime Minister Margaret Thatcher's all-out war on the working class, symbolised by the crushing of the miners' strike. When the Berlin Wall fell in 1989, it should have been a moment of triumph for capitalism and its cheerleaders on the political right. Thatcher's famous dictum of TINA – 'There Is No Alternative' – reverberated across the world, as the guillotine went down on all debate about whether things could be done differently. The American political theorist Francis Fukuyama suggested that we had reached the 'end of history', in which liberal democracy may come to constitute the 'end point of mankind's ideological evolution' and the 'final form of human government'.[10] The age of political, economic and social alternatives to the advanced capitalist societies of the West was over. This was it.

But it was a strange, ambivalent victory. Amidst the cultural optimism surrounding the postwar economic boom, the grey conformity of the Soviet Union was frequently counterposed to the technicolour freedom of the West, a consumer paradise in which all thoughts and things were possible. By the late Seventies, the grey seemed to have spread to Western societies; by the Eighties, it seemed to seep into their soul.

As the historian Philip Jenkins puts it in *Decade of Nightmares: The end of the sixties and the making of eighties America*, the quest for personal freedom that had come to define the Spirit of the Sixties gave way to a 'marked change in the national mood', bringing with it 'a much deeper pessimism about the state of America and its future, and a growing rejection of liberal orthodoxies'. Throughout the Eighties, many of the 'social and political victories' won in the Sixties had become mainstream; but these coexisted with an aggressive foreign policy agenda, a crippling fear about the dangers posed by drugs and terrorism, and imagery that suggested 'a nation under siege'.[11]

This 'darkening vision' was not, Jenkins suggests, 'the result of a deliberate policy of any particular group or agency', but a consequence of a narrowing political debate and historical imagination. 'At home and abroad, the post-1975 public was less willing to see social dangers in terms of historical forces, instead preferring a strict moralistic division: problems were a matter of evil, not dysfunction,' he writes.[12] In place of the clashes of ideology that had dominated the early part of the twentieth century, we had the 'culture wars' of the 1980s: bitter, entrenched battles over 'family values', questions of personal morality, education and the raising of children. Generationalism leapt into the void left by the end of politics – not to present the younger generation as the vanguard of cultural and political change, but to blame the Sixties generation for screwing up their kids.

'During the 1980s and 1990s debates in Britain about social, political and economic affairs have been heavily circumscribed by the discourses of the New Right, which has made for a heightened public discussion of children and childhood,' wrote Jane Pilcher and Stephen Wagg in 1996, in their introduction to a collection of essays about 'Thatcher's Children'. The New Right's representation of children often had them appearing 'to hover between Heaven and Hell', in a rhetoric that drew on wider political and cultural motifs:

> In Heaven, the male head of their nuclear family, doubtless an entrepreneur now liberated from state control and trade union interference, provides them with love, discipline and selective education. In Hell, children are menaced by a gallery of social demons: single mothers, absent fathers, muddle-headed social workers failing to detect abuse, drug pushers, paedophiles, 'do-gooders' reluctant to punish young offenders, 'trendy' teachers, doctors providing contraceptives for young girls, media executives purveying violent and sexually explicit material, and so on.[13]

In the New Right iconography described by Pilcher and Wagg, the Sixties generation was associated with the Hellish vision of permissive morality and a decline in the authority and autonomy of the family. But conservative moralism was only one side of the argument. The political Left had become defensive – unhappy with the 'liberalising' economic forces associated with the Sixties, and conflicted about the narrative of individual freedom that seemed to justify a fragmentation of collective solidarities and the institutions of the welfare state.[14]

What Jenkins terms 'the politics of children' gave a framework through which a range of anxieties about the present and the future were aired, both on the Right and the liberal Left. While the

Right painted young people as amoral drug-takers and pregnant teenagers, the liberal Left had them standing in unemployment lines and sinking into misery, the disaffected victims of a world that doesn't care. On some issues, such as sexual violence and pornography, radical feminists and conservative moralists found themselves to be strange bedfellows; on others, like the morality of abortion or the acceptability of divorce, they were poles apart. But all sides seemed to agree that the kids were somehow in crisis, and just about everything that they did – or didn't do – was offered up as evidence of this fact.

This was the context in which Generation X came of age: a time of downbeat uncertainty, in which a lot was said about them, but nothing much expected of them. In early adulthood, as in birth, it became a generation defined by what it was not – not the Baby Boomers, but nothing else either; a generation more done to than doing.

The book that came to define that generation, and gave it its label, was Douglas Coupland's 1991 novel *Generation X*. This book, wrote music journalist Jon Savage in 1993, seemed to define 'a new generation of middle-class anomie: the twentysomething slackers, who dropped out of work just as the early Eighties yuppies celebrated it. Its characters seemed narcoleptic, drifting through a world of pop culture references devoid of all meaning, postmodernism anthropomorphised.'[15] It was this sense of aimless drifting that gave Generation X its other moniker – the 'slacker generation' – and came to define ideas about youth in the 1980s and 1990s.

The apparent reluctance to grow up was as frustrating to commentators and academics as the careless cynicism with which Xers refused to look or behave like innocent kids. The Boomer stereotype, of carefree young people with flowing silk scarves and flowers in their hair, strumming guitars while sharing a joint and pondering a world of peace and love, stood in stark contrast to the self-destructive self-absorption apparently exhibited by the generation that came next: the Baby Busters, whose orientation to the world was negative. 'Today's teenagers, early victims of Eighties economic cutbacks and late-Eighties recession, have almost no values in America,' wrote Savage. Musically, the anthem of the early 1990s was Nirvana's 'Smells Like Teen Spirit', which also spoke directly to disenchantment. Like the Californian slackers of Coupland's novel *Generation X*, Nirvana spoke to a particular, middle-class sensibility associated with the Nineties generation: 'the artier, more nihilist Seattle groups are more popular with students', wrote Savage, 'while the real dead-end kids prefer the heroic, damaged bombast of Guns N' Roses'. Neither the tragic brilliance of Nirvana's Kurt Cobain, nor the meaningless antics of Coupland's characters, were actually representative of the generation as a whole. But in the symbolic web of generationalism, these cultural icons spoke to the alienation experienced by a section of middle-class youth towards the end of the twentieth century, and reflected a wider sense that society had somehow lost its children.

'"Smells Like Teen Spirit",' wrote Savage back then, was the 'harbinger' of a generation gap 'between the 25 and 45-year-old baby-boomers whose taste had dominated the record industry and the 15 to 24-year-old "baby busters"'. When the Baby Boomers suddenly returned to centre stage, with the election of President Bill Clinton in 1992, it was to a sense of palpable relief: the hangover was over, and the party could begin again. But as Savage astutely commented:

> Clinton's election may have created a climate of hope, but these oblique, shadowy messages from the baby-busters pose an awkward question for a president so associated with the baby-boomer generation, a president at whose inauguration Stevie Wonder, Aretha Franklin and Bob Dylan all sang. How is the first pop-culture president going to involve today's teenagers in the society they will inherit?'[16]

As generationalism got political, that turned out to be the biggest question.

Generation as a political identity

'[U]ntil the election of Bill Clinton as President of the United States, the sixties generation promised only to disappoint on the playing field of politics,' began a lengthy editorial in the *Guardian* in 1992. The editorial argued that '[n]o other generation had, in its youth, wrought such a profound change on the cultural landscape of the western world' – that was partly to do with 'sheer numbers', and partly to do with its 'remarkably radical and innovative' ideas:

> This was the generation that gave sudden birth to the first serious critique of the post-war welfare society – to gender politics, to personal politics, to environmental politics, and to generational politics as well.[17]

Clinton's election marked the point at which generationalism became institutionalised, as a way of discussing political problems and solutions. Until the 1990s, the impact of the Sixties generation had been mainly cultural; it came to be known for pursuing its vision of a better world through cultural institutions of education and the arts, as '[t]he revolting students of the 1960s' became the 'revolting teachers' of the 1980s, 'reproducing themselves by teaching as received wisdom what they furiously asserted against the wisdom received from their own teachers'.[18] Believing that 'the personal is political', the radicals of this time sought to change ideas and conventions through their actions and behaviour in society, seeking a 'permanent fusion of the everyday and history' that stood in stark contrast to the aloof institutions of representative democracy.[19]

When Clinton came along, generationalism suddenly shifted gear. His election in 1992 was reported far and wide as symbolising a new generation in politics;[20] a time of 'Woodstock in Washington', when 'the baby-boomers' coming of age is being proclaimed everywhere, George Bush is gloomily handing over the office of president to a man young enough to be his son and a sticky wave of Sixties nostalgia is sweeping the nation'.[21] For those who saw themselves on the liberal left – and many still hovering uncertainly around the political right – the sense that Sixties radicalism was now taking the reins in the most powerful nation in the world was greeted with cautious optimism. Clintonism seemed to mark a break from the exhausted political framework of the Cold War years, with a novel set of policies that appealed neither to the market-first approach of the Right, or the statist solutions of the Left.

Clinton's 'Third Way' – the approach later taken on by Tony Blair's New Labour Party in the United Kingdom – was a self-consciously pragmatic, centrist vision that offered a way to live within the confines of capitalism by curbing some of its excesses. The optimism came from a sense that yes, something had to change. The caution was about what, exactly, that change would involve – and the kind of people who were promising to do it. 'The sixties generation was, above all, one of critique and opposition' opined the *Guardian*:

> It was a rebellion against 1945, against the long boom, consumer society, social and moral conservatism, and the Vietnam war. It may have defined new cultural mores, but it failed to define a new political agenda. It came from the Left, and saw itself as being vaguely on the Left, but its rebellion was fundamentally against the Left and its achievements, against the edifices of post-war social democracy. The sixties generation laid siege to both the Labour Party and the Democratic Party. It felt scant rapport with the post-war Left; and yet it had nowhere else to go. It was a generation which came to live in a political diaspora.[22]

An article in the *Mail on Sunday* put it more succinctly: 'Now it's their turn to rule . . . but what, you might wonder, do you do as a sequel to 12 years of protest?'[23]

'What you do', it turned out, is to re-make politics in your own generational image. 'Bill Clinton (b. 1946) is touchingly proud of being the first baby-boomer candidate for the White House,' wrote Peter Stothard. 'He wants "generational change" and the election of the first president of the 21st century: himself.'[24] The generation talk that was central to the Clinton election firmly established that old was bad and young was good; that the past was another country and the future could only be paved by the new, Third Way. Politics underwent a cultural makeover, bringing issues of identity and lifestyle to the fore, and pushing the old politics of class firmly into the background.

In a similar fashion, Clinton's British acolyte Tony Blair (b. 1953) rode to prime ministerial power in 1997 on a platform of being anything but 'old'. Under his radical midwifery, the Labour Party was reborn as 'New Labour', on a mission to build a 'Young Britain'. Pop stars were invited to 10 Downing Street to showcase 'Cool Britannia', and a host of young, female Members of Parliament were brought in to make up the face of this new dawn. Central to New Labour's modernisation agenda was a determination to put the politics of class firmly behind it, consigned to the dustbin of twentieth-century history.

The transformation of Labour into the preferred party of the middle class is a well-documented story, beginning with Blair's highly symbolic ditching of 'Clause Four' of the Labour Party constitution back in 1995. This sent a clear signal about the kind of politics New Labour would pursue – not a commitment to socialism by means of the 'common ownership of the means of production, distribution, and exchange', but commitment to capitalism by means of a 'dynamic economy'.[25] It also sent a clear message about the kind of people it wanted to engage with. In New Britain, trade unions and flat caps were out; lawyers, networks and journalists were in. New Labour set itself up as a thinking person's dinner party, far more concerned about spinning to the media than talking to the electorate. Over the years, its original working-class base has peeled off – some to the Tories, some to the anti-immigration UK Independence Party, and some to the shadows of non-representation. The more recent Labour Party makeover, under Jeremy Corbyn, may have the party flying the Red Flag of re-nationalisation, but its base remains decidedly middle class.

Across the Western world, politics has been transformed into a centrist, managerial process. There are many insightful critiques of this historical moment, and its implications for democratic institutions in the twenty-first century – all raising the kind of questions that have been slammed back on the table with the rise of populist movements aiming their fire at the 'liberal elites' that have shut their doors and minds to working-class people and the problems they face. But just as blaming the Sixties generation for the Sixties accords the kids of the counterculture far too much influence over their historical moment, blaming the Baby Boomer generation as a whole for Clinton, Blair and everything that has happened to politics subsequently is decidedly unfair.

The Clinton and Blair administrations played the generation card in setting themselves up as the new, young brooms. This resonated with a wider political and media narrative that sought to make sense of the new landscape, and saw in the mythology of the Sixties a way to give shape and glamour to the hotch-potch of policies and prejudices that made up the 'Third Way' of the Nineties. The Sixties generation became fused with the outlook and policies promoted by a suddenly powerful 'liberal elite' – a political identity that drew its authority from a generational location, rather than from established ideologies or party-political loyalties.

The presentation of Clinton as the symbol of the Sixties generation consolidated a simplistic set of cultural memes about this particular generation unit, consisting of student protests, soft drugs, New Left politics, self-obsession and sexual promiscuity, and sought a direct continuity between the Sixties zeitgeist and the politics promoted by the White House in the Nineties. Many actual Baby Boomers, of course, were bemused by the idea that Clinton was somehow their generational mascot. 'On the issues, he'll more than "do" – he's almost a neo-liberal's dream,' wrote Mickey Kaus in

1992. Kaus explained that he would vote for Clinton because he would be a better president than his opponents – but, he wondered aloud, 'Why him? I mean, we marched, we took drugs, we dodged tear gas – and this is our contribution, this non-inhaling, student-body president?'[26]

In a context already heavily influenced by personality politics and the culture wars, the construction of a generational identity around the spirit of the Sixties played well, at least at first. The hope that greeted Bill Clinton's win in 1992 was at least prompted by a desire for a new kind of politics, represented by a new 'type' of politician emerging from a generation that had come to stand for something. But when the music stopped, it brought the other Baby Boomers down as well.

Backlash against the Boomers

'I am not now nor have I ever been a Clintonite, but when Jeb Bush reportedly said . . . that "if someone wants to run a campaign about '90s nostalgia, it's not going to be very successful," I think he was being wishful,' writes a nostalgic Kurt Andersen in the *New York Times*, in an article on why the 1990s was 'the best decade ever'. From a growing economy to the prospect of world peace, from the technology boom to the *Harry Potter* novels and the 'sudden availability of excellent coffee', the Nineties was 'simply the happiest decade of our American lifetimes'. 'Were there real problems in the '90s?' wonders Andersen. 'Of course. But they weren't obvious, so . . . we were blissfully ignorant!' For example:

> When the House and Senate passed by overwhelming bipartisan majorities and President Clinton signed the Financial Services Modernization Act of 1999, doing away with the firewalls between investment banks and commercial banks, the change seemed inevitable, sensible, modern – not a precursor of the 2008 Wall Street crash. When a jihadist truck bomb detonated in the parking garage below the north tower of the

World Trade Center in 1993, we were alarmed only briefly, figuring it for a crazy one-off rather than a first strike in a long struggle.[27]

Andersen's nostalgia-trip gives a wry reminder of what the success story of the Nineties was really all about. The 'end of history', brought about by the defeat of any economic alternative to capitalism, allowed for a hiatus in historic tensions and the emergence of a tentative sentiment that Western society's many problems could be peacefully managed. Newly financialised economies and the dot.com boom meant that there was cash floating around to pay for shiny regeneration schemes, and with the Baby Boomers in the driving seat it seemed to many that this was the Sixties coming around again. 'It was a great decade to be young,' reminisces gallerist and club owner Alex Proud in the *Daily Telegraph*:

> We had cool music. We had cool drugs. We had (sort of) cool politicians, some of the time. We thought history had ended in a good way. Anything seemed possible. Dare I say it, the Nineties were our Sixties.[28]

But history never repeats itself – and the desire to see the Nineties as an echo of the Sixties reflected the exhaustion of political life, rather than the start of a new economic boom or cultural revolution. As the century turned, ushering in a new era of terrorism and economic crisis, grandiose claims that Clinton's arrival in the White House had marked 'the political legitimation of the cultural advances ushered in by the Sixties'[29] quickly gave way to a suspicion that the Clinton-Blair administrations had merely been playing at politics and economics. They had bought into the fantasy of postmaterialism, relying on the chimera of finance capital and the never-never of national debt to keep the bubble afloat.

In the United States, Bill Clinton stood exposed as sexually feckless and ideologically compromised. In Britain, Tony Blair went from being applauded as the fresh face of 'New Britain' to being despised as a 'Tony Bliar', a fake, 'perma-tanned freeloader'[30] who had put the economy in hock and followed Clinton's successor George W. Bush (another Baby Boomer) into a bloody, hopeless war in Iraq. And the Baby Boomer generation, so recently hailed as the hope for the future, now stood demonised as the cause of the problem.

To some extent, this was the predictable flipside of the 'generational politics' promoted by Clinton and Blair. Having drawn on the mystique of the Sixties generation to give energy and credibility to their shallow, managerialist brand of consensus politics, they set the whole generation up as the focus for blame when the politics went wrong. Hence Bruce Cannon Gibney's broadside against the Boomers' 'generational representatives' in Congress who, for 'purely selfish reasons . . . unraveled the social fabric woven by previous generations' – and who, by the 2016 Presidential election, were so determined to consolidate their generational domination that they were prepared to ignore the public entirely:

> That Clinton and Trump were the two most unpopular presidential candidates in decades, if not since the Civil War, deterred the Boomer machine not a whit, because they all agreed on what mattered.[31]

Of course, there was a lot wrong with the Clinton and Blair administrations. As discussed in Chapters 7 and 8, the continuing inability of mainstream parties to come to terms with the failure of the 'Third Way' and to present a credible alternative is having some deeply destabilising consequences across the Western world. Yet this is not the Boomers' fault – and attempts to peg the current political malaise to the apparent pathology of a whole generation is as illogical as it is unfair. On the one hand, Boomer politicians are blamed for embodying the 'liberal elite' that voters are kicking off against; on the other, they are blamed for being the grumpy old gits in Hillary Clinton's 'basket of deplorables'. They can't win either way.

And tempting as it is to blame the generational politics card played by Bill Clinton and Tony Blair for the cult of all-round Boomer-bashing, this is only part of the story. In a previous study, I analysed how the British media has discussed the Baby Boomers over a period of time, from the mid-1980s to 2011.[32] I found, to some surprise, that although some have moaned about the Boomers for a long time, it was not until around 2006 that generation chatter reached the level of negativity that we have seen in recent years. This was not because the Baby Boomers had done anything new, but because of the ease with which political elites reached for generational arguments to evade confronting the crises of the moment.

The developing sentiment of generational grievance had two significant catalysts, in the big crises of the early twenty-first century – in 2001, the terrorist attacks of 9/11, and the global financial crisis of 2007–8. These events had a particular, and profound, impact on the young people coming of age in this fearful new dawn. The 'spirit of the Sixties' – experimental, freedom-loving, boundary-pushing – had never seemed so ethereal. And those who embodied that spirit were no longer cast as the bright beacons of the counterculture, but seniors teetering on the brink of retirement, and about to drain what little was left of the national wealth with their greedy houses, rapacious pensions and inflated Social Security entitlements.

9/11, and the bombings and shootings that followed in major cities around Europe, brought to the surface a whole number of lurking fears that went way beyond the danger to individual lives. Commentators freely proclaimed the existential threat posed to Western societies by Islamist terrorism, and politicians responded by launching air strikes against countries in the Middle East and repressive 'anti-terrorist' initiatives in their homelands. Rather than responding with an assertion of the importance of freedom and democracy, politicians and commentators worried aloud that these aspects of Western civilisation had made societies not only vulnerable to jihadist attacks, but also somehow responsible for them. The populations of America and Europe were cajoled to watch out for suspicious talk or behaviour amongst their Muslim colleagues, neighbours and children, and at the same time were warned not to criticise Islam for fear of sparking resentment and reprisal. Commitment to freedom was recycled as a quest for 'freedom from fear', whereby citizens were cajoled to trade in their liberties for protection from the shadowy threat posed by random, disaffected groups or individuals coming both from abroad, and from within our own communities.

The effect of the 9/11 attacks was to concretise many anxieties that were already lurking. For the generation coming of age at the turn of the Millennium, the defining event of their youth was presented as a problem of open space, open borders and a surfeit of freedom: all things that had once been positively associated with the Sixties generation.[33] Where the Sixties generation put themselves at the vanguard of change and demonstrated noisily against war, censorship and authoritarianism, 9/11 seemed to bring about a new world that was out of everybody's control.

The second big event was the global financial crisis, sparked by a crash in the US sub-prime mortgage market. The depth of this crisis, and the speed with which it spread, revealed the underlying weakness of advanced economies and shone a spotlight on the parasitical workings of finance capital. Aside from the effect on jobs, wages and public spending, the role played by the housing market in this crisis massively heightened people's sense of insecurity. Governments scrambled to limit the repercussions by imposing austerity budgets on public spending, and adjusting expectations downwards. Problems of economic and social policy were reframed as natural problems of an 'ageing' society, in which scarce resources were being depleted by having too many old people greedily hanging onto their current standard of living.

The consolidation of a sentiment of limits and fear has given the pessimism of the early twenty-first century a darker and more enduring hue than at any point in the postwar period. The British journalist Yvonne Roberts, born in 1948, sums up the difference between the spirit of that age and our current 'cross-generational pessimism' about the prospects of the young. 'Pessimism is not new,' she writes, noting that '[i]n the 1970s and 80s, inflation reached 21%, three million people were on the dole, poverty was soaring and Thatcherism had laid waste to manufacturing and industry'. Even so, back then 'life, money and opportunities had an elasticity that they lack today'. She recalls:

> On a full grant, and from a working-class background, I was one of the 8% who went to university, charged up with notions of (women's) liberation, revolution and an envy of Mary Quant's unaffordable wardrobe. My best friend had left school at 16 and moved up the managerial ladder, earning what our mothers called 'a good wage'. Pessimism was the national trait but we all had hope. I was 28 and single when I put a deposit on a tiny flat; my parents were in their late 40s before they took out a hefty mortgage on a modest bungalow.[34]

Today, argues Roberts, 'the escalator that for decades ensured the younger generation had a better standard of living than their parents has stalled', and 'Britain – along with Greece – is now the most pessimistic among the advanced economic countries, a mood that has potentially catastrophic implications for a country's well-being and resilience'. The effects of stalling social mobility, along with other features of economic stagnation, on young expectations and opportunities is discussed in the next chapter, and Roberts is right to suggest that this contributes to the widespread sentiment of cultural pessimism, with its envy of the 'lucky, cocky' Sixties generation who at least had dreams of a better future. But in endorsing the 'invaluable work' of the Intergenerational Commission, Roberts buys into the representation of deep-seated economic conflicts as a problem of generational inequalities.

For Millennials, '[e]ven at a time when unemployment is at its lowest and inflation minimal, aspirations of having a home, a fulfilling job and a higher income than the generation before are being extinguished', writes Roberts. In contrast:

> Some of us baby boomers, newly retired, are apparently living in an experiential paradise – cruising the globe, contemplating buying a second home – albeit dazed at how good pensions, secure employment and the fluke of buying at the outset of a period of rapid house inflation has catapulted us so much further, financially, than many of us expected to travel.[35]

Roberts argues that the Intergenerational Commission's policy agenda will help to 'repair the damage done to confidence, trust, wellbeing and optimism by a situation where 90% of people manage on increasingly less, while the other 10% rapidly accrue more and more'. But the Baby Boomers are not the wealthiest 10%, and it is hard to see how the cause of 'trust, wellbeing and optimism' will be served by evasive campaigns to blame Grandma's holidays for young people's difficulties. If the best idea we have for reducing economic inequality is to boot a few lucky old people out of their 'experiential paradise', we really do have something to worry about.

Passing the buck

In the following chapters, I challenge the claims made about the Boomers as a massive, monolithic voting bloc, whose disproportionate power has come to put 'democracy at risk',[36] and the idea that this greedy, entitled gang of wrinklies gambled away our economic future. Neither of these charges stands up to scrutiny: they are myths that have been propagated to deflect the blame for bad political decisions and deep-rooted economic problems. But they have had a powerful effect on the way in which we have come to think about the Millennials: the key players in the generational drama of our present times.

In her insightful review of 'what the world calls millennials',[37] Kate Lyons finds that the labels differ according to the economic and cultural circumstances that preoccupy the opinion-formers in different countries. In Spain, they are nicknamed 'Generación Ni-Ni, a demographic driven by national economic ruin into a limbo of neither work nor study – ni trabaja, ni estudia'. In Germany, Millennials have been called Generation Maybe, 'a group who are well educated, highly connected, multilingual, globally minded, with myriad opportunities, but who are so over-whelmed by the possibilities available to them that they commit to nothing'; in Sweden, parental overprotection has been presented as the defining characteristic of 'the Curling Generation, named for the sport in which teammates furiously sweep the ice in front of their stone to make sure its journey is smooth and unhindered'. Millennials' parents, claim their critics, have 'cleared any obstacles from their children's paths . . . refusing to set boundaries, defending them to teachers who try to discipline them, even going with them to job interviews'.

The Millennials, writes Lyons, are also 'Generation Terror':

This, after all, is a group of people whose defining geopolitical moment was 9/11 and the 'war on terror' that followed. Terrorism is to them what the threat of nuclear war was to boomers and older members of Gen X. Instead of armaggedon pamphlets and sirens, they have airport security, metro lock-downs and constant warnings to report suspicious behaviour. They have grown up with images of mass murder – in universi-ties, nightclubs, army barracks, trains, buses, museums, cafes, beaches and city streets – and therefore have everywhere to fear.[38]

Lyons's article, unlike so many of the commentaries desperate to nail 'the thing' that is different about Millennials, neatly demonstrates that the ongoing debates about Millennials and their predicament are really a discussion about us. The things that are highlighted by the various labels – economic woes, demographic changes, terrorism and fear, a drift away from commitment, a culture of what has been called 'intensive', 'hyper', or even 'paranoid' parenting – represent genuine problems of the world today. But when viewed through the distorting lens of generationalism, they appear as features that are peculiar to young people, and which affect them and them alone.

This is a problem emphasised by Christian Smith and colleagues in their unsettling study of young American adults, *Lost in Transition: The dark side of emerging adulthood.* Smith criticises the commonly held assumption that 'whatever problems youth have are entirely *their* problems, unrelated to the adults around them'. By perceiving young adults' problems as evidence of some kind of deficit of maturity or attitude, he argues, proponents of 'this well-worn cultural script' evade the discomfiting fact that 'most of the problems in the lives of youth have their origins in the larger world into which the youth are being socialized', whether these be the 'problems of the adults in their immediate lives – their parents, relatives, teachers, family friends, and so on', or, more broadly, 'the priorities, values, practices, and institutions of the larger adult world they inhabit – schools, mass media, shopping malls, advertising, and the like'. The reality, argues Smith, 'is that emerging adult problems are ultimately problems of our entire culture and society'.[39]

Acknowledging that so-called 'Millennial problems' are really problems confronting all of us should not mean that we discount the particular ways in which younger people understand and experience their lives. On the contrary: if we know anything about generations, it is that people born in different times come to understand the world in different ways, because their relationship to the events that frame their experience is historically distinct. Although it is fair to criticise the historical ignorance embedded in claims that, for example, the Baby Boomers are all (and were always) lucky and rich, it is not fair to criticise young people for not truly understanding what it meant to grow up through the Sixties, Seventies and Eighties, when the world was quite a different place. 'Teenagers think they are the first people ever to have had these problems,' I once told my daughter, then aged 12, as I offered the wisdom of my experience to resolve some random friendship issue. Quick as a flash, she corrected me: 'It's the first time *we* have ever had these problems.' And, of course, she was right.

Understanding the specific ways in which today's young people work up their experiences means engaging with the deeper reasons why. This means acknowledging that young people are not growing up in a perfect world; they, like their elders, are living in uneasy times, where there is no blueprint as to how things will go. Whereas older people at least have a memory of other difficult moments in history, which were muddled through and sometimes resolved, the young have no such anchor – and increasingly, it seems that their elders are refusing to give them a steer. By pandering to the panic and self-pity narrated through the cultural script of Millennial angst, and inciting young people to under-stand the problems of the world through the distorted prism of generational grievance, Boomer-blamers are attacking the only thing that gives young people any sense of security and stability in this uncertain world: the conversation between the generations.

CHAPTER 6

Millennial fears

'As a group, Millennials are unlike any other youth generation in living memory,' wrote Howe and Strauss in their 2000 book *Millennials Rising*:

> They are more numerous, more affluent, better educated, and more ethnically diverse. More important, they are beginning to manifest a wide array of positive social habits that older Americans no longer associate with youth, including a new focus on teamwork, achievement, modesty, and good conduct. Only a few years from now, this can-do youth revolution will overwhelm the cynics and pessimists. Over the next decade, the Millennial Generation will entirely recast the image of youth from downbeat and alienated to upbeat and engaged – with potentially seismic consequences for America.[1]

Howe and Strauss are widely credited with coining the label 'Millennials', and their upbeat predictions about 'the next great generation' were widely shared in the mid- to late 1990s. In contrast to the wasters of Generation X, the kids born in the early 1980s were imagined to be optimistic, pragmatic, constructive and creative. They may have been the 'Echo Boomers', but not so troublesome as the Sixties generation; less interested in rebelling than in getting with the programme. Initially, and unimaginatively, labelled as 'Generation Y', the 'Millennials' moniker seemed to capture something positively future-oriented.

But this was all written before 9/11, before the global financial crisis, and before the Boomers became so clearly perceived as Bad. Once the twenty-first century actually started, the script assigned to the Millennials lurched wildly in the direction of pessimism. They were fearful, depressed and impoverished, the victims of 'generational theft' and social media, and their inability to cope with the world was evidenced by rocketing rates of mental illness. Rather than coming along to save the world, they were condemned to be perpetually victimised by it: not a glowing alternative to Generation X after all, but the next chapter in the dystopia. They were 'Generation Me', wrote Jean Twenge in her explanation of 'why today's young Americans are more confident, assertive, entitled – and more miserable than ever before'.[2] (As the 'Me Generation', of course, Millennials have merely inherited a label that was routinely applied to their Boomer parents.) They were the 'Snowflake Generation', fragile and over-sensitive, all highly aware of their own, individual specialness. But they were also the 'Jilted Generation' or 'Generation Debt', whose future had been 'sold out for student loans, bad jobs, no benefits, and tax cuts for rich geezers'.[3]

So what are we to make of the Millennials, these kids about whom such a lot has been said – much of it contradictory, all of it one-sided, and most of it said by people old enough to be their parents? This chapter looks beneath the hype and the horror that characterises Millennial myth-making, and explores the reality that confronts young people in their struggles with education, work and housing. Their experience, like that of the generations before them, is a mixed one. In some respects, they have more opportunities, more stuff and more choices than young people have ever had; in others, their lives, aspirations and freedoms are extraordinarily constrained.

As ever, young people's outlook is shaped by wider factors, including their social class and where they live. The metropolitan, middle-class voice of Millennial angst that dominates the head-lines is no more representative of the generation as a whole than claiming that the nihilism of Nirvana represents all members of 'Generation X'. And as my students remarked, there seems to be a world of difference between those Millennials who grew up in the shiny Nineties and came of age just before 9/11, and those reared in the fear and austerity of the early twenty-first century. But they can be plausibly seen as a distinct generation, nonetheless. The wider social context that shaped the Millennials is different from that which shaped the Generation X that preceded them, and the Baby Boomers that bred them. The descriptor 'Millennial', writes Shaun Scott in *Millennials and the Moments that Made Us*, is not only a 'noun that refers to an age cohort':

> It is also an adjective that refers to a historical situation defined by the technology, politics, and pop culture of the 21st century. One can speak of 'Millennials' as a group, and also refer to a 'millennial' era that previous generations are also living through. Not everybody is a Millennial, but we're all passing through a millennial moment in history.[4]

What is distinct about growing up in the early twenty-first century is not the experience of economic hardship, the prospect of violence and war, or even the confusion and anxiety experienced by young people in early adulthood, as they struggle to make sense of themselves and the world around them. Compared to the spectre of global destruction that stalked the world during the two world wars, or the nuke-induced Armageddon that weighed on young people's imaginations during the Cold War, the present-day fears of crazed gunmen, suicide bombers and murderous van drivers does not seem like something that, in itself, should define a generation. The much-discussed elements of Millennial angst that relate to depressed wages, insecure jobs, inflated housing costs and student debt can similarly be compared to the difficulties faced by young people at various points throughout history, and declared to be nothing particularly new, or even all that bad. 'Stop whinging!' say the grown-ups. 'You've got iPhones!'

But Millennials experience these problems as *new to them*, and in a particular context. They have grown up at a time when cautious hopes for the future jostle with a heightened sense of fear; when 'the young' are hailed as the answer to questions that nobody has quite worked out; when a prevalent generationalist outlook presents young people's problems as a direct consequence of the mistakes made by their parents' generation, which they are expected to suffer from rather than overcome. These features of our 'millennial moment' affect both how young adults make sense of the zeitgeist, and how they express it.

Millennial angst: What are they moaning about?

The 'Millennial voice' that finds its way into media debates about generational conflict is invariably cherry-picked from a particular kind of young person, saying a particular kind of thing. These appointed, or self-appointed, voices of youth tend to be the epitome of middle-class success – articulate, well-groomed and so confident in their privilege that they continually apologise for it. They issue the same list of complaints – the cost of education and housing, the insecurity of jobs and the unfairness of unpaid internships – and blame their parents for helping them navigate these difficulties, thereby preventing them growing into independent, well-rounded adults.

A painful example of Millennial angst is provided by the journalist Francesca Angelini, writing in the *Sunday Times* under the headline 'Trapped in Kidulthood: No job security. No pensions. No hope of being better off than our parents. No wonder my generation won't grow up.'[5] Angelini describes her 'alarm' upon returning from a month-long backpacking trip in 2008, having diligently ignored news of the global financial crisis, to find the UK government's 'social mobility tsar' claiming that 'for the first time in a century, the current generation of middle-class children will be worse off than their parents'. This sets her worrying about the difference between the future opportunities she believed to be her birthright, and the future that is now forecast for people like her:

> I grew up in a four-bedroom house in Blackheath, southeast London. My twin brother and I went to good schools and we spent summers lolling about on a beach in Italy. My parents run their own businesses in the arts world and since I have never had any ambitions to work in the lucrative fields of law or finance, I had always assumed that my lifestyle would be similar to theirs.
>
> It is not turning out that way, however.
>
> Like most of my generation who graduated into the worst recession since the Second World War, I do not have a foot on the housing ladder. I do not even have a secure job, let alone a pension. I am saddled with thousands of pounds of student debt, and my father still pays my phone bill.

Angelini contrasts the free higher education and subsidised accommodation enjoyed by her Baby Boomer mother with the debt accrued by her own 'five pleasant years' at Oxford University. By her late 20s, not only was Angelini's mother 'earning enough to save money each month, but there were few stresses in the job market'. This, suggests Angelini, might account for her mother's reaction ('that is ludicrous') to her demand that 'I needed her to support me through unpaid journalism internships'. Although Angelini has now secured her job, she tells us, 'my income in real terms is less than my mother's at my age'; and '[f]ar from having a stress-free existence, as she did, the uncertain employment market makes me anxious about my lack of job security'.

Angelini, at the age of 27, has no savings. (What 27-year-old ever did?) She tried, she says, but 'I realised it was futile and blew the money on a trip to the Burning Man event in Nevada so

I could hang out with other disenfranchised, anxiety-riddled, middle-class freelancers'. The prospect of owning a property 'remains a distant dream' – compared to her mother, who, at the same age, had jumped on the ladder 'thanks to a convenient loan of £10,000 from her father', and proceeded to upgrade property and prices throughout her adult life. House prices are 'continuing to increase out of all proportion to average earnings', complains Angelini, and '[t]o make matters worse, all the buying power resides with the baby boomers who, like my mother, have watched their equity balloon since the 1970s'. Rising rents mean that 'one-third of us under-35s are living at home with our parents, sneaking one-night stands out of the back door and helping ourselves to fine cheeses that we definitely did not buy'.

Having rented in London for three years, Angelini has now bitten the bullet and is 'in the fortunate position of renting the flat my mother owns at London Bridge'; she spends just over one third of her monthly income on rent ('which goes towards my mother's mortgage'). The overriding effect of all this on Angelini's generation, she says, is ' "kidulthood": we are not coming of age'. 'Deprived of commitments and responsibilities, it is not surprising that, like most of my contemporaries, I am stuck in a state of "adultescence", making plans that extend only as far as the weekend,' she muses. And although she acknowledges that sociologists have pointed to deeper, cultural reasons that have blunted young people's aspiration to independence, she clearly doesn't believe that. 'Perhaps it is time to grow up,' she concludes bitterly:

> And if I want to have it all, that might mean gritting my teeth, forgetting feminism and financial independence, and marrying a red-trousered banker with a signet ring and a three-bedroom house in a posh part of London.[6]

If, by this point, you are wanting to shake Angelini out of her cynical self-absorption with a few choice reminders about history, you are not alone. Angelini's tirade against the better-off Baby

Boomers is followed by a spirited riposte from her mother, who notes that '[i]n many ways, you have it very good and far better than we did, especially as a woman'.[7] Although 'the economy looks gloomy and perhaps your future seems bleak', she reminds her daughter that 'we also lived through belt-tightening years in the late 1970s and early 1980s so you are not unique'. Young women 'have access to jobs today that were almost impenetrable for women in 1980', the Sixties generation 'fought long and hard for equal opportunities and you are reaping those rewards'. Angelini, says her mother, is 'mostly unaware of the meteoric rise in the standard of living that has taken place over the past decades', illustrated by the wide range of leisure and travel opportunities, consumer goods, new technology, and much better food:

> There has been a tidal change in eating habits and foods available. When I called you last week, you couldn't talk for long because you were too busy cooking a Lebanese chicken dish with exotic spices. When I was your age, my diet largely consisted of quiche, jacket potatoes, hundreds of kilograms of baked beans and pink blancmange (a gelatine dish filled with those additives you avoid). An 'avocado pear' was a luxury, buffalo mozzarella unknown and garlic suspicious.

Angelini's mother concludes, affectionately, that 'perhaps you need to stop worrying and complaining about baby boomers, and realise you're actually quite lucky'.[8]

This daughter-mother exchange, clearly stylised for the media, speaks to many of the themes in the 'generation wars' narrative. Social problems – primarily, those to do with the economy – are swiftly internalised and repackaged as individualised, existential issues. The kind of problem that would once have been seen as a social concern, to be debated and changed through some kind of political action, is reframed as a one-dimensional problem of generational injustice. This is reinforced by a stubborn reluctance to acknowledge where the situation for young people – particularly, bright young middle-class women – is actually more favourable than it was back when avoiding unwanted pregnancy and getting a university degree were hurdles enough for many women.

As we have seen, the 'voice of generations' that has been heard throughout history – from the First World War poets to the student radicals of the Baby Boomer generation and the slackers of Generation X – comes from a particular section of middle-class youth. It is not surprising that the generation unit conjured up in ideas about 'the Millennials' is steeped in both the privileges and anxieties of the relatively wealthy. To counter the notion that this voice is not representative of all young people's experiences or attitudes is as easy as it is correct and necessary. But to dismiss Millennial angst as the entitled whinging of a privileged sub-group of young adults would be to miss what this particular form of Boomer-blaming is trying to say. It is not really that they blame their parents for everything – how could they, when they rely on these same parents to do everything from fund their education to provide them with material about how the Baby Boomers had things better? A far more powerful driver of Millennial angst is disenchantment – with the way things are at the moment, and the promises with which young people were raised. And this is a disenchantment that their parents often share.

Middle-class dreams – and nightmares

Generation Debt, by Yale University graduate Anya Kamenetz, is an eight-chapter plaint about how the strains of living in twenty-first-century America are allegedly making it impossible for young people to grow up. At its core, the book rages against the economic landscape for American college graduates – one defined by 'job erosion, temp hell, the intern trap, low pay, no benefits, and the uncertain quest for a fulfilling career'. These problems, Kamenetz argues, are driven by 'structural changes in the economy', which mean that 'stable living-wage jobs' are harder to come by for recent graduates – and well-nigh impossible for those from poor backgrounds without college degrees. 'In income and occupational prestige, young adults are behind where their parents were at their age,' she writes. 'Unless something changes soon, entry into middle-class comfort is far from guaranteed for most of us.'[9]

The assumption that young adults should have guaranteed 'entry into middle-class comfort' is the kind of Millennial-speak that really winds older people up. It speaks to a sentiment of entitlement – the idea that you should be given an adult life that falls in line with your expectations, rather than the more prosaic reality that life is what you make it through your own work, achievements and efforts, albeit in the wider context of the circumstances into which you were born. And it is articulated through making childish, one-sided and ahistorical comparisons with where young adults' 'parents were at their age' – a marker that, as Francesca Angelini's mother points out, is deployed highly selectively.

As a working-class grammar school girl, my own Baby Boomer mother benefited from 'free' higher education and a student maintenance grant. But given that only about 8 per cent of young British people went to university in the 1960s, compared to almost 50 per cent today, she had to work pretty hard to get there. When my parents graduated, they married in a Register Office followed by sandwiches in the pub. Their first home was a rented flat on the Kent coast, where my father studied for his Master's degree. That year, my mother worked for a pittance in a local factory, followed by a London hospital; with no central heating, they dried clothes over newspaper and lost much of their disposable income to an electricity meter rigged to gobble up change as fast as you could put it in (to this day, Mum refers to Herne Bay, rather unfairly, as 'the coldest place on earth'). Mum gave birth to me at the age of 27, and was referred to in hospital as an 'elderly primigravida'. She went back to work as a full-time college lecturer when I was 9 years old and my sister 7; in the small Midlands village where my family had landed, this was daring and exotic. As these kids of the Swinging Sixties entered adulthood, parties revolved less around sex, drugs and rock-and-roll than the 'Watney's Party Seven', a famously impossible-to-open tin of draught ale (seven pints!) that did the rounds of practically every house party in the early 1970s.[10] My parents bought a house in their mid-20s, but not without a certain amount of scrimping and financial anxiety; not least during those times when rapid spikes in interest rates sent the cost of mortgage payments sky high.

As I write this, I can imagine the Millennial eye-rolling. Yet another homily about how much harder the Boomers had things! And it is true that my parents' tale, like those of many middle-class Baby Boomers, is a far cry from both the gilded affluence imagined by the Boomer-blaming playlist, and the relative comfort in which middle-class young people today actually live. But this is only half the story. The Boomers – particularly those, like my parents, who were born just after the Second World War and came of age in what Marwick calls the 'high Sixties' – may not have been individually affluent, optimistic or even particularly happy. The kids of the student protest movement spent their young adult years raging and rebelling, worried about the end of the world and pitting their dreams and idealism against 'the system'. Yet they were rich in their dreams and hopeful in their idealism – a reflection of the dynamism and optimism of the system they raged against. For all their problems and contradictions, the movements that defined that era – for civil rights, for women's equality, against war – were built on the belief that a better society was possible, and that people could bring about that change.

The economic boom helped, of course – jobs were relatively plentiful, the expansion of cultural and economic institutions provided an outlook for graduates looking for 'meaningful work', and people didn't turn their noses up at 'real work' either. When the dark days came, in the 1970s and 1980s, people's frustrations were channelled through political anger; nobody blamed the old guys for 'stealing their future', but came to blows over the question of what kind of world we wanted in the here and now. The Millennial generation has grown up in an entirely different context. Whereas the Boomers were hell-bent on shaping the future, the Millennials were born at the 'end of history' – the point at which it seemed everybody wanted to shed their ideological baggage without replacing it with any new idealistic gear. The proliferation of smart phones and frothy coffee offered limited compensation, particularly when the economy went bust as well. As fond as the Millennials are of their shiny gadgets and designer trainers, they, like every generation before them, are painfully aware that you can't buy meaning.

When the Millennial dilemma is reduced to a generationalist competition over 'who had it worst', the debate quickly degenerates into a game of tit for tat, where lines are drawn, sides are taken, and everybody avoids the issues at stake. In one 2016 Twitter-war, sparked by the hashtag #HowToConfuseAMillenial [sic], older tweeters took aim at Millennials for their 'unpractical' university degree choices, their laziness and sense of self-entitlement.[11] 'Tell them their French History degree will get them a job at Target,' mocked one. 'Tell them the irony of people wearing the same coloured t-shirt with the slogan "Dare To Be Different",' suggested another. 'The world doesn't revolve around you; and, unsurprisingly: You are owed nothing,' spat yet another. Although the spite of these initial tweets was disturbing, particularly striking was the vitriol thrown back by Millennial counter-tweets, which escalated intergenerational bitching to a sentiment of absolute betrayal. 'Destroy the environment, kill the economy, make education so expensive we have lifelong debt, call us lazy'; 'Say nobody is entitled to anything but demand a senior discount; a discount just for being old'; 'Whine about the way millennials behave when you were the ones that raised us'; 'Invent participation trophies so you don't feel like a shitty parent, mock millennials for getting them' . . . you get the gist.

What is being said here is far more than a complaint about the difficulties of getting a well-paid job and a place to live. It is a howl of existential anguish, which centres on the question, 'what do you want from us?' Our present society is failing to answer this question.

It is true that nobody is entitled to a future of 'middle-class comfort'. But as citizens of wealthy, advanced economies, they are entitled at least to see this as a realistic possibility, so long as they follow the rules of the game. The great fear, for middle-class Millennials *and* their parents, is that the rules have become both more demanding and more arbitrary. This seems to be the case at every level. Education is increasingly presented as a high-risk, zero-sum game, where failure to achieve high scores at any stage in school or college will damage a child's opportunities for life. 'In the shadow of this high-stakes rat race, childrearing has gone from harm prevention to risk elimination,' argues Malcolm Harris (born 1988), author of *Kids These Days: Human capital and the making of Millennials*. 'It's no longer enough to graduate a kid from high school in one piece; if an American parent wants to give their child a chance at success, they can't take any chances.'[12]

What 'not taking chances' means, in Harris's view, is engaging children in a relentless process of 'upgrading'. This takes the form of education, but it is not about education as it has traditionally been understood – rather, it is a highly rationalised process of building human capital, while hiding behind what Harris calls 'the pedagogical mask'. '[S]o far we seem only interested in *how much* we can count on producing, rather than what the hell it is we're growing,' he writes:

> To adopt the scholastic euphemism 'enrichment', America is trying to refine our kids to full capacity, trying to engineer a generation of hyperenriched 'readers, writers, coworkers, and problem solvers'. Parents, teachers, policymakers, and employers are all so worried that their children won't 'meet the demands of a changing world' that they don't bother asking what kind of kids *can* meet those demands, and what historical problems they're really being equipped to solve. The anxious frenzy that surrounds the future has come to function as an excuse for the choices adults make for kids on the uncertain road there.[13]

Harris is right that something very strange has happened to the culture of parenting and education in the last couple of decades. These time-honoured encounters between the generations, which historically focused on gradually inducting children into the adult world through socialisation, education and work, are now routinely presented as intensive, all-consuming, expert-guided exercises in 'concerted cultivation'.[14] Harris's claim that these developments have resulted in 'drastic changes in the character of childhood' may take things too far – kids are still kids, after all. It is clear, though, that the competitive obsession with raising children to succeed in the modern world is not driven by parental over-ambition so much as by fear of what might happen if they fail; a fear that has been internalised by Millennial angst.

Back in 1989, when the generation wars were little more than a twinkle in policymakers' eyes, the celebrated social critic Barbara Ehrenreich published *Fear of Falling*, an insightful study of 'the inner life' of the American middle class. When Millennials complain that 'entry into middle-class comfort is far from guaranteed'[15] for most of their generation, they are echoing the malaise that Ehrenreich attributes to this 'insecure and deeply anxious' section of society, which 'is afraid, like any class below the most securely wealthy, of misfortunes that might lead to a downward slide'.[16] In the middle class, though, there is 'another anxiety: a fear of inner weakness, of growing soft, of failing to strive, of losing discipline and will' – an anxiety that, in recent years, has been amplified by the parental-educational project of concerted cultivation. 'Whether the middle class looks down toward the realm of less, or up toward the realm of more, there is the fear, always, of falling,' wrote Ehrenreich – astutely prefiguring the restless dissatisfaction behind the 'high-stakes rat race'[17] of modern childrearing.

When the voices of Millennial angst bemoan the cost and pressures of higher education, the apparent lack of career pathways that reward their hard work and academic achievement, their inability to afford to buy a house and their reluctance to start a family of their own, they are expressing a dislocation between the aspirations and behaviours that have framed their middle-class upbringing, and what the world looks like to a graduate emerging from the cocoon. 'Many college kids,' writes Kamenetz, 'have an expectations problem':

> We were raised to dream big. While we face real challenges, our chronic dissatisfaction can itself be a stumbling block. We spend too much time and borrow too much money shooting for the stars.[18]

But 'dreaming big' is not really the problem here. Beneath the shrill sense of entitlement articulated by middle-class Millennials lies a more complex set of emotional responses: the fear of falling; confusion, about what society wants from them; and resentment, at having pounded the treadmill of educational achievement to find that none of it is enough.

Their 'fear of falling' is partly to do with what 'middle-class jobs' have become, and what it takes to get them. One consequence of the 'upgrading' described by Harris is that Western societies are funnelling increasing proportions of young people through higher education, propelled by a belief that education up until the early twenties should be a necessary precondition to gain a decent job. One predictable effect of this is that the so-called 'graduate premium' – the higher earnings generally accrued by graduates compared to non-graduates, trumpeted by British policy-makers as an incentive for young people to pay for a university degree – is shrinking. Noting that the rapid expansion of the UK's higher education sector has not been matched by an increase in high-skilled jobs, the Chartered Institute of Personnel and Development argues that 'graduate over-qualification is a particular problem', with a large proportion of the country's graduates working in 'non-graduate jobs'.[19] The more graduates there are, the more jobs are 'upgraded' to graduate jobs, simply because you need a degree to get one. This has led to a situation where, some argue, young people find themselves 'running up a down escalator of devalued qualifications',[20] needing to collect more and more credentials, just to stay where they are.

'Bad jobs' and work ethics

In February 2016, a disgruntled 25-year-old English Literature graduate, Talia Jane, published an 'Open Letter' to the CEO of the reviews and reservations hub, Yelp/Eat 24. Having graduated with little experience of work, apart from 'freelancing and tutoring', and a dream of pursuing a career in the media, she explains:

> I felt it was fair that I start out working in the customer support section of Yelp/Eat24 before I'd be qualified to transfer to media. Then, after I had moved and got firmly stuck in this apartment with this debt, I was told I'd have to work in support for *an entire **year*** before I would be able to move to a different department. A whole year answering calls and talking to customers just for the hope that someday I'd be able to make memes and twitter jokes about food. If you follow me on twitter, which you don't, you'd know that these are things I already do.[21]

What follows is a litany of complaints about poor wages, which don't cover the cost of renting accommodation or eating food in the San Francisco Bay area where Jane was living; unsociable working hours and with few paid holidays; and (what seems to wind Jane up the most) the company's determination to ignore her ideas for how things could be improved. Once she put all these ideas and criticisms down in a blog post, Jane was fired. 'This was entirely unplanned (but I guess not completely unexpected?)' she wrote – before giving details of her PayPal and other accounts so that the readers of the post could provide her with 'any help until I find new employment'. In the furore that followed, Talia Jane was 'called everything from an entitled millennial to a champion of the living wage'.[22]

Thirty-year-old screenplay writer Stefanie Williams, who had also graduated with an English major, posted a blistering response to the saga on *Huffington Post* under the title 'The Problem With Millennials and Work Ethic'.[23] Williams recounts her own struggles to work her way up through a restaurant job, where she 'made the sacrifices and sucked up my pride in order to make ends meet and figure out what I wanted to do and how to do it'. '[Y]ou are a young, white, English-speaking woman with a degree and a family who I would assume is helping you out at the moment,' Williams tells Jane:

> And you are asking for handouts from strangers while you sit on your ass looking for cushy jobs you are not entitled to while you complain about the establishment, probably from a nice laptop. To you, that is more acceptable than taking a job in a restaurant, or a coffee shop, or a fast food place. And that's the trouble with not just your outlook, but the outlook of so many people your age.

Williams is 'utterly disgusted' by Jane's attitude, and by her attempt to pose as a warrior for impoverished workers. '[T]urning this girl's inability to work for what she wants into a conversation about poverty' she writes, 'is utter bullshit': the real story is about 'this girl's personal responsibility to be an adult and find a job', and her attitude of entitlement.

In the Talia–Stefanie catfight, whose side would you take? The immature, self-obsessed Millennial who believed that slating her employer on a high-profile social media platform might result in the Yelp CEO sending her 'an email or something', or the company politely asking her to take the article down – not to censor her, 'more like, "We hear you. We're intervening so we don't have to do this in public"'?[24] Or the smug Millennial who wants to tell the world her own success story, and thinks that the problem for everyone else is that they don't share her graft and talent? Talia Jane thinks that her own dissatisfaction makes her emblematic of a whole section of society ('the issues I outlined here are the result of much larger problems within the gig economy', she states). Stefanie Williams dismisses that self-aggrandising claim, yet states that Jane's 'disgusting' outlook is also 'the outlook of so many people your age'. Jane believes that she has the right to shout her problems to the world; Williams thinks she needs to lower her expectations and recognise that she's lucky to get whatever job she can.

Both these young women endorse the terms laid down by the phoney generation wars, whereby life is either seen to be peculiarly terrible for young people, or young people are seen to have a terrible attitude. The self-righteous grievance articulated by the Millennials trying to make a name for themselves by bemoaning their predicament is exacerbated by the accusation that they are spoilt brats making much ado about nothing. Jane signs off, in an update to her open letter, by defending herself against,

> those looking to scold and/or blame me. . . . And if you really think someone working full time shouldn't point out that it's insane that a full time job isn't enough to support a single person just doing their best (when the minimum wage was established to support a family of three and has failed to keep up with [the] skyrocketing cost of living), you're being willfully stupid and that's not my problem. But if you really need to call me a whiny entitled millennial just to feel superior and/or less afraid of the reality of our world, have at it. I don't give a shit.[25]

Jane's belief that her brief excursion into the murky underbelly of what Kamenetz calls 'bad jobs' qualifies her as a critic on the 'reality of our world' is somewhat fanciful, but she is right about the level of evasion involved in debates about the labour market. Middle-class graduates are castigated for their lack of discipline, work ethic, and their overblown sense of entitlement, as though their quest for a career is unreasonable and unrealistic. As the historian Jacqui Shine put it, in her review of Harris's *Kids These Days*:

'We were promised something and we didn't get it' is not just a millennial refrain: it's a shared American delusion. But a dream is not an entitlement. The idea that entry into a stable middle class is some sort of American national birthright is ahistorical; that it ever seemed possible may prove to be epiphenomenal. The American middle class to which we were supposed to aspire was vanishingly short-lived, and it was certainly never uniformly accessible.[26]

It is true that, as Ehrenreich pointed out, the American middle class was never stable, and that entry into this layer of society was never a given. It is also true that, as social critics have argued for decades, many claims about meritocracy and social mobility conveniently ignore the role played by class background in skewing the distribution of both 'merit' and reward. But the idea that expectations of a middle-class life are 'delusional', even 'epiphenomenal'? That takes the demand for 'realistic expectations' to a whole new level of unreasonableness. Telling young people that decent jobs never existed in the first place is patronisingly dismissive, and as ahistorical as the assumption that people once had their dream career handed to them on a plate.

The fear of falling that lies behind much of Millennial angst comes not only from an anxiety about where they might fall from, but a terror about where they might fall to. Kamenetz's *Generation Debt* quivers with indignation, not only about the fate that might await fellow Yale graduates, but the working lives of young people who have never glimpsed the inside of an ivory tower. Researching the book, she says, made her realise 'just how lucky I am', belonging to that privileged quarter of the young population who holds a bachelor's degree, and that truly fortunate 'one-third of four-year college graduates without loan debts'.[27] This made the chapter on low-wage jobs 'especially difficult to write':

For all the other issues in this book – the rising cost of education, the growth of debt, the decline in employment benefits, budget deficits, and changing families – I can plausibly make common cause with young people of very different backgrounds. These changes affect us all. But when you're talking about poor and working-class young people . . . who don't finish, or even begin, college, too-easy comparisons are worse than useless.[28]

Kamenetz's outrage reflects a certain naivety: throughout history, working people have faced very similar struggles over pay, conditions and job security. The idea that today's young people are suddenly, uniquely disadvantaged compared to previous generations is based as much on 'too-easy comparisons' as is the idea that all Millennials are in the same, sinking boat. 'By talking about "the millennials" as a disadvantaged group, we're in danger of obscuring other, more fundamental differences between young people,' write Steven Roberts and Kim Allen. 'The portrayal of millennials as victims has allowed the experience of the squeezed middle class to take centre stage.'[29]

Roberts and Allen are right to highlight the partial and divisive character of generationalism, and to emphasise that 'long-standing, ongoing inequalities relating to class, race and gender' are much more significant problems than the alleged disparity of fortunes between the generations. But dismissing the concerns of the 'squeezed middle class' as a distraction from focusing on those who are 'really at a disadvantage' does not get us very far either. By refusing to focus on anything more profound than the question of who deserves a relatively bigger share of a shrinking pie, political elites around the Western world have spent years evading the problem of economic stagnation. Until they start addressing this problem, the possibility of society becoming better, or fairer, for anybody will recede further into the future.

Running scared from the zombie economy

'Perhaps one of the most fitting names for this generation . . . is the Echo Boomers,' writes Kate Lyons in her review of global

Millennial name-calling. This label derives partly from their demographic size (about the same as the Boomers), and partly because the two generations 'share many of the same values':

> While millennials don't want to repeat the boomers' failings and are scathing of them for hoarding wealth and ruining the environment, in reality they want many of the same things: in Britain or Australia, that's homeownership; in the US, to escape debt; in Spain and Greece, to have a job and any sense of a future.
>
> It seems that what millennials want, as well as flexibility, fairness, and tolerance – all touted as strengths of this generation – is for capitalism, which they think worked so well for previous generations, to fulfil its promise to them.
>
> 'The difficulty the Spanish (and many European) youth face to mobilise is that they want to live like their parents, in a world of consumer capitalism,' writes Spanish academic Antonio Alaminos. 'They do not want to end it; it is capitalism that has broken up with them.'[30]

Not all brands of Millennial angst overflow with love of consumer capitalism. Some, like Malcolm Harris, are self-consciously left wing. The Australian columnist Eleanor Robertson describes herself as a 'writer, editor, rowdy whinger', as well as a communist.[31] In her version of twenty-first-century communism, the Baby Boomers are positioned as the evil bourgeoisie, and the Millennials the proletariat brainwashed by false consciousness. The 'Boomer mentality', she writes, is one that tells young people that if they fail to get a well-paying full-time job, a stable partner, a house, a car, and a child, they are lacking in moral fibre. 'Of course, it's all a trick,' Robertson states. 'The global conditions that enabled a middle-class existence are evaporating, and are being replaced by an economic system whose function is the transfer of wealth to the lucky few.' But this pernicious, all-pervasive 'Boomer mentality' encourages young people to buy into the con:

[N]ever mind that the point of this ideology is to discipline young people's behaviour through weaponised self-loathing. Instead of demanding better, we engage in futile competition over crumbs. Instead of questioning why life often feels meaningless, why we feel so alienated and inadequate, we turn these beliefs inward. Instead of using this shared experience to build solidarity with each other, we feel shame.[32]

Most other 'Echo Boomers', however, would recoil at this wild-eyed vision of a Boomer conspiracy, whimpering that they just want a little bit more of what their parents had. 'I don't think it's America's self-image that's wrong,' says Kamenetz. 'It's the gulf that has grown up between ideal and reality. Mom, Dad, listen up: Things have changed. We're not doing as well as you did. And if something doesn't change soon, it's unlikely that we ever will.'[33]

'We're not doing as well as you did.' In this, Kamenetz is not entirely wrong. Although, as we have seen, direct comparisons between generations in terms of house prices or living standards don't stack up, today's economic reality is very different to that which framed the post-war boom. The economist Phil Mullan observes that the tempo of economic growth in the Group of Seven leading Western economies fell sharply between the 1960s and 1970s, from 64 per cent to 39 per cent, and has since 'tailed off stealthily, decade by decade', reaching 14 per cent in the 2000s.[34] These figures are startling – not because they have resulted in mass immiseration, but because they haven't. 'The fact that many people have continued to experience rising living standards over recent decades reflects how economic decay is neither absolute nor uninterrupted,' writes Mullan. The pattern, he suggests, is not one of 'unmitigated decline' but rather one in which 'an underlying dynamic of decay interacts with offsetting bulwarks of resilience, occasionally even producing bursts of vigour'. Globalisation, financialisation and periodic recessions have contributed to the resilience of the system, while periodic 'windfalls' such as energy booms and the 1990s dot.com bubble have provided mature economies with 'temporary respite' from their pattern of overall decline, as well as 'the opportunity to avoid tackling fundamental problems of investment and productivity'.[35]

Economic resilience has been helped by the political situation of recent decades, where the big conflicts – Left vs Right, labour vs capital – have been constrained and contained. Throughout the 1990s, many economists and politicians presented a trade-off – the relative stability of sluggish economic growth without the eviscerating effects of severe recession; an attempt to contain the risks associated with the classic economic cycles of 'boom and bust'. 'Third Way' politicians across the United States and Europe saw economic policy as a technical, managerial issue: something that was best left to financial experts and regulators, and essentially out of control of governments. In Britain, one of the first moves made by the Blair government was to grant operational independence to the Bank of England – a clear statement that economic policy was seen to lie in the lap of the gods, beyond all political debate and control.

But resilience has come at a cost – and as time goes on, the effects of what Mullan describes as a contained, Long Depression, are making themselves intimately felt. He describes a situation of economic and political atrophy, in which sluggish growth in mature economies is compounded by attempts to evade discussion of this problem, and a reluctance to formulate solutions. As a result, Mullan argues:

> [S]tandards of housing and transport, education and health have continued to lag behind popular expectations. Social problems, from mass unemployment among young people to those arising from the needs of an ageing population, appear to multiply beyond the capacity of public intervention.[36]

In this respect, the evidence relentlessly marshalled by generation warriors with regard to stagnant wages, insecure employment, overpriced housing, and the problems confronting the welfare state is not plucked out of thin air. It speaks to a situation of chronic economic stagnation. Since the 1990s, economic policy has actively evaded tackling the problems of low productivity, under-investment and slow growth, opting instead for buffers against youth unemployment, in the form of the relentless expansion of education; taking false comfort in bubbles provided by housing shortages or the financial markets; or propping things up through public spending. Embroiled in perennial crisis-management, the state has become intimately intertwined with business, encouraging the survival of what Mullan terms the 'zombie economy' at the expense of confronting reality and formulating the kind of bold initiatives that could have a hope of nurturing economic growth.

The failure here is not just economic, but political and cultural. Politics has turned its face away from grappling with the causes of our economic malaise, desperately seeking ways to mitigate the crisis by clawing back cash from people who currently have some, and lowering expectations across the board. This is why 'intergenerational equity' policies designed to squeeze apparently wealthy pensioners are enjoying so much elite attention, and why they are so damaging for young and old alike. They are presented as pragmatic measures, designed to promote greater 'fairness' in a time of growing inequality. But they are driven by a powerful fatalism, which discourages any discussion of a more hopeful future.

Fearful futures

In *The Minimal Self: Psychic survival in troubled times*, published in 1984, the American thinker Christopher Lasch described a culture of 'survivalism', in which the goal of history becomes little more than the management of one's personal life in an uncertain present. 'People have lost confidence in the future,' he wrote back then:

> Faced with an escalating arms race, an increase in crime and
> terrorism, environmental deterioration, and the prospect of

long-term decline, they have begun to prepare for the worst, sometimes by building fallout shelters and laying in provisions, more commonly by executing a kind of emotional retreat from the long-term commitments that presuppose a stable, secure, and orderly world.[37]

Lasch wrote that 'the end of the world has loomed as a hypothetical possibility' since the end of the Second World War, the 'sense of danger' greatly increased since the mid-1960s. This was partly, he argued, because of the objective instability of social and economic conditions, but also because of a sharp decline in 'the hope of a remedial politics, a self-reformation of the political system'. 'The hope that political action will gradually humanise industrial society has given way to a determination to survive the general wreckage or, more modestly, to hold one's own life together in the face of mounting pressures,' he observed bleakly. 'The danger of personal disintegration encourages a sense of selfhood neither "imperial" nor "narcissistic" but simply beleaguered.'[38]

The Millennial generation, for all the opportunities afforded by a world of open space and personal liberty, was raised in a culture that was already closing down. With the 'end of history', political and economic alternatives were off the table for discussion. The question confronting young people coming of age at the Millennium was not the one that preoccupied the Baby Boomers – how people could come together to change the world – but how to navigate a world that seemed to be spinning out of all control. Sociologists have termed this uncertain terrain a 'risk society', in which individuals stand alone and exposed to the forces that beleaguer them: able to make any number of lifestyle choices, but unable to influence much beyond that.[39] When the twin shocks of 9/11 and the global financial crisis struck, it seemed to confirm that this was the price for our decades of fun, freedom and relative peace. Tough luck, the kids were told. The party's over – and you not only missed it, you've got to pay for it too.

As noted in Chapter 3, the presentation of the Sixties as an irresponsible party, the toxic consequences of which will have to be borne by younger generations, has been going on for some time. 'Others have had their little binge, their little drug-debt-and-divorce debacle, their little overconsumption party,' wrote Howe and Strauss in their 1993 book about the '13th generation' (their label for Generation X). 'Now it's time for history's great clean-up brigade. That's not a pretty job, but somebody's got to do it.'[40] But however downbeat Generation Xers might have felt about their future, at least they were expected to have one. There was still the possibility that they could deal with the hangover, and move on.

In recent times, the so-called Boomer 'party' has taken on a significance of epic, almost mythical, proportions. Generation warriors paint a picture of the Sixties as a time of unparalleled affluence and greed, and the Boomer generation as the gluttonous guest that keeps on drinking. The part cast for the Millennial generation is that of a victimised packhorse, robbed of the opportunity to make a half-decent life and burdened with the responsibility of atoning for their parents' many sins. Whether they view capitalism as an evil 'trick' or as a good system that just needs to work better for them, the angst-ridden Millennials parading their anger and sense of entitlement across the comment pages have one thing in common: they want something more than our present society is able to offer them. The way this is articulated can be partial, self-centred and downright brattish – but so what? It is the task of older generations to encourage young people to think and act beyond themselves.

When Kamenetz entreats her parents to acknowledge that 'we're not doing as well as you did', she articulates both the understandable frustrations of today's vocal Millennials, and how hobbled their hopes and aspirations have become. Their desire for a better life is expressed by looking backwards, to a selective account of the relative prosperity of previous generations, and feeling aggrieved by their own relative misfortune. This is a consequence of the way in which they have been encouraged to view their predicament: as punishment for the greed and good fortune of their parents. And rather than listening to what the kids are trying to express, political elites have simply appropriated and manipulated the voice of Millennial angst, pretending it says what they want to hear.

CHAPTER 7

'Youthquakes' and the politicisation of generational identity

The script of Boomer-blaming has formed the basis for a new political narrative, which has come to view generational conflict as an alternative frame to the class-based politics that dominated the twentieth century. This latest phase of generationalism overstates the importance of generational characteristics and difference, and threatens to turn them into a brittle form of generational identity, deliberately setting old and young against each other. A set of ideas about the 'younger generation' – the kind of people they are, the politics they support, the vision they hold of the future – has been marshalled to narrate political events and promote particular outcomes. Older generations, meanwhile, are positioned as standing in the way of the interests of the present – voting too much, voting the wrong way, daring to have a say on the future of a society in which they will soon be dead.

This indicates the opening of a grim new chapter in the generation wars. An ongoing dialogue between the generations is fundamental to the healthy functioning of a democratic, civilised society. By seeking to separate the interests and aspirations of those who are currently young from those of their elders, generation warriors are promoting a narrow, sectional vision that privileges a particular voice – provided, of course, that it says the right kind of things.

Youthquake: What's in a word?

Beneath the vaulted ceilings of Union Chapel, a North London church that multi-tasks as an entertainment venue and charity drop-in centre, crowds of young people sway as if to a concert. But they are making the music – 'Oh, Jeremy Corbyn . . .'. The star on stage is a grey-whiskered man who led the British Labour Party to a smaller-than-expected defeat in the 2017 General Election, and gained a short-lived cult following as a result. A few weeks later, JC addressed an audience of tens of thousands at the UK's biggest music festival, Glastonbury, introduced as the 'hero of the hour' by Michael Eavis, the festival's founder. Festivalgoers wore his face on T-shirts, flags and leggings, and were 'quick to launch into impromptu "Oh, Jeremy Corbyn" chants at the most unlikely occasions: during a silent disco, in the dance area Shangri-La, or in the middle of Radiohead's headline set'.[1]

Welcome to the 'youthquake' – the moment when the politics of generational division seemed to come of age. So significant was this moment that the Oxford Dictionaries crowned 'youthquake' as the 'Word of the Year 2017'. The dictionaries' editors noted a fivefold increase in usage of the term in 2017 compared to 2016, beginning with discussion of the United Kingdom's general election and spreading to New Zealand, where the 'use of youthquake to discuss young people's engagement in politics was rapidly picked up by politicians and the press alike during the country's general election . . . setting youthquake firmly on its way to become a fixture of political discourse'.[2]

There was certainly a lot of talk about a youthquake in 2017 – but before declaring a seismic shift in the political landscape, we might want to consider what the apparent upsurge in political engagement amongst young people was really all about. Scratch the surface of the 2017 youthquake, and it becomes obvious that there are two things going on: what young people are thinking, saying and doing, and what pollsters, pundits and politicians *want them* to be thinking, saying and doing. The tendency to collapse the two has become one of the most distorting examples of generationalism in recent years.

The 2017 'youthquake' was an over-excited attempt to draw meaning from an event that wobbled all over the place. Prime Minister Theresa May had called a General Election to gain legitimacy for her premiership as she pushed through Britain's withdrawal from the European Union (EU), and to consolidate the Conservative Party's hold over Parliament as the Labour Party crumbled into division and disarray. Right up to the moment the election result was called, the mainstream of the Labour Party and their friends in the commentariat regarded Corbyn more as a liability than a leader, spawning a series of toe-curling *mea culpa*s when election night turned a surefire Labour loss into a near win.[3]

Into this mix wandered an extraordinary spectacle – young people actually talking about the election. This came on the back of decades of concern about the problem of 'youth apathy', with low electoral turnout overall and especially among younger age groups illustrating a growing detachment between political institutions and the people whom they represent. More immediately, it followed the divisive EU referendum, the result of which was widely presented as a 'betrayal' of young people. A broad, informal coalition of Corbyn supporters, Corbyn-loathing Labour supporters, Labour-wary anti-Brexiters, and those who just wanted to see Theresa May get a bit of a kicking, was open to any means of snatching a symbolic victory from the jaws of electoral defeat. In this context, the idea that politics had been shaken up by a 'youthquake' played very well.

The statistics seemed to bear it out, at first. A post-election poll by Ipsos MORI suggested that turnout amongst 18–24-year-olds went up by 16 percentage points compared with 2015, and by 8 points among 25–34-year-olds.[4] YouGov reported an increase in youth turnout to 57 per cent of 18–19-year-olds and 59 per cent of 20–24-year-olds,[5] and Labour MP David Lammy tweeted his congratulations to 18–24-year-olds for achieving a turnout of 72 per cent – although the source of this statistic remains dubiously unknown.[6]

But the youthquake was a myth. That was the conclusion drawn by the British Election Study (BES), widely regarded as the most reliable source of data on electoral turnout (which is notoriously hard to measure, let alone to predict). In January 2018, the BES team reported that while the 2017 election had probably resulted in 'a small increase in turnout across a large age range, with a slightly larger rise for those aged 30–40', they could be confident that 'there was no dramatic surge in youth turnout of the sort suggested by some other surveys. In short, there was no "youthquake"'.[7] The Election Study's findings met with howls of protest, but the analysts stood their ground. 'When we embarked on this exercise we expected to see evidence of a youthquake but the data did not support it,' they stated, in a published reply to their critics. 'As social scientists, our duty is to report what we see.'[8]

What they saw was something very telling about our political moment. In attempting to explain why the idea of a surge in youth turnout took hold, the BES suggested that 'in part it is because political commentary is prone to believing that what politicians set out to do is effective, even if there is no concrete evidence that it is':

Increasing youth turnout was part of Corbyn's political strategy. As Labour did unexpectedly well, it is not unreasonable to think that strategy might have paid off, even though this turns out not to be the case.

Although 'Labour also *was* more popular amongst young people than old people in 2017' – as it had been in previous elections – and its share of the youth vote did increase, 'this is not the same as a surge in youth *turnout*'.[9] Starry-eyed with wishful thinking, those rooting for a Labour win had ended up finding evidence that their own campaigns had worked. The music magazine *NME*, for example, had been pushing the idea that 'young people will decide this year's election' in advance of claims that they had done just that. 'This is, after all, not just about individuals but about whole generations,' the *NME* insisted, promoting its 'plus one' campaign cajoling readers 'to take a mate to the polls'.[10]

Even if turnout amongst younger people had increased substantially, talk of 'youthquakes' seems peculiarly dramatic. The Oxford Dictionaries define 'youthquake' as 'a significant cultural, political, or social change arising from the actions or influence of young people'. We might assume a revolution, or a cultural uprising – something that is more visible and enduring than whether a slightly higher number of young people than previously vote for a particular party or candidate on one occasion. The cultural origin of the term – first used in the January 1965 edition of *Vogue* magazine to 'describe the youth-led fashion and music movement of the swinging sixties, which saw baby boomers reject the traditional values of their parents'[11] – has more to it than its insipid 2017 version.

And let's not forget the last time we saw a youthquake, in the 2008 campaign to elect Barack Obama as President of the United States. Corbyn's youth campaign was a self-conscious echo of the slogan of 'Hope' with which Obama led a campaign blazed by bright-eyed college kids.[12] Commentators then, too, sought to draw wider messages from the moment. 'At the time, young people's key role in bringing Obama to power was often referred to as a "Youthquake",' explains Martin Wattenberg, professor of political science at the University of California:

> Furthermore, many observers were ready to proclaim that the 2008 election had ended the era of youth apathy and signified the beginning of a new era of youth-based activism that would keep progressives solidly in power for the next generation. As Michelle Obama famously told a large crowd at the University of California, Los Angeles during the 2008 campaign, 'Barack will never allow you to go back to your lives as usual, uninvolved, uninformed'.[13]

It is widely accepted that Obama did inspire youngsters out to vote – and turnout in general reached a high point in the 2008 election. But the hyperbole quickly turned to dust, as 'youth turnout plummeted in the Democrats' disastrous midterm performance in 2010'.[14] The trouble with hope is that it quickly fades when it fails to deliver. Obama quickly lost the excitement and support among young people that had helped him to gain him the presidency; and when it came to the 2016 election, Millennials were widely blamed for allowing Trump into the White House. 'As disheartened as young Americans might feel today, it may well be that their lack of enthusiasm to go out and vote cost Hillary Clinton the presidency,' wrote Niall McCarthy for the Statista website. 'Even though Millennials backed Clinton at the polls, their turnout rates have been historically dismal. In 2012, only 46 percent of eligible Millennials went out and voted and this year, the number could be similarly low.'[15]

The ongoing chatter about youthquakes, youth apathy, what young people vote for and why, have strikingly little to do with young people themselves. Rather, they represent a continuation of twentieth-century generationalism, where elites turn to the idea of generations to make sense of confusing times. 'Our choice of language illuminates our preoccupations,' stated Oxford Dictionaries – but it does more than that. Casper Grathwohl, President of Oxford Dictionaries, gave a candid account of how this worked out in the decision to choose 'youthquake' from the other shortlisted 'words of 2017':

[M]ost importantly for me, at a time when our language is reflecting a deepening unrest and exhausted nerves, it is a rare political word that sounds a hopeful note. Hope that the damage we've done to our institutions will enable the next generation to rebuild better ones. Hope that our polarized times are creating a more open-minded electorate that will exercise its voice in the times ahead . . . As the *annus horribilis* of 2017 draws to a close, a year which many of us feel we've barely survived, I think it's time for a word we can all rally behind. A word we can root for and collectively empower as the Word of the Year.[16]

The reason why 2017 should be labelled a 'horrible year' is seen to require no explanation: presumably Grathwohl was talking about Brexit in Britain, Trump in the USA, various European election shocks – and assuming that readers of Oxford Dictionaries would agree with him. In this respect, the 'youthquake' was not expressing a hope that youth would lead the way, so much as an assumption that young people would vote in a particular, 'open-minded' way.

Talking up youthquakes, and fantasising about the healing powers of Millennial voters, reveals a gap between the present political elite and voters of any age. The notion that 'generation' denotes some kind of political identity is not only misguided – it is manipulative. And the consequences of attempting to manipulate the youth vote into a demand for a particular result are proving deeply destabilising. 'Wait . . . did you just feel that? I think it's the beginning of a *youthquake*,' asks Grathwohl, sensing the reverberations of his own rhetoric. But if it's stability he is after, Grathwohl might want to be careful what he wishes for.

Voting the wrong way

The obsession with the 'youth vote' is selective and contradictory, often serving as a mask for preoccupations that political elites do not feel able to confront. Over the past couple of decades, discussions about the importance of boosting youth turnout in elections have had a routine quality, as though this is something that politicians should care about, and young people should just do. Attempts to 'include' young people in the election process have tended to involve, on the one hand, craven proposals such as lowering the voting age, doing stuff with social media, putting polling booths in shopping malls, and on the other, excuseniks claiming that democratic institutions need to adapt to the fact that young people 'do politics differently', as though signing an online petition or sharing a Facebook meme is equivalent to exercising the voting rights that our ancestors fought so hard for.[17] At its extreme end, the argument that participating in elections is less a right than a duty takes the form of compulsory voting systems, where those who fail to give a 'valid and sufficient' reason for not voting are required to pay a penalty fine. But even in Australia, where voting is compulsory, there is ongoing teeth-gnashing about the 'missing youth vote'.[18]

This sentiment, that young people should be engaged in voting 'just because', has run alongside a general trend in sluggish turnout for elections, declining membership of political parties, and overall lack of enthusiasm for politics and politicians. This has provided political elites with both an opportunity and a problem. The opportunity is that policy can be decided in the Westminster or Washington bubble, without coming under too much pressure from the awkward sods out there in the constituencies. The problem is that disengagement with politics provides an implicit challenge to the legitimacy of the people and institutions claiming to represent us. If they held an election and nobody came, it wouldn't be democracy, but oligarchy. And while the political rulers of Western societies might like oligarchy in practice, they are not (quite) at the point where they are prepared to argue for it in principle.

The excitement generated around Obama's election campaign, and articulated by many of the young people on the campaign trail, was genuine. Like the brief, British moment in 2017, when it suddenly became cool for twenty-somethings to pay more than a glancing interest in a General Election campaign, it seemed to shift the entrenched idea that political choices were irrelevant, a tired board game played by other, older people. And of course, this is important. Whether young people vote or not, and whoever they cast their votes for, a sense that voting actually matters and can bring about some change is crucial for democracy to work. Otherwise, we may as well get rid of the public elections and give ourselves over to a benevolent dictatorship controlled by whoever can be bothered to do the job.

The problem for political elites is that, for all their talk about wanting to increase turnout for elections, they don't always like it. They don't like who people are currently voting for (not one of them), what people are voting for (the 'wrong' kind of ideas), and what people are voting against (the political elites). They didn't like it in France, when in the first round of the 2017 Presidential election around one quarter of voters aged 18–34 reportedly backed the Communist-allied candidate Jean-Luc Mélenchon, while a similar proportion backed the far-right candidate Marine Le Pen.[19] They didn't like it in Italy, where the Five Star Movement attracted younger voters away from the traditional parties.[20] Some have raised fears that as, across Europe 'anti-establishment parties are taking votes left, right and center from the traditional power players . . . it has become all but impossible for the establishment to govern on its own'.[21]

Discomfited members of the so-called 'liberal elite' are trying to take refuge in the belief that the 'youth vote' is a vote for their own point of view, and if they can be enticed out to the polls next time, the 'youthquake' of Oxford Dictionaries' imagination can be shaken into action, enabling the 'next generation' to rebuild better political institutions and provide us with 'a more open-minded electorate'.[22] But here again, they may find themselves disappointed. Age is far from a determining factor: whether people vote for left-wing or right-wing politicians or parties depends on the wider mood of the times. Even in the recent wave of unpredictable elections, where age has been reported as 'the biggest political divide',[23] social class, geographical location and political beliefs play a more significant role than birthdays.

In the USA, the Clinton campaign made the big mistake of taking the kids for granted. 'Although Clinton had failed to do well with young people in the 2008 primaries against Obama and again in 2016 against Bernie Sanders, they were optimistic that the stark choice between Clinton and Trump would propel them to support

Clinton in overwhelming numbers,' writes Wattenberg. This optimism was misplaced: youth support for the Democratic nominee plummeted, especially in some of the Midwestern states, and many would-be Democrat voters gave their votes to a third-party candidate instead. 'If the Clinton campaign could not believe how bad the numbers were among young people, I can sympathize; I am still shocked every time I see them,' Wattenberg admits.[24]

Support for Clinton among young voters was tepid at best – with some reporting feelings of outright frigidity. Wattenberg reports that '[a] third of young voters gave Clinton a rating of 15 or below on the feeling thermometer, meaning that they had either very cold or quite cold feelings about her'; less than half reported 'any degree of warm feelings toward her', and 'just 7% gave her a rating of 85 or above, meaning they had either very warm or quite warm feelings about her.'[25] Trump gained a smaller share of the youth vote than Clinton, but as the Brookings Institution reported:

Overall, Trump won one-third of young voters, a greater number than pre-election polls suggested he would. Notably, 32 percent of these young Trump supporters were excited by the prospect of a Trump presidency while only 18 percent of young Clinton supporters reported being excited about their candidate.[26]

In Germany, the assumption that young voters would plump for the established 'liberal elite' candidate also turned out to be misguided. In the run-up to the 2017 election, it was widely reported that the youth vote would put a fourth term in the bag for Chancellor Angela Merkel, of the centre-right Christian Democratic Union (CDU). 'They are the Merkel generation,' reported the *Washington Post*, citing a poll claiming that 57 per cent of first-time voters favoured the chancellor, compared with 21 per cent who preferred her Social Democratic rival, Martin Schulz.[27] Conrad Clemens, the 34-year-old national secretary of Junge Union, the youth organisation of the CDU, told the UK *Independent* that the apparent surge in support from young people was a 'unique and spectacular' development. Ms Merkel had become 'a cool, international leader who modernised the CDU', he said, and 'young people don't pursue leftist ideologies as much anymore'; they have adopted 'more conservative attitudes'. Above all, he said, young people wanted stability in a 'world in turmoil', an antidote to Trump, Brexit and the rise of right-wing populist movements across Europe.[28]

When it came to election day, the German people didn't want stability, and the 'Merkel generation' didn't all come to *Mutti*. Merkel narrowly made it into her fourth term to head a fractious coalition government in which all the major parties of the centre-left and the centre-right recorded some of their worst results, with voters shifting allegiance to the right-wing nationalist Alternative für Deutschland (AfD) and the liberal Free Democratic Party (FDP). Meanwhile, Germany's relatively small Left Party, reported the British *Financial Times*, did not change its overall vote share by much but 'under the surface it has gone through an astonishing metamorphosis'. The Left appears 'no longer to be the party of the working class', losing votes in poorer, eastern areas and picking up gains in areas with 'more younger voters and more people in high-quality jobs'. 'This points at the party becoming younger and more of a leftist option for professionals, which is comparable with the transformation of Labour in the UK,' the *FT* concluded.[29]

It turns out that electoral turnout is different to political *mobilisation* – and this is where the events of 2016 and 2017 have proved to be most disorienting for political elites sheltering beneath the comfort blanket of 'voter apathy'. In the UK's referendum on membership of the EU, 72 per cent of the electorate turned out to vote – a higher proportion than in any general election since 1992.[30] Not only that: people were actively engaged in the referendum debate, in a campaign that came to divide constituencies, polarise regions, and upgrade family mealtime bickering into heated debates about the issues. In the end, the mandate for Britain to leave the EU was given by over 17 million people – and swept up in this excitement was a significant number of young people.

The mythology of the EU referendum has it that this was a decision made by old people at the expense of the young, deploying both their vast numbers and their greater propensity to vote in order to steal the vote. As I discuss below and in the next chapter, this myth is both empirically dubious and politically propagated. Estimates of the turnout among 18–24-year-olds for the referendum have varied wildly, putting it anywhere between 36 per cent and 64 per cent;[31] while we may well never know the exact figures, what we do know is that this was not an event that somehow just passed young people by. For the political elite, however, the problem that revealed itself at the referendum was not about who didn't vote, but who *did*.

According to Sarah Birch of the University of Glasgow, the referendum appeared 'to buck the well-documented trend of increasing differences in turnout between young and old'. One reason for this was precisely the divisive character of the event: the sense that a clear choice was there to be made, and that what you did with your vote mattered. Birch observes that:

> The opening of new divides is typically associated with the political mobilisation of previously disengaged groups, and this is what we appear to have observed with the EU referendum vote. Political cleavages can be highly divisive when they threaten to rend the fabric of society, yet they also have the capacity to interest people in politics.[32]

The 2018 edition of the *British Social Attitudes* (BSA) report found that 43 per cent of those who claimed to have no interest in politics at all, and 65 per cent of those who claimed 'not very much' interest in politics, voted in the referendum, up from 30 per cent and 54 per cent respectively in the 2015 general election. Turnout for voters under the age of 35 increased by nine percentage points, compared to five points amongst those aged 65 and older. However, the BSA report adds some important caveats. It remained the case that 'those with "a great deal" or "quite a lot" of interest in politics were much more likely to have voted than those with no interest at all'; and 'younger people were much less likely to vote than their older counterparts, even though it might be felt that it was their futures above all that would be affected by the outcome of the referendum'.[33]

The elite panic provoked by the 'political mobilisation of previously disengaged groups' is a curious and contradictory thing. Despite fears our intensely divided society is causing the 'left-behinds' to rise up and revolt against established political institutions, figures on turnout don't really bear this out. The EU referendum mobilised all sections of society to get out and vote: the 'disengaged' were more likely to vote than previously, but less likely than the already-engaged. In the US Presidential election, turnout reached a '20-year low', as many voters apparently found themselves caught between two equally unappealing candidates.[34] Throughout these tumultuous elections, there was no popular uprising; just people voting for choices that some sections of the elite really don't like.

On the other hand, the dramas that have characterised recent elections – established political parties losing ground to parties situated on the extremes of left and right, centre-left parties accused of representing a narrow, sectional interest of the 'liberal elite', pollsters and pundits finding it impossible to predict how any election will go – represent a significant shift in the status quo. The referendum gave voice to ideas and aspirations the Westminster bubble has attempted for so long to contain and ignore, along with the kind of people that centrist, dinner-party politics have effectively managed to keep firmly downstairs. A similar pattern has been seen in the USA, with people electing a President whom political leaders across the Western world had deemed unelectable, and is repeated across Europe with voters upsetting the applecart every time an election is called. When the disengaged become mobilised, it turns out that 'turnout' is far from the comfort blanket of legitimacy previously imagined by the political elite.

How do we make sense of the role played by 'youth' in these recent events? The divides that have revealed themselves have been driven far more by social class, opportunity and ideas about the future than by the age of the person marking their ballot paper. It seems that young people may turn out to vote or not, and when they do, they might vote for the Left or the Right, for the status quo or against it. The one thing that all the recent electoral shocks had in common was that they represented a reaction against the established political elite. This was not a clash of generations, so much as a clash of values.

Divided generations

'When the UK voted for Brexit, British pensioners were three times more likely than younger voters to want to cut ties with the European Union,' wrote Niall McCarthy in an analysis titled 'Young Voted Clinton, Old Voted Trump'. In Britain, 'the majority of young Remain voters still blame older people with secure jobs and pensions for depriving them of the freedom to live and work in Europe', while in the USA Donald Trump 'also profited from the older generation', appealing to 'an older cohort who are proud and nostalgic about their nation's history as well as being less dependent on jobs and education'.[35]

This kind of simplistic summary of the 'age divide' in politics has become widely aired. And yet, like the chatter about 'youthquakes', it does not tell us very much about the way that older and younger generations have voted in recent events, let alone the reasons why they voted the way that they did. Contradictions and nuances are glazed over in order to present evidence that the needs and desires of the future are being held back by the values of the past.

The role assigned to the Baby Boomer generation in all this is a curious one. As discussed in the previous chapter, generational politics in the 1990s consolidated a particular idea about the 'Sixties generation' as the 'liberal elite' represented by the Clinton and Blair administrations. To the extent that political events of recent years have represented a reaction against socially liberal values and the policies of the 'Third Way', it would be logical to see these events as a reaction against the Baby Boomers. But they have been more widely reframed as a reaction *by* the Baby Boomers, against the hopes and dreams of young people.

'This is not the first time our generation has suffered this kind of treatment,' complained Philip Bronk from London on the *Independent*'s letters page, echoing the well-established script of Boomer-blaming:

> The baby boomers subsidised their lives with massive public borrowing, then voted for austerity; they enjoyed final salary pension schemes, then abolished them; they enjoyed free university education, then voted to abolish that too; they enjoyed public utilities, then sold them off; and now, after enjoying a lifetime of EU citizenship, they've voted to take it away from us – not even to save money, but simply to give them a nationalistic thrill. Enough is enough![36]

Amidst the raw outrage that followed the Brexit vote, the Boomers found themselves to be a particular target. Headlines such as 'Baby Boomers, You Have Already Robbed Your Children of Their Future. Don't Make it Worse by Voting for Brexit,' and ' "This Vote Doesn't Represent the Younger Generation Who Will Have to Live with the Consequences": Millennials vent fury at baby boomers for voting Britain OUT of the EU',[37] drew on an already established image: hordes of wealthy, powerful Baby Boomers, engaged in a generational conspiracy to do everything possible to rob the young of their rightful future. In the USA, headlines such as 'Baby Boomers Have Been a Disaster for America, and Trump is Their Biggest Mistake Yet' showed how quickly the blame for this divisive election settled into the groove of the generation wars.[38]

The rush to blame 'the Boomers' for Brexit and Trump relies on the assumption that they all voted one way, and that younger voters were 'outvoted' by the vast number of old people. But neither of these myths is true. In the US election, it has been estimated that 44 per cent of voters aged 45–64, and 45 per cent of voters aged 65 and older, voted for Clinton, while 53 per cent of all those over 45 voted for Trump. For voters aged 18–29, Clinton picked up 55 per cent of the vote and Trump 37 per cent; of those aged 30–44, 50 per cent voted for Clinton and 42 per cent for Trump. Age certainly made a difference – but it was hardly as binary as 'Young Voted Clinton, Old Voted Trump'.[39]

A similar prejudice informed the simplistic reporting of the 'generational divide' in voting during Britain's EU referendum. Despite the ire directed at Baby Boomers for swinging the Leave vote, about two-fifths of this cohort are estimated to have voted Remain. And despite the assumption that young people who came out to vote would automatically see their future lying with Remain, around one-third of Millennials are thought to have voted Leave.[40] *Generation Remain*, an insightful study produced for the Intergenerational Foundation, notes:

> In terms of the number of voters, the data suggest that there were as many voters who voted Remain among the Baby Boomer generation as there were among Millennials (potentially more if, as seems likely, turnout among Millennials was lower); these data also suggest that more Millennial voters may have actually voted for Leave than did voters who belonged to the pre-1945 generation because there were many more of them.[41]

The report's author, David Kingman, points that that 'for all the talk of Brexit being an intergenerational conflict, young people did not vote homogenously'.[42] *Generation Remain* identified four different 'tribes' of Millennial voters. About one third of its sample were 'Eurosceptics', 'the most disaffected subset of Millennials, those who feel that modern British society and its economy has relatively little to offer them, for whom Brexit was an opportunity to rebel against the status quo'. They were predominantly white

British and of relatively low educational attainment, who feel a strong sense of national identity, report high levels of satisfaction with UK democracy, and are greatly concerned about immigration. Most of this group voted Leave.

Those young people who voted Remain did not do so with one voice, or because of one set of interests. The report identified three other 'tribes' of Millennial voters, all of whom wanted to stay in the European Union. The first were 'Left-Wing Europeans' (32.1 per cent), economically disadvantaged young people who lean to the Left politically, report 'extreme dissatisfaction' with UK democracy, and whose support for Remain 'appears to be rooted in a concern for the environment and social justice, and a hostility to the nationalist and anti-immigration rhetoric surrounding the Leave campaign'. A further 28 per cent were 'Affluent Pro-Europeans', highly educated and well-off young workers, mainly living in London and the southeast, who are 'broadly satisfied with the economic and political status quo'; and 8 per cent were 'Celtic Pro-Europeans', residents of Scotland and Wales, who 'view the EU as a way of counterbalancing England's dominant role in relation to the rest of the UK, as suggested by their weak sense of British national identity and dissatisfaction with UK democracy'.[43]

In insisting that politics has become divided between generations, generational narratives ignore the inconvenient fact of divisions *within* generations. The polarised battles of Clinton versus Trump, and Remain versus Leave, were driven by something far deeper than polite disagreements over strategy and policy, and went to the very heart of people's sense of identity and belonging. In attempting to fit these struggles into a generationalist narrative, both younger and older generations have been robbed of their voice as individual citizens, who vote different ways and with different reasons for doing so.

Deep stories and generational identities

A commonly heard story about the current political moment is that modern Western societies have become divided, not only by people's experiences of the current economic situation but also by their attitudes to recent social and cultural changes. Bluntly speaking, more affluent, educated people tend to welcome the opportunities offered by migration, multiculturalism and lifestyle diversity. They benefit from migrant cleaners, builders, and nannies, who work hard for low wages; they relish the ease of living, studying, and holidaying in a Europe without borders; they cherish the ability to experiment with one's sexuality, gender and personal living arrangements as a human right.

The other side of the divide is one which, until recently, has been skilfully airbrushed from the picture, as politics has come to focus more on issues of culture and identity than on social class and public policy. These are the people who live outside affluent, metropolitan areas in regions that have been left behind by the post-industrial world: the 'Red States' in the USA, or in the UK, the North, the Midlands and Wales. For these voters, jobs have been lost or made more insecure; wages have been depressed; and everywhere they are confronted with the admonition to put up, shut up, or be replaced by somebody who is prepared to get with the programme. As the economic situation has undermined their sense of financial security, the cultural turn taken by politics has become hostile to their own sense of identity.

This sense of cultural hostility is skilfully described by the sociologist Arlie Hochschild, in her 2016 book *Strangers in Their Own Land: Anger and mourning on the American right*. Hochschild spent five years talking and listening to Tea Party supporters in Louisiana – a 'red state' wracked with poverty and pollution, with low levels of education. Her aim was not just to find out what people said about politics, but to understand what they *thought and felt* about the current moment. She wanted to 'scale the empathy wall' that has been erected between people like her – highly educated, self-styled liberals living in coastal states, who eat organic food, recycle their garbage, use public transport and work in public or non-profit sector jobs – and the people for whom Donald Trump became the more appealing presidential candidate.[44]

In Hochschild's view, what drives people to take sides in political conflicts goes much deeper than a particular opinion about, say, immigration policies, or the extent of environmental regulation. Rather, it relates to how a particular view of the world connects with people's sense of themselves and where they are headed, or whether it is experienced as an assault on their way of life and sense of self. At play here, explains Hochschild, 'are "feeling rules", left ones and right ones. The right seeks release from liberal notions of what they *should feel* – happy for the gay newlywed, sad at the plight of the Syrian refugee, unresentful about paying taxes. The left sees prejudice.'[45] By dismissing people's rejection of orthodox 'feeling rules' as mere prejudice, the Left fails to understand 'the emotional core of right-wing belief', which is rooted in social, economic and cultural factors that are far more significant in framing people's outlook.

At a time when the liberal elite has become shrill and defensive, Hochschild's research is an invaluable contribution. The visceral reaction that boiled up and over in the past couple of years has forged a messy crack in the carefully constructed facemask of managerial politics-as-usual. All of a sudden, the economic policies and cultural assumptions that underpinned the 'Third Way' appear to stand in question. It is no longer enough for elites to assert the benefits of immigration, sexual and cultural diversity, labour market flexibility and economic fluidity: these things have to be argued for, against people who remember a different way of doing things. But making this positive case has proved remarkably difficult to do.

In the run-up to Britain's EU referendum, campaigners for Remain – including the British government – resorted to bullying the electorate with dark threats of what would happen if they voted the wrong way. Quickly dubbed 'Project Fear', it backfired in a spectacular fashion. In the United States, Clinton's assumption that women and young people would vote for her meant that she failed to engage in the arguments to why they *should* vote for her, and subsequent attempts to cast blame for 'what happened' anywhere but at her own campaign, indicate a continued refusal to acknowledge that people might have rational reasons for voting another way.

The recent upheavals are about politics: competing views of the society in which we want to live. But they go deeper than a disagreement about ideas. For the first time in its political reign, the so-called 'liberal elite' has been confronted with an alternative. This is not a positive, revolutionary alternative of the kind that propelled societies towards the pursuit of liberty, fraternity, equality, democracy and progress; nor is it the kind of economic and political alternative represented by the Soviet Union during the Cold War years. It is a romanticised alternative that draws on the norms and values of the recent past to provide an alternative sense of identity and belonging, in a world where it seems that the rules of the game are constantly changing. Attachment to the nation state, the church, and ideals of cultural homogeneity have come to the fore, in direct opposition to the 'twenty-first-century values' that have been relentlessly promoted for the past two decades.

Hochschild approaches this alternative identity through what she calls 'a "deep story", a story that feels as if it were true'. The 'deep story' narrated by the Tea Party is essentially one of loss: an estrangement from the values associated with the liberal elite. Partly, it is about making sense of the realities of life for many working-class Americans, which are now finally coming to light: insecure jobs, stagnant wages and debilitating working conditions. But more than that, they include having little control over the world around you and being despised for doing your best to support your family and community. In this deep story, Hochschild writes:

> You turn to your workplace for respect – but wages are flat and jobs insecure. So you look to other sources of honor. You get no extra points for your race. You look to gender, but if you're a man, you get no extra points for that either. If you are straight you are proud to be a married, heterosexual male, but that pride is now seen as a potential sign of homophobia – a

source of dishonor. Regional honor? Not that either. You are often disparaged for the place you call home. As for the church, many look down on it, and the proportion of Americans outside any denomination has risen. You are old, but in America, attention is trained on the young. People like you – white, Christian, working and middle class – suffer this sense of fading honor demographically, too, as this very group has declined in numbers.[46]

Age does not shape all of this deep story – but it is a significant part of it. The generational dislocation arising from the sense that 'you are old, but in America, attention is trained on the young' is a response to the way in which older people feel cut off both from the norms and values through which they were socialised, and the norms and values that are appreciated today. It is not only that young people are more likely to have rejected these traditional values: it is that public spaces and institutions across society now seem to be repelled by them – and by the people who hold them. The authority that once came with being old has been replaced by a sentiment of marginalisation, as the whip hand is held by those who identify with 'youth'.

A similar sense of dislocation is suggested by David Goodhart in *The Road to Somewhere*, his account of the 'populist revolt' in Britain and beyond. For Goodhart, the faultlines that have opened up in recent years can best be understood, not as a clash between left and right or between rich and poor, but between 'Anywheres and Somewheres'. 'Anywheres' are those who have developed their identity within the framework of twenty-first-century values – socially liberal, university educated, often living in urban areas and happily globetrotting for work or leisure. 'Somewheres' are those who remain attached to a particular place or community; they tend to be socially conservative, live in rural areas, less highly educated. Goodhart suggests that 'Somewheres' make up about half the population; 'Anywheres' up to a quarter; and the remainder can be classified as 'Inbetweeners'.[47]

Although there are limitations to Goodhart's analysis, it takes us beyond the pat diagnoses of the Brexit vote as racist, nationalist, or simply an expression of anger and frustration by the dispossessed against the political elite. The 'Anywhere/Somewhere' fault-line relates to a deeper sense of identity and belonging; the sense of whether you are embraced as part of the modern world or kept at a disdainful distance. And again, age and generation has come to play a significant role in this.

Contradictions of belonging

In explaining the 'generation gap' apparently revealed by the EU referendum, many suggested that the reality inhabited by young people is just different to that inhabited by their elders: youth represent the new, future-oriented reality, while older generations represent 'the past'. The Remain campaign successfully conveyed the idea that the desire for national sovereignty involved buying into an identity that means very little to many young people in Britain today, who have grown up in an increasingly globalised culture. They are used to mingling with people of different nationalities, whether in the playground at school or on social media. The internet provides unprecedented access to culture and media across the world, and schools continually emphasise the importance of knowing about other cultures and religions. Travelling, working and volunteering abroad have become quite normal features of teenage life, for those with the resources to do it. A cultural world constrained by national borders is, for many, unimaginable and unappealing.

The globalist outlook held by many young people accounts, at least in part, for why they experienced the Brexit vote as devastating and disorientating. Younger generations have been socialised into an outlook that presents the cultural values of the present day as several evolutionary steps ahead of those that dominated their grandparents' youth, when marriage was for life, gender was something you were born with, and teenagers were expected to respect their elders and fight for their country. In their own 'deep story', an orientation to 'Anywhere' does not represent a threat to a cherished set of values: it is simply the way things are, and probably better than the way things were.

In this sense, there does seem to be a generational difference in political outlook. But this is not caused by generational location alone, and young people have had to negotiate some profound contradictions in their orientation towards an 'Anywhere', twenty-first-century identity. Youth is not a clear-cut category – young people are also working-class people, unemployed people, university students, and so on. While young people are presented with an idea about an experience of the world, or a 'life of opportunities', that revolves around the notion that they should be flexible, well-travelled ambassadors for global citizenship, this can jar with many of the values and experiences that they have grown up with, and the commitments they hold dear.

This became particularly apparent during the recent political upheavals, in cases where young people found themselves at odds with their parents, and struggling to reconcile their own affection for, and experience of, their family with the stereotypes of the kind of people that might vote for 'That'. Despite all the talk about intergenerational conflict, most indicators suggest that young people today are generally emotionally close to their parents, often financially dependent on them, and see their families as a source of stability and support in a world where other commitments seem increasingly difficult to make.

This is a reality that has simply been invisible to elite campaigners inciting young people not only to vote the 'right way', but to guilt-trip their elders into toeing the line. Two months before the EU referendum, the campaign group Britain Stronger in Europe launched the 'Talk to Gran' initiative, encouraging young voters to pester their elders with postcards pleading, 'Please vote Remain so I can enjoy a life of opportunities in the EU (though I promise I'll be back for Sunday lunch)'; 'Nan, I know I should call more but . . . I want you to know why I'm voting to stay in Europe', and 'Gran, let's sit down for a cuppa, a slice of Battenberg and . . . A chat about why my future's in the EU'.[48]

The aim of this campaign was shameless manipulation. 'Research shows that people are more likely to listen to someone they know,' claimed the campaign video; and because your parents and grandparents 'want the best for you', you can persuade them that voting Remain is the way to achieve that. The real problem with older people, as presented by this campaign, was that they are more likely to vote than their children and grandchildren. So it did not encourage more young people to vote, or even to talk directly to the older generations about why they should change their minds; instead, it demanded that young people deploy emotional blackmail and pester-power against their elders.

'Talk to Gran' was a naked attempt to politicise family interactions – to make the conversation over Sunday lunch, or 'a slice of cake and a cup of tea', a vehicle for politicians to inculcate the electorate into particular ways of thinking, while bypassing political engagement and debate. It exemplifies the process discussed in the next chapter, where the views of older voters are dismissed as outdated and problematic, and the 'voice of youth' is co-opted to drive through the preferred politics of the current elite. The patronising stereotypes on which this campaign were based – and for which it received a well-deserved kicking, even from supporters of the Remain cause – were based on particular assumptions about old and young people alike, which simply failed to acknowledge the context in which people of all ages were deciding which way to vote, and the importance of genuine discussion between the generations.

In any case, breezy claims about the 'life of opportunities' offered by the current situation jar with the other complaints articulated by Millennial angst: for example, that the enforced flexibility of the labour market, and the excesses of the housing market, are conspiring to make it difficult for young people to grow up and settle down. As the Intergenerational Foundation's *Generation Remain* report observes, attempting to reconcile the apparent generational divide in the referendum with the 'plethora of evidence' showing that young people 'have suffered the most from the negative effects of recent economic trends such as stagnant wages and higher housing costs, while the majority of older people have enjoyed rising living standards' presents 'a very interesting conundrum':

> If the Brexit vote became a means for economically disadvantaged groups to register their anger and frustration with the status quo, then why didn't young people support Brexit?[49]

When it came to Brexit, the majority of young people plumped for the values and structures offered by the EU. But not all of them made what they were told was the 'obvious' choice – and around Europe young people are going in all kinds of political directions. In the USA, as we have seen, attempts to second-guess the youth vote on the assumption that the kids will do 'the right thing' have made the fatal error of ignoring young people's lack of enthusiasm for the thing itself.

The so-called generation gap in politics has not been created either by the backwardness of old people, or the new forms of political engagement practised by young people. It is a gap that has been constructed by the so-called 'liberal elite', in an attempt to gain moral authority for the values they want to promote. Rather than make a positive case for the values of today, this elite narrative has systematically set out to discredit the values of the past – along with the people who are presumed to embody them. One consequence of this has been to flatter a sense of generational grievance among younger 'Anywheres', who are incited to blame older people for voting against 'the future'. Another has been to provoke a backlash amongst older 'Somewheres', who are encouraged to see the threat to their values and ways of life as coming from intolerant, whining 'Millennials'.

In this, the politicisation of generational identity that began with the 'Baby Boomer elections' of the 1990s has taken a bigger, and more regressive, step. Clinton and Blair used and abused the language of youth to justify the need for a 'new' politics, situated beyond the left–right polarisation that underpinned the main parties of the twentieth century. Obama got out the youth vote by playing to a substance-lite rhetoric of youthful idealism. Since then, the elixir of youth seems to have been pickled in the spirit of self-righteous grievance: not 'Yes We Can!' so much as 'No They Can't'. Claims about the problem of allegedly under-represented groups, and the need to listen to those who don't vote, have been used to throw doubt on the legitimacy of the votes cast by those who do; and the 'younger generation' has been marched out as a stage army to undermine the authority of other people's votes.

CHAPTER 8

'Democratic deficits' and the tyranny of 'future generations'

'A gang of angry old men, irritable even in victory, are shaping the future of the country against the inclinations of its youth,' the respected novelist Ian McEwan told the two-day 'Convention on Brexit and the Political Crash' in 2017.[1] Arguing the case for a second EU referendum, he surmised:

> By 2019 the country could be in a receptive mood: 2.5 million over-18-year-olds, freshly franchised and mostly remainers; 1.5 million oldsters, mostly Brexiters, freshly in their graves.

McEwan, born in 1948, presumably doesn't see himself as the kind of angry old man who should pop his clogs for the greater good. Nor, one suspects, do his hopes for 'freshly franchised' teen-agers extend to those 18–24-year-olds who voted for Brexit in the 2016 EU referendum. In McEwan's fictional universe, 'youth' means good and 'oldster' denotes the bad, Brexit guy. Having failed to win the argument the first time round, he hopes that the Remain camp can wait a couple of years and let demography do the dirty work.

Amidst the bitter acrimony generated by the Brexit vote, one of the most disturbing developments was a systematic attempt to de-authorise the vote of older people, while investing the youth vote with greater worth. This was graphically illustrated by a widely reproduced table indicating how many years certain voters had left to 'live with the decision'.[2] According to this grim hourglass, voters aged 18–24 have a life expectancy of 90, and an average of 69 years to live with the decision to leave the EU, although the majority voted to Remain. Voters aged over 65, the majority of whom voted Leave, have a life expectancy of 89, and an average of 16 years to live with the decision.

The message was clear. Older generations have no business participating in big decisions that will affect the future: they have had their time, and should now shut up and let the kids get on with it. 'The wrinkly bastards stitched us young uns up good and proper,' wrote Giles Coren in *The Times* just after referendum day. 'We should cut them off. Rewrite the franchise to start at 16 and end at 60 and do this thing all over again.'[3] Coren claimed that his article was meant as satire, but many didn't get the joke: probably because the tone of his article was indistinguishable from others earnestly proclaiming the unfairness of a system that gives every adult an equal right to vote.

'Having overwhelmingly voted to remain, many feel betrayed by an older generation who turned their backs on Europe but who will not be around to see the damage wreaked,' reported Emma Graham-Harrison in the *Observer*.[4] She noted 'bleak jokes across social media, driven by a powerful anger at being sacrificed for the short-term self-interest of people who would not have to face all the consequences', including one teenager who remarked on Facebook that 'the older generation voting to leave the EU is the same as your mate picking the film then leaving 20 minutes in'. Graham-Harrison also quoted 18-year-old Phoebe Warneford-Thomson, who complained 'I feel quite bitter that the older generation can celebrate victory, while young people have suffered such defeat and will have to live longest with this decision'; and 25-year-old Celeste Houlker:

For my generation, our future is quite bleak. We're told you may not have a pension, there are going to be no jobs, no houses for me and my friends to buy, we are going to rent for the rest of our lives. And now I'm not a European . . . We feel we have to live with these choices we haven't made. They are being made by people who have already lived their lives.

The idea that older people, who have 'already lived their lives', should have no say in the future of our society, expresses the toxic impact of generationalism on political debate. In their determination to present political conflicts as a clash of interests between old and young, generation warriors promote a version of citizenship that is as anti-democratic as it is anti-social. A tangled web is woven from dubious statistics, barely veiled prejudices and contradictory arguments, to promote a particular kind of political and policy agenda. In the previous chapter, we saw how the manipulative flattery of the youth vote bears little relation to the votes cast by young people. The 'youth vote' has become a symbolic vehicle for pushing through a certain set of values, by a section of the elite that finds itself on the defensive and lacking in popular support. The flipside of this artificial promotion of the youth vote is the denigration of the 'senior' vote – and the people who cast it.

Even before the upset caused by recent political events, generation warriors were arguing that democratic systems have become biased in favour of older people, and that something must be done to redress this alleged generational imbalance. They have made the case that young voters are outnumbered by older voters, leading to policies that benefit older people at the expense of the young. They have complained that the Baby Boomer generation is particularly culpable, because it is a large cohort that has been particularly active, selfish and greedy in pursuing the policies that it wants. They have argued that younger voters lack the will and the clout to vote for their own interests, and so they need intervention from those who will guard the interests of the younger generations today and in the future. And in all of these arguments, generation warriors have implied that the future has already been written – therefore, democratic processes need to be tidied up and tamed in order to bring the political choices made today in line with the world as it will be tomorrow. Swept along on a tide of Boomer-blaming, generation warriors have rhetorically stripped older voters of their right to citizenship and appropriated the voice of younger generations to serve their own agendas.

Wishing their lives away

'In Germany, it's the older generations who decide the government,' wrote Sandro Schroeder for *Deutsche Welle* in 2017.[5] That 30 per cent of the German electorate is above the age of 60 while the under-30s represent 'just 15 percent', and that half of the electorate is over 50 years of age, has, Schroeder argues, raised fears of Germany becoming a 'pensioners' democracy': a term used by the late former German President Roman Herzog in 2008, when he complained: 'We have an increasing number of older people in Germany, and all the parties are disproportionately playing to them.'

Nowadays, generation warriors around the globe are busy coming up with statistics designed to prove just how far the institutions of democracy are weighted in favour of older people, leading a number of commentators and campaigners to ask how 'free and fair' elections really are.[6] 'We already know that older voters (over-65s) don't have any problem turning out to vote,' the *NME* told its readers just before the 2017 UK General Election:

> But for decades, the youth turnout has been significantly lower. Following the result of last June's EU referendum, many wondered how active, older voters could decide a policy that would shape younger generations' futures. The way to combat this is simple – turn up to your local polling station, stick a cross in the ballot paper, job done.[7]

At a time when political campaigners have long been obsessed with capturing the votes of 'key demographics', it's not surprising that politicians are out to get the youth vote – especially when the

Millennials are now overtaking the Boomers in terms of their cohort size.[8] The idea that elections have to be won or lost by particular promises made to particular demographic groups is a pretty miserable reflection of the lack of wider vision at the heart of our democratic institutions. Even so, in this context, there is nothing wrong with politicians trying to get out the youth vote in the same way they try to get out the Black or Latino vote, or the Grey vote. The more people at the ballot box the better, right?

Except that this is not the way the discussion is going. Instead, we hear calls to 'even up' the franchise by giving young people a louder voice, and shutting older people up.

A central argument deployed by the intergenerational equity lobby has been that older generations – specifically, the Baby Boomers – have a monopoly on voting power, which leads them to have disproportionate political influence. But more than a cursory glance at this claim shows that the numbers don't stack up. Peddling this argument requires some creative accounting, which generally takes two forms: collapsing together the categories of age and generation, and calculating democratic weight according to past turnout estimates.

Some of the 'democratic deficit' claims focus on the problem of 'older people' versus 'younger people' – a niftily elastic categorisation that means boundaries can be drawn wherever best makes the point. In this vein, the UK's Intergenerational Foundation has warned of 'The Rise of Gerontocracy', which means that '65 year olds have seven times more voting power than 18 year olds'. Apparently, 'large cohorts of older voters are creating a "democratic deficit" in the UK'.[9] In a later report, published in 2016, the Foundation warned that at the next general election 'the median voter will be 49 years old . . . despite the fact that people in their late-20s and early-30s will then be among the most populous cohorts'.[10] By 2030, things will be even worse:

[T]he median voter will be 50 years old. There will be more potential voters in their 60s (with an average single-year cohort size of 867,000) than in their 20s (with an average of 847,000), while potential voting power will generally be concentrated among people in their 30s and 40s.[11]

The argument that there are more older voters than younger ones obviously depends on how you define your categories. If young is defined as 'aged 18–24', or even as 'aged 18–30', it stands to reason that there will be fewer voters in this category than in the over-50s, or even in the over-65s. If, when it comes to 2030, 'potential voting power will generally be concentrated among people in their 30s and 40s',[12] how is this proof of an all-powerful 'gerontocracy'? Talk about kids being old before their time.

Whether voters in their 30s or 40s are defined as part of the problematic old or the hopeful young seems to depend on the point that campaigners and pundits want to make. One news report from 2017 stated that: 'The "youthquake" behind Labour's general election surge extended to the under-45s'.[13] But it seems fairly obvious that any attempt to talk about the problem posed for younger generations by larger, older cohorts is not going to favour the Millennials for very long. As the 'Echo Boomers', Millennials are already assumed to embody the very features that have made the Boomers so problematic: a relatively big cohort, a greedy desire for more, a sense of entitlement that makes them reluctant to settle for less. Once they grow out of the small and cuddly '18–24' category, as most of them have already, Millennials will be well on their way to facing the same charge that has long been levelled at their parents: large, old and mean.

This has already happened to Generation X, the generation now mooching into middle age. In terms of cohort size, Generation X remains relatively runty; but when it votes the same way as the Boomers, its numbers are quickly added to the problem. An article by Bonnie Greer in *The New European* – a periodical quickly established in the wake of the EU referendum to give voice to the defeated '48 per cent' – is headlined 'Is Generation X to Blame for

Brexit?' Although the Baby Boomers have rightly taken a lot of the blame for the Brexit and Trump votes, argues Greer, 'the real rage comes from elsewhere':

> It's Generation X – the second biggest voters for Leave. Nobody's talking about them. But just picture that moment in *Gladiator* when Russell Crowe takes off his helmet and snarls: 'I will have my vengeance!'

What Generation X wants vengeance for, suggests Greer, is a whole range of things: the 1970s, Margaret Thatcher, the decline of the welfare state and the rise of individualism. But above all, they are bitter, selfish and vindictive. 'There is an aspect of Gen X that has do with rage: the rage about being male and feeling shafted,' she writes. 'Pissed off and angry Gen X guys are the shock troops driving the Trump Train in the States. And they are fuelling Leave here.'[14]

Poor old Generation X. Until fairly recently, this was the cohort most clearly positioned as the victim of Baby Boomer self-ishness – dwarfed in size, neglected in childhood, robbed of the opportunities that the Boomers allegedly took as their collective birthright. But now they are sprouting grey hairs and belligerence, they are apparently joining forces with those bad Boomers. Never mind, of course, that the Gen X vote for Leave, or Trump, was split almost down the middle – they are old enough to be casti-gated for voting the wrong way, rather than pitied or patronised like the Millennials.

The claim that large numbers of older people have brought about a 'democratic deficit' makes no sense in its own terms. It only makes sense if we presume that older people will vote a particular way, for policies that will disadvantage younger people. In other words, it's not a claim based on the number of voters, but the (presumed) content of their votes. This is where Boomer-blaming, that now-familiar narrative of generational grievance, is brought into play.

Mobilising generational grievance

'Democracy at Risk as Baby Boomers Dominate Voting,' warned the *i* newspaper in 2016, as the Intergenerational Commission told of a 'democratic imbalance' caused by the 'ballot box advantage' enjoyed by Baby Boomers.[15] The central claim made by this report was that in the 2015 UK General Election, '67 per cent of baby boomers voted, compared to 56 per cent of generation X and just 46 per cent of millennials of voting age'. By combining turnout estimates with the impact of their large cohort size, the Commission claimed that there is 'a four million person ballot box advantage for the baby boomers over the millennials'.[16]

But hang on a minute. As a bewildered letter to the newspaper pointed out:

> How exactly do 'baby boomers dominate voting'? Through corruption, threats, nepotism, skulduggery? None of the above. We just vote, that's all, while too many people from other generations don't bother. That isn't 'democracy at risk', it's democracy. If non-voting millennials feel aggrieved by baby boomers' alleged electoral advantages, then the answer is in their own hands.[17]

If young people did share the *NME*'s concern that 'active, older voters' were deciding policies that would shape their futures in a bad way, it is true that the solution is simple: go out and vote. For all the emphasis on the great size of the Baby Boomer cohort, it is now beginning to dawn on commentators that as older Boomers die and the Millennials come of age, they are rapidly becoming outnumbered by the young ones. And though turnout rates tend to be higher among older people, a count of the votes hardly supports the idea that older people dominate. According to the Pew Research Center, Millennials and Generation Xers cast 69.6 million votes in the 2016 Presidential election, a slight majority of the total votes cast, while Boomers and older voters 'represented fewer than half of all votes for the first time in decades'.[18]

When the Boomer and Millennial cohorts are defined according to the birth dates used by the Intergenerational Commission, they turn out to be about the same size; and as the ageing Boomers begin to die off, any demographic 'advantage' will quickly fall to the Millennials. So where does the extra 'four million' come from? In a classic case of an argument in search of evidence, its report comes up with the scientific-sounding concept of 'generational democratic weight', which 'can be thought of as reflecting the combination of relative turnout and cohort size'.[19] Explaining that the Boomers have scored 'consistently highly on the former' and also 'dominate on the latter, due to both high birth numbers and longevity improvements', the Commission combined the demographic size of birth cohorts with their voting *behaviour*: a variable that, as we have seen, is not static, and can depend on individual motivations as well as wider political factors.

According to the Intergenerational Commission's analysis, factors behind the 'generational turnout gap' include the 'decline in voting when first eligible, and the simultaneous strengthening of the relationship between past and future turnout', meaning that 'young people are less likely to vote first time round, and this effect gets amplified because getting into the habit takes relatively longer than it did in the past'.[20] So this 'democratic imbalance' between the generations is framed not simply as an analysis of past trends in voter turnout, but as a projection of a particular crisis to come. Through attempting to establish not only that Millennials are less likely to vote than Boomers because they are young, but that they will *always* be less likely to vote, the Intergenerational Commission positions the Boomers not just as having a malevolent and determining effect on political decision-making in the here and now, but warping the very shape of democracy.

There are a number of empirical problems with the claim of a 'Boomer ballot-box advantage'. Most obviously, such rigid interpretations of voter behaviour don't hold up when things seem to have changed: meaning that the very same explanations for low turnout morph into arguments for why young people might suddenly be politically engaged. In a blog post published just before the 2017 UK General Election, the Commission's Laura Gardiner, author of the 'ballot box advantage' report, argued that young people are less likely to vote because they don't own their own homes.[21] Yet in the aftermath of the election and amidst all the 'youthquake' chatter, the Commission's Torsten Bell claimed that young people's sense of generational grievance had turned into a force for mobilisation, rather than demoralisation. In a post wishfully headlined 'The Millennials and Politics: Are they getting into the swing of it?', Bell stated that the 'rise in engagement amongst young people' was driven by 'the fact that their future looks bleaker than . . . any of us expected it to', exemplified by the way in which 'young people have seen the dream of home ownership pushed further out of reach'.[22] So young people don't vote because they don't own houses, therefore young people's struggle to get on the property ladder is encouraging them to vote. Oxymoron, anybody?

The Boomers' alleged 'ballot box advantage' is further deployed as evidence that policy has become skewed around the interests of the Boomers, at the expense of younger generations. 'The superficial correlation between generational voting blocs and the tax and benefit policies being implemented this parliament, which deliver a net benefit to those aged 55–75 set against large losses for those aged 20–40, is evident,' writes Gardiner.[23]

The assumption that people vote according to their immediate generational interests is a favourite weapon in the Boomer-blamers' arsenal: and given the consumerist character of political campaigning in recent decades, it seems to hit home. Politicians chasing votes are shamelessly eager to pander to the biggest numbers – whether that is the 'Grey vote' of the Boomers, or the 'youth vote' of the Echo Boomers. But just because politicians think they need to appeal to people's sectional, generational prejudices, does not mean that the electorate sees things the same way. 'As a first time voter, one thing struck me in particular, and that was the polarisation and patronisation of the electorate, and the damage this can do,' said Rhianna Voice, an A-level student from Staffordshire, when asked by the *Huffington Post* what she thought about the result of the UK's 2015 General Election, in which candidates from all parties tried to outbid each other in their attempt to capture the youth vote.[24] Voice continued:

> The polling booth is perhaps the only place where nothing can separate us – be it race, gender, age or sexuality – and that is what makes [voting] so great a privilege. By suggesting that any one group has its own particular issues, and insinuating, or outright advocating, that these should be considered in isolation to the electorate as a whole, we are harming our democracy.

This young woman intuitively grasped what all the politicians shamelessly chasing the 'youth vote' or the 'grey vote' have got so wrong. Education, jobs, housing, healthcare, taxation, pensions and anything else that politicians might be concerned with are issues that affect young people just as much as everybody else – if not immediately now, then in relation to their families, and certainly in relation to their own future. The idea that social policy provision can be split up and billed to whichever group is currently directly affected by it is as nonsensical as it is divisive. As the 'dementia tax' furore of 2017 revealed, people's lives and concerns across the generations are intertwined. Demanding money with menaces from old, sick people not only threatens them, but impacts upon the younger generations in their family. In any case, today's young people are tomorrow's pensioners. The historian Arthur Marwick put it well back in 1970, when he noted that 'there is probably always one final sanction on the power of youth: the process of growing older'.[25]

Attempts to buy young people's vote through promises of reductions in university tuition fees, or a bit of cash to put towards buying a mean, overpriced, 'affordable' apartment, are the flipside of attempts to shore up the grey vote through policies affirming social security entitlements. But it is worse than that. Pensions, healthcare and social care – like education, child care and housing – are things that we, as a whole society, want and need. If politicians are discouraged from cutting funding for these provisions because they don't want to annoy the 'greedy' Baby Boomers, at least we get to hold onto them. The kind of initiatives that pander to aggrieved youth offer very little for young people, at the expense of chipping away at the genuinely social provisions of the welfare state.

In May 2018, the Intergenerational Commission issued its twenty-third and final report, grandly titled *A New Generational Contract*.[26] Its most widely reported proposal was the introduction of a 'citizen's inheritance' payment of £10,000 for 25-year-olds, 'a restricted-use asset endowment to all young adults to support skills, entrepreneurship, housing and pension saving': a bizarre initiative that reveals what low aspirations the proponents of 'intergenerational equity' policies have for the younger generation.

As the Commission's own reports have spelled out, the big problems confronting young people come from a combination of low wages and the spiralling costs of housing – whether buying or renting. The energy and expertise engaged by the Commission over the two years of its work could have been directed at a serious attempt to resolve these problems – but it wasn't. Because right from the start, its aim was to shoehorn complicated questions of economic and social policy into a divisive and penny-pinching rationale for plundering Grandma's assets.

As well as encouraging young people to swap their expectations of a decent working life for a welfare handout and a sentiment of generational grievance, the Commission's proposals included replacing inheritance tax with a 'lifetime receipts tax that is levied on recipients with fewer exemptions', increasing 'property-based contributions towards the cost of social care' (a recycled version of the unpopular 'dementia tax' proposed in the Conservative Party's 2017 election manifesto), and the introduction of a '£2.3 billion "NHS levy" via national insurance on the earnings of those above state pension age and limited national insurance on occupational pension income'. In other words – get old people to pay for their 'own' policies, and find more creative ways to shave cash from pensioners' assets, in order to prop up the zombie economy.

The argument that politics and policy has been weighted in favour of older people, and now needs to be 'rebalanced' in favour of the young, is usually interpreted as a move to privilege the interests of a particular section of the population over the conflicting needs of another. Proponents of policies that promote 'intergenerational equity' see this as a necessary and righteous move – not just on the pragmatic grounds that we can no longer afford to pursue the good life for all, but on the principle that a particular section of the population does not deserve to have its interests represented. As an editorial for the *Guardian* newspaper put it, when welcoming the Intergenerational Commission's proposals for 'A New Generational Contract' that 'would reshape the burden of taxation in favour of the young and at the expense of many of the old':

> Much of this is a very direct challenge to recent political orthodoxy, because older voters – more pro-leave and pro-Conservative – would be expected to do more than at present to finance the life chances of young ones – more pro-remain and pro-Labour.[27]

The idea that policy provision necessarily involves taking from one group to give to another, lies at the core of the intergenerational inequity cause. As numerous scholars have shown, this argument is not only divisive but dishonest: robbing old Peter to pay young Paul invariably means that Paul gets a cut in wages too. And as we saw in Chapter 3, campaigners for such policies are driven by the conviction that 'intergenerational equity' should be high on the political agenda not only despite lack of public support, but *because* of it. The idea is that the electorate just doesn't get it and needs to be subjected to a relentless programme of 'generational thinking', which holds that selfish older voters have a moral obligation to subsume their own interests under the presumed best interests of younger voters.

But the young do not benefit from policies that take away from the old. The consequence of generationalist politics is to weaken the expression of political interest by all people, of any age. The 'grey vote' is stripped of its authority, the 'youth vote' stripped of its relationship with actual, young voters, and greater power is invested in the hands of self-appointed guardians of the needs of 'future generations'.

Demographic cleansing

In the wake of Brexit and Trump, the idea that the older generation, those 'old white men' with their backward ideas and old-fashioned values, are standing in the way of the future has become a prominent theme in the conceit of generational politics. The assumption here is that the values of the future have already been determined, and are embodied in the younger generation: not only their voting preferences, but their very existence.

According to William H. Frey, author of the Brookings Institution report *The Millennial Generation: A demographic bridge to America's diverse future*, the most significant feature of this generation is 'its racial and ethnic diversity'. 'By the mid-2040s, racial and ethnic minorities are projected to make up over half of all Americans, but the 2020 census will show that the postmillennial generation – people who are younger than millennials – will already be minority white,' writes Frey. 'This means that millennials, now 44 percent minority, will pave the way for the generations behind them as workers, consumers, and leaders in business and government in their acceptance by and participation in tomorrow's more racially diverse America.'[28]

The demographic shift in the ethnic diversity of Western populations is striking and significant. But in discussions about the generational quality of this shift, what is more striking is the attempt to invest it with an urgent, missionary quality: as though it is constantly under threat from those who were not born to be a part of it. A combination of more fluid migration and the ongoing decline in segregationist attitudes means that younger generations have grown up in a world where ethnic diversity is not only normal, but welcomed as a positive virtue. For this, we might give some credit to the civil rights movement of the 1960s, or the immigration policies of the 1990s, or the TV and internet for bringing access to other cultures to our living rooms. These endeavours were all brought about by people of previous generations – not least, the Sixties generation who, as 'the first global generation', experienced the world as 'an open space' to be travelled, explored and communicated with, and played no small role in transmitting this ideal to its Millennial progeny.[29]

Yet now, the Baby Boomer/Sixties generation is cast as a threat to all that, which can only be diffused by their children who, it is hoped, will help 'to close the racial and cultural generation gap that, as recent politics have shown, is dividing the nation'.[30] Too many older people, said Liberal Democrat leader Vince Cable, were driven to vote for Brexit by 'nostalgia for a world where passports were blue, faces were white and the map was coloured imperial pink', and 'it was their votes on one wet day in June which crushed the hopes and aspirations of young people for years to come'.[31] It is as though the Boomers who lived through racial tensions, fought against racist policies and preached the virtues of diversity have suddenly turned into senile bigots, stuck forever on the wrong side of Frey's 'demographic bridge to the future'. The superiority of the Millennials, meanwhile, is seen to result not from anything they have said or done, but from just being who they are.

Frey acknowledges that the Millennial generation 'will face both opportunities and challenges' in fulfilling its mission, including the problems caused by disparities of race and ethnicity in education attainment, family formation, income and housing. He recognises some of the over-simplification that goes with his generational analysis, not least the extent to which it does not account for the fact that 'local contexts for the social and economic opportunities available to millennials differ widely across the country'. But all the important differences between Millennials apparently pale into insignificance compared to their naturalised, demographic characteristics:

> The millennial generation, over 75 million strong is America's largest – eclipsing the current size of the postwar baby boom generation . . . While much attention has been given to this generation's unique attributes – its technological savvy, its tolerance and independence, and its aversion to large institutions – one aspect of millennials is most relevant to its future impact on the nation: its racial and ethnic diversity.[32]

The hope that Millennials will drive through twenty-first-century values just by being who they are is reflected in assumptions about their voting choices in the years to come. 'Millennial support for Remain could be a generational effect rather than an age effect,' argues the Intergenerational Foundation's report *Generation Remain*:

> If this is the case, then the growing share of the British population which is university educated and non-White British could push public opinion in a more pro-European direction over the coming decades.[33]

Given the visceral and formative character of the EU referendum and the commentary that followed it, the 'generation effect' – certainly for Millennials – could well hold true across their lifetimes. Because of the context in which this generation has developed their ideas about the world, the presumption that to be 'pro-EU' is the morally correct stance might stay with them. But then again, it might not. As we have seen, the divides revealed by the current moment go much deeper than a generation gap; and even within generations, there are differences in outlook that are obscured by the generalisation of 'young versus old'.

And while the EU referendum may have been a formative political moment for Millennials, it may not hold the same resonance for the younger 'Generation Z'. The 'voice of a generation' is not the same as 'the voice of young people for all time'. History moves on, and people form different ideas and attachments. Generational location has to contend with other contradictions of belonging, which are not so easy to manipulate away. Deep down, the political elites currently looking to the Millennial vote to save them from the effects of older people voting the wrong way, know this. That is why, rather than simply leaving demographic trends to run their course and assuming that, as the older generations die off the kids will build their own 'bridge to the future', political elites are engaged in an increasingly desperate attempt at project management.

Hiding behind the children

To argue that democracy is being put 'at risk' by people voting is not only a strange argument – it is one with some serious implications. The basis of democratic institutions and processes in the United Kingdom is that all adult citizens (with some specific exceptions) hold one vote, and that each vote counts equally. Although we are well aware that power, influence and access to resources is not distributed equally in society, any allegation that voting rights are unequally distributed strikes at the very basis of citizenship. But such a redefinition of citizenship is the explicit goal of many generation warriors, who seem to want to 'save democracy' by establishing that some votes are more equal than others.[34]

The Intergenerational Foundation's report *The Rising Tide of Gerontocracy* allows that 'young people do not speak with one voice', and that 'the extent to which governments' apparent favouritism towards older people is responsible' for the 'intergenerational democratic deficit' is 'contestable'. Nonetheless, Berry and Hunt argue:

[W]e have to consider the possibility . . . that the intergenerational democratic deficit undermines one of the key 'unwritten rules' of representative democracy, that is, that those who will be affected by the outcomes of the democratic process for longest should have the greatest representation at the ballot box.[35]

Given that the key 'written rule' of representative democracy is that each adult holds one, equal vote, it takes a particular circumlocution of the imagination to perceive the 'unwritten rule' that those who have longer to live should have the 'greatest representation'. On one level, of course, if we consider voters as they actually are – people who make decisions about the future of society as a whole, rather than as individual consumers of policy who can only be engaged with through the sale of policies that are immediately relevant and personally beneficial – then it is possible to see how this unwritten rule might work in practice. Any good policy that is voted in will last the longest for people who live the longest.

That view, however, relies on assuming that people are willing and able to vote for a common good. And that is the opposite of the assumption made by the authors of *The Rising Tide of Gerontocracy*, who see voting as the expression of particularistic interests. For Berry and Hunt, the 'unwritten rule' of greater representation for the young is made impossible by the biological ageing of the population. 'There has never been an authentic democracy in any large society without a pyramid-shaped age distribution – yet we are moving rapidly, and unavoidably, towards a much more dome-shaped age profile,' they write. 'The improvements in longevity that are bringing about this development are arguably one of the great successes of democracy, but nevertheless the implications for the future of the democratic process must not be ignored.'[36]

In the name of rescuing the 'future of the democratic process', generation warriors propose measures that are directly anti-democratic. One idea, which gained momentum in the wake of

Britain's EU referendum, was that votes should be weighted, in proportion to how long individual voters had to live – a clear message that the interests of those who have less long to live should count for less than the interests of those who have many years of productive life ahead of them.

Maja Založnik, a demographer from the University of Oxford, conducted a thought experiment to see what would have happened had that been the case in the 2016 referendum.[37] She crunched together the available (and not always reliable) data about the number of votes for Leave and Remain, broken down by age, with turnout data, voter registration data, population counts and life expectancy estimates. She then calculated how many 'years left to live' belong to each age group, and used them to weight the results. In this experimental voting system, she suggested, the votes of the youngest age group would account for 19.6 per cent of the overall votes, while the votes of those over 65 account for 8.2 per cent.

So, asked Založnik, 'with this new, "fairer" weighting of votes, would the result be radically overturned?' Yes – in that Remain would win with a two-point margin. But because of the relatively small youth turnout, a much greater proportion of 'votes' would be lost to 'voter apathy'. She concluded:

The more our societies age, the more self-serving voting behaviour will translate into inter-generational warfare. To those who would argue that this would also be an ageist system: in fact, over an individual's lifetime, everyone would get the same number of votes, so it would even out in the end.

Založnik argued that this thought experiment was 'not as fanciful as it may seem' – it is already being seriously considered by political scientists in Japan, where society is ageing even more drastically. But she also acknowledged that 'blaming the older generations for voting as they do, when the young don't make use of their voting rights, is disingenuous at best'.[38]

The very suggestion that voting should be weighted according to age is based on a number of dubious, and downright dangerous, assumptions. Besides the idea that decisions about the future direction of society are driven by individuals' immediate, 'self-serving' desires, and that these are somehow given by their generational location, it speaks to the transformation of citizenship into a technical process whereby people's interests are balanced and managed on their behalf. Rather than citizens having an entitlement to one, equal vote, democratic rights are recast as something that should be rationed and distributed according to the worth accorded to a particular group of citizens at a particular moment.

This paternalistic presumption is even more clearly encapsulated in the longstanding suggestion that the right to vote should be given to children. In most cases, this is limited to the argument that the franchise should be extended to 16-year-olds, as it already has been in a handful of countries – and was in Scotland, for the purpose of the 2014 referendum on Scottish independence. Even so, this would amount to a considerable infantilisation of voting rights. At least in Scotland, young people are still allowed to leave school at 16 – in England, they are compelled to stay in education or training until the age of 18.[39] Students in compulsory education, who are still ensconced in an environment where their daily routines, behaviours and ideas are subject to monitoring and correction by adult authorities, are, to all extents and purposes, still kids. They might have all kinds of ideas about how they want society to go – but as they haven't yet reached the first rung of the independence ladder, how could we even pretend to assume that these views are their own, rather than a proxy for some other voice?

This, for some, is the point. 'The younger a person the more time they have to spend in formal education, where they can develop their civic knowledge and recognise the importance of political participation – including voting,' argue New Zealand academics Bronwyn E. Wood and Nicholas Munn, in their discussion of 'how lowering the voting age to 16 could save democracy'.[40]

This logic also informs the Intergenerational Foundation's call for lowering the voting age to 16 in Britain. Such a move would not only 'reduce the median age of the electorate, giving politicians more of a reason to pursue policies which will help young people' – it would also 'be easier to educate young people about the political process and to help them engage with it while they are still at school, leaving them better-equipped for life as politically active citizens'.[41] According to this viewpoint, it is young people's very dependence on authority that makes them best placed to vote responsibly: presumably, once they are grown up, they are more likely to fall prey to their own ideas.

In Germany a number of parties, including the SPD, the Greens, and the Left Party reportedly supported lowering the voting age to 16. Wolfgang Gründinger, the Millennial author of two books on generational politics, *Alte Säcke Politik* (*Old Grumpy Men Politics*) and *Aufstand der Jungen* (*Youth Uprising*), is an active member of the Foundation for the Rights of Future Generations (FRFG), an environmentalist organisation established in the late 1990s, which has close links with the British Intergenerational Foundation. 'Every young person should have the right to vote as soon as they want to,' says Gründinger. 'Most would probably start exercising that right from the age of 12 or 13. But in principle, there should not be [an] age limit for young people – there's no age limit for old people either.'[42] The Intergenerational Foundation has noted approvingly the FRFG's argument that there should be no minimum age for voting, and suggests:

> One way to handle this is for parents to vote on behalf of minors until the children are old enough to exercise this democratic right themselves, whilst another approach is to allow children and teenagers to register for voting whenever they think they are ready to vote.[43]

The assumption that the voting credentials of a pubescent child, who has experienced nothing of the world beyond their own lives, can be put on a par with those of an octogenarian who has lived through broad swathes of social history, reveals the extent to which our idea of democratic citizenship is becoming detached from the most basic distinction between adults and children. Politics is, fundamentally, a means for individual adults to have their say in the way society works; an opportunity to have their interests recognised and represented. Why did the Chartists and the Suffragettes fight so long and hard to get the vote? Because otherwise, there was no way for women and working-class men to have their interests represented by Parliament. Why was the denial of Black people's right to exercise their vote such a disgrace in the USA? Because it presumed that the interests of the Black community were not worthy of political recognition.

In previous eras, the denial of votes to women, Black people, and working-class men was symbolic of their infantilised status. They were not regarded as independent citizens who knew their own minds and could be trusted to vote in their own best interests, or those of society as a whole. In fighting for the right to vote, they demonstrated the lie of this presumption. Even when, in the 1970s, the age of majority in the UK and USA was lowered from 21 to 18, it was informed by the sentiment that 18-year-olds, as adults, could and should be trusted to know their own minds and take responsibility for deciding their own personal and political futures. It came about as part of a wider political and cultural turn against paternalistic authority, in what came to be known as the 'permissive' society.

Calls to give the vote to children represent a resurgence of paternalism, with a very twenty-first-century twist. Adults are not denied the vote, but the status of their vote is undermined by the claim that this ignores the interests of a more deserving group, who have the 'longest to live' with policy decisions. Children, meanwhile, are presented as the group that most deserves a voice, precisely because they are not capable of exercising their rights independently and need somebody to speak on their behalf.

Forespeaking the needs of 'future generations'

By putting their words into the mouths of disenfranchised youth, generation warriors aim to present their agenda as radical, edgy and forward thinking. But at its core, the desire to preserve what is called the generational contract has deeply conservative roots. It was most famously articulated by the eighteenth-century political theorist and philosopher Edmund Burke in response to the French Revolution. Burke was appalled by the spectre of citizens rising up against the stability and authority of a society based on hereditary ancestry, and warned against the dangers of democratic rule, which he felt would destroy the moral and spiritual values that had been gathered by centuries of tradition. Society, argued Burke, should be understood as a 'contract' to be looked upon with 'reverence':

> . . . because it is not a partnership in things subservient only to the gross animal existence of a temporary and perishable nature. It is a partnership in all science, a partnership in all art, a partnership in every virtue and in all perfection. As the ends of such a partnership cannot be obtained in many generations, it becomes a partnership not only between those who are living, but between those who are living, those who are dead, and those who are to be born.[44]

In Burke's view, the need to preserve the generational contract was a powerful argument against radical change. He feared that by tearing up the institutions and traditions of the past, society would lose its moorings, cutting future generations adrift. It was the stability and authority of the past that provided the foundation for the conservative case against experimentation and change.

Present-day generation warriors often repeat Burke's statement of the partnership 'between those who are living, those who are dead, and those who are to be born' – but in a revised form. Like Burke, they are looking to shore up the status quo. But rather than anchoring the generational contract in the authority of the past ('those who are dead'), they project it forwards, to a future organised around the interests of 'those who are to be born'. This shares with Burke a fear of change, but with an important difference. For better or worse, the past has already been played out, by political actors working through problems and making decisions about where they want their societies to go. The future, by definition, is still to come. We cannot know what problems our future societies will deal with, or how they will be resolved. There is no future blueprint that can guide our actions in the present.

For David Willetts, Burke's appeal to government 'as a custodian of the contract between the generations' is a 'beautiful statement' of the central theme of his own book, *The Pinch*. Yet in re-stating the generational contract, Willetts flips it around. Willetts insists that the problem with British social policy today lies in its failure to attach 'sufficient value to the claims of future generations'. His argument is premised on a particular diagnosis of the problem of the Baby Boomer generation, which, he claims, has monopolised economic, social and cultural resources, and thereby 'weakened many of the ties between the generations'. Willetts presents the Baby Boomer problem as emblematic of:

> [A]n intellectual failure: we have not got a clear way of thinking about the rights of future generations. We are allowing one very big generation to break the inter-generational contract because we do not fully understand it. . . . [This] is where politics comes in . . . Good politics is about a contract between the generations in which the interests of the present generation should not automatically come first.[45]

But who can speak on behalf of 'future generations'? Not older people, whose stubborn commitment to their own interests is seen to be standing in the way of the sacrifices that need to be made. Not young people either, who are cast as weak and powerless in the face of the problems that have been stored up by decades of generational greed. Compared to the moral authority with which 'future generations' are endowed, the kids of today have very little clout. By default, guardianship of the interests of 'future generations' rests, not with democratic politics, but with an elite charged with making higher-order decisions. The conceit that politics is too short-termist to be left to people deciding their futures in the here and now, recasts decision-making as a technical risk-management project. This risk-averse projection of today's problems onto a pre-determined future is already having a profound effect on public policy around pensions, healthcare, housing and education – where the imperatives of 'austerity', 'sustainability' and 'fairness' are deployed to justify driving down expectations and provision in the here and now.

From the austerity ballads performed by campaigners for inter-generational equity policies to the dark Year Zero fantasies harboured by those awaiting a reckoning and 'great awakening', generation warriors are propelled by the belief that our actions, in the recent past and in the present, are leading inexorably to a future crisis. This has some profound consequences for the way in which social policy, and political action, is conceived. Generationalist politics assert that public policy should focus on the intricacies and intimacies of relations between the generations, rather than social problems that affect us all. This outlook presupposes that relations between old and young should be re-ordered around the presumed demands of an already-imagined and constrained future.

In this bleak outlook, adult society is presented as having a destructive impact on the younger generation, rather than one that is constructive and protective. Young people, meanwhile, are positioned, not as political actors, but as pawns; not as a solution to the problems of the future, but as part of the problem. In this respect, the generational determinism that has come to frame the Millennials' existence has gone a long way to consolidating the sense of beleaguered, minimal selfhood that Lasch wrote about back in the 1980s. What is at stake here is not only young people's conception of themselves as political citizens, but the aspiration to grow up, and become part of the adult world themselves.

CHAPTER 9

Ambivalent adulthood

Millennial angst is underpinned by the refrain of economic crisis. But the sense of betrayal and anomie articulated by these tracks – 'I don't give a shit,' says Talia Jane to her critics – comes from a deeper, darker place than the struggle to find a decent job. Nor is it just about the disenchantment that younger generations, in different times, have variously articulated with the world into which they are growing up. An increasingly prominent strain of complaint focuses on the problem of growing up *itself* – and the ways in which the Boomers have allegedly made that so much harder to do.

Younger people, complains Rhiannon Lucy Cosslett in the *Guardian*, 'are frequently portrayed as existing in a Neverland of kidulthood, a world of selfish entitlement and cereal, of onesies and bum selfies'. This analysis, she counters, 'conveniently ignores' the ways in which younger people are being priced out of 'the traditional rites of passage to adulthood – leaving the parental home, eventually buying property, stable employment, starting a family'. She continues:

> Far from relishing a prolonged adolescence, many people in their mid to late 20s and 30s would like nothing more than some semblance of stability. From the couples who desperately want to have a baby but can't imagine doing so in a shared

house, to those who long to leave the parental home but will be prevented from doing so by the removal of housing benefit for 18 to 21 year-olds (if they are lucky enough to have a parental home in the first place), young people are actually crying out for adulthood. The idea of proper, grownup stability has taken on the feeling of a fairytale, a children's story murmured comfortingly to send you off to sleep.[1]

The Baby Boomers are blamed not only for creating the problem of rising house prices and unstable employment, but for refusing to understand their children's pain. 'I'd like to offer a plea to boomers,' writes Cosslett. 'Next time you catch us "whining", or accuse us of never wanting to grow up, try mentally listing all the policy blockades that are stopping us from doing just that.' Anya Kamenetz is also 'really angry' when she sees 'the Boomers in charge of the media and other powerful institutions attributing the problems young people are going through to nothing more serious than a lack of initiative'. The media portrays Millennials as 'slackers, overgrown children, and procrastinators, as though we're intentionally dragging our heels to avoid reaching adulthood'. Yet, she complains, 'it's arguably our elders who are taking more than their fair share'.[2]

Given the scattergun vitriol that blames the Boomers for everything, it is perhaps not surprising that delayed adulthood should be framed as their fault too. But there is a curious tension between the thwarted desire to grow up that Millennial angst tries to exude, and the content of this aspiration. Millennials may rail against being 'trapped in kidulthood'[3] – but it is far from clear whether they actually want to escape it.

Emerging adulthood – and then what?

At the turn of the Millennium, the American psychologist Jeffrey Jensen Arnett coined the term 'emerging adulthood'[4] to describe what he saw as a 'new and historically unprecedented period of the life course', experienced by young people who were 'neither adolescents nor young adults but something in-between'; who were 'taking longer to grow up than young people had in the past, as measured by their entry to stable adult roles as well as their own self-perceptions of not-fully-adult status'.[5] In developing his account of 'the winding road from the late teens through the twenties', Arnett discussed a range of social, economic and cultural changes, including the experience of work and higher education, relationships with parents, religious beliefs and values, and later ages of marriage and parenthood.

All these are broad trends, which have been widely discussed with reference to Western societies as a whole – particularly in the extent to which they reflect a decline in traditional sources of commitment, solidarity and meaning.[6] They are not unique to young people, and they are not necessarily trends that young people welcome, or lifestyles that they choose. But the notion of 'emerging adulthood' has caught on, spawning a veritable industry of books, articles, text books and even an academic journal.[7] This concept is widely interpreted as illuminating a positive social development, which allows young people more 'freedom of exploration' than in times past. 'Their society grants them a long moratorium in their late teens and twenties without expecting them to take on adult responsibilities as soon as they are able,' writes Arnett. 'Instead, they are allowed to move into adult responsibilities gradually, at their own pace.'[8]

As the concept of 'emerging adulthood' has developed, so have its critics. The idea of this new life stage as a period of 'freedom of exploration' focuses on the experience of middle-class, college-educated youth; as Arnett acknowledges, not all young adults 'have an equal portion of it', and many are living in circumstances that provide them with 'severely limited' opportunities.[9] Even for the privileged, the notion of 'freedom' encapsulated here is one that is relatively regulated and constrained. In reality, emerging adulthood is neither perceived nor experienced as a time in which young people can merely enjoy being footloose and fancy-free, but as a series of semi-structured exercises in preparing for an adult life that has yet to begin.

For example, a study by Anika Haverig and Steven Roberts of the 'Overseas Experience', a New Zealand term for an extended overseas working period or holiday, finds that young people who participate in the 'OE' experience it less in terms of unmitigated freedom and boundless opportunity, than as an endeavour framed by 'constraint, restriction, and . . . notions of perceived normalised behaviour'.[10] Higher education, gap years, internships and other station stops along the 'winding road' are increasingly becoming normative activities in which young people are expected to engage in order to learn 'adult' skills: with the implication that they are not considered fit for adulthood unless they have gone through the programme of exploration first. In this respect, many features of the 'emerging adult' experience have become formalised, to compensate for a deeper confusion about what it means to be an adult anyway.

'In recent years, the transition to adulthood has grown more protracted and problematic as acquisition of the traditional markers of adult identity – marriage, childbirth, and entry into a full-time career – are delayed into the late twenties,' writes the historian Stephen Mintz.[11] But he also notes that young adulthood has been viewed as a time of 'aimlessness and indecision' for well over a century; in this sense, many of the worries aired with regard to kidult Millennials are not that distinct after all. A far more significant change is the kind of adulthood that young people emerge into: not a stable identity, but a time of ongoing 'flux and mutability'. 'Instability, uncertainty, and a desire to grow, but not grow up and settle down, persist into adults' thirties, forties, fifties, and sixties,' he explains. 'A script that shaped expectations of adulthood through much of the twentieth century has unravelled.'[12]

Historically, 'becoming an adult' has been framed as something to celebrate – receiving 'the key to the door', as my grandfather put it. For sure, that milestone has always meant the end of playtime; for older generations, who left school at 14, 16 or 18 to start their working lives, spontaneity would already have been long gone and a 'personal growth' regarded as something that might need lancing by a surgeon. But young adults also saw themselves as pushing open a door to something bigger than themselves; working through the frustrations of daily life to pursue the ambitions and commitments that were reserved for grown-up society.

Today, Mintz writes, 'many young adults view the traditional markers of adulthood with suspicion and contempt, associating adulthood with weighty, unwelcomed responsibilities, closed-off options, and stultifying, button-down conformity'.[13] Arnett, too, suggests that young people are at least as aware of the downsides of growing up – 'the dreary, dead-end jobs, the bitter divorces, the disappointing and disrespectful children that some will find themselves experiencing in the years to come'[14] – as they are positive about the responsibilities of adulthood. '[M]any emerging adults are ambivalent about reaching adulthood,' he writes:

> Yes, it is nice to have the freedom to run your own life, and it is satisfying to be able to handle adult responsibilities competently. But mixed with their pride in reaching adulthood is dread and reluctance.[15]

Arnett cites a national poll conducted by himself and a colleague in 2012, in which 35 per cent of 18–29-year-olds agreed with the statement, 'If I could have my way I would never become an adult'. In part, he suggests, this ambivalence stems from 'a realization that adult responsibilities can be burdensome and annoying'. But another source of ambivalence is that 'they associate becoming an adult with stagnation': in this view, reaching adulthood means 'the end of fun, of spontaneity, of personal growth'.[16]

Even where adulthood is not perceived as something to be avoided for as long as possible, its meaning is often reduced to a set of technicalities or competencies, which do little to inspire. Arnett states that in a number of studies from across the United States, people consistently list the following as the top three criteria for adulthood:

1. Accept responsibility for yourself.
2. Make independent decisions.
3. Become financially independent.[17]

Couched in these terms, the life stage once described as 'adulthood' is reframed as a particular skill-set that enables individuals to navigate the demands of everyday life and work. While these skills may be necessary, they hardly capture what it means to grow up, or why young people should want to do so. Yet some aspects of Millennial culture have embraced this competency-based model of adulthood, constructing a whole new term – 'adulting' – to denote 'the practice of behaving in a way characteristic of a responsible adult, especially the accomplishment of mundane but necessary tasks'.[18]

Adulting, as Katy Steinmetz explains in *Time* magazine, can partly be seen as a self-deprecating reflection of the 'delayed development' of emerging adults. Millennials, as we have seen, are adept at constructing witty hashtags out of people's criticisms; and turning 'adulting' into a discrete activity could be merely a neat contraction of the finger-wagging admonition to behave like adults. But it also connotes a wider sentiment that growing up might be a state of being that young people want to avoid while they have the choice:

> [T]his jokey way of describing one's engagement in adult behaviors – whether that is doing your own taxes, buying your first lawn mower, staying in on a Friday, being someone's boss or getting super pumped about home appliances – can help those millennials acknowledge *and/or* make fun of *and/or* come to grips with that transition (or how late they are to it).

The trouble is that being an adult is not an activity, but a state of being – and growing up is not something that can be done only on days when you feel like it. Steinmetz observes:

To say you are "adulting" is to, on some level, create distance between you and what are implied to be *actual* adults who are adulting 100% of the time and therefore have little reason to acknowledge it. Or if they do, they might instead use phrases like 'going about my normal day'.[19]

Growing up, growing old

The sentiment that growing up comes with a downside is not new – think of that hackneyed phrase, 'schooldays are the best days of your life'. But it has become strikingly pronounced in recent times. Much of the blame for this has come to rest on the Baby Boomers (again) for the 'cult of youth' spawned by the Sixties, a culture pithily documented by Christopher Booker in *The Neophiliacs*, which emphasised novelty and experimentation at the expense of authority and tradition.[20] As previous chapters have discussed, the Boomers were as much of a product of their time as its protagonists – Booker's *Neophiliacs* was first published in 1969, reflecting on upheavals to social life and convention that were already taking place in the 1950s. During the early 1960s, when the eldest Boomers were still in high school, sociologists and anthropologists were engaging with new tensions that were emerging around the socialisation of 'youth',[21] growing up in a world of crumbling conventions and rapid social change.

Even back then, the emergent 'cult of youth' was perceived as unsettling, as well as exciting. The status of adulthood as something deserving respect received a slap in the face with that catchy student protest slogan, 'don't trust anyone over 30'. The protagonists of the permissive society threw over the kind of adulthood that was conventionally represented – marriage, house, children, the same 'job for life' – in favour of something less dreary and more experimental; a period in which fun, spontaneity and personal growth could continue over the whole life course, rather than stop short once adult life began.

This was not merely a cultural shift. One influential theory, formulated by Ron Lesthaeghe and Dirk van de Kaa in the mid-1980s, was that developed societies in the post-war period were undergoing a 'second demographic transition', characterised by 'sub-replacement fertility, a multitude of living arrangements other than marriage, a disconnection between marriage and procreation, and no stationary population'. Populations would age and shrink, relying increasingly on new migrants to sustain them.[22] Smaller family sizes, an increase in childlessness, women having children at a later age, women having careers, people forming long-term partnerships at a later age, young people staying in education for longer and living at home with their parents until they are pushing 30, increased longevity, increased migration – all these have affected the traditional milestones on the way to adulthood.

These demographic changes have also brought with them a shift in ideas about adulthood and childhood – which are not fixed categories, but concepts that develop in relation to wider social changes. During the first demographic transition from the eighteenth century onwards, where modernising societies underwent significant declines in death rates and birth rates, 'the decline in fertility was "unleashed by an enormous sentimental and financial investment in the child"' – what Philippe Ariès, in his seminal analysis of the history of childhood, termed the 'king child era'. During the second demographic transition, explains Lesthaeghe, the motivation is 'adult self-realization within the role or life style as a parent or more complete and fulfilled adult'.[23]

Following this insight, we can see that changing milestones on the journey to adulthood form only part of a bigger story, about changes in the meaning ascribed to adulthood itself. Whereas the first demographic transition is considered 'as anchored mainly in the stage of the realization of basic material needs', the background to the second is described by Lesthaeghe in terms of 'a Maslowian preference drift' towards a focus on the 'development of higher-order, non-material needs and of expressive values', such as freedom of expression, participation and emancipation, self-realization and autonomy, and recognition.[24] This gave rise to an ideal of growing up that seemed to be premised as much on a rejection of the norms and expectations of adult life as it was based on a positive desire to embrace them.

Mintz notes that the phenomenon of delayed adulthood is happening at the same time as 'growing numbers of those at midlife refuse to act their age.' 'Instead, they wear youthful fashions, eschew activities previously associated with middle age, and actively resist the ageing process,' he writes. 'In the age of Future Shock, the settledness that many assumed characterized the mature years has broken down.'[25] The 'traditional markers of adult identity' not only take longer to acquire, but are culturally framed as inadequate sources of individual fulfilment. Personal identity is projected as something distinct from, even at odds with, adult identity.

The restless pursuit of individual self-realisation throughout midlife, starkly expressed in the concept of the Third Age formulated by Peter Laslett in the 1980s to describe the life stage between the Second Age of 'independence, maturity, responsibility and earning' and the Fourth Age of 'final dependence, decrepitude and death', has caught on in the Western world.[26] The Third Age, Laslett argued, 'is the interlude . . . when the goal of the individual life plan is realised':

> This goal, which can itself be plural, lies outside the earning career for all but the really great achievers, and for others in a position to attain their personal objectives during that earning career, and persist in this way until the onset of the Fourth Age. Hence a chosen point in the personal age of the individual, rather than a point in his or her calendar age, or biological age, or social age is the occasion of the onset of the Third Age for her or for him.[27]

Like the concept of 'emerging adulthood', Laslett's thesis has been criticised on the basis that life, for many Third Agers, is not some freewheeling moment of self-actualisation, but a more prosaic reality shaped by low income, ill health and family pressures.[28] The US writer Susan Jacoby has slammed 'the myth and marketing of the new old age', which blithely presents getting older as a state of mind that can be overcome by adopting a youthful, active, can-do mindset, as 'a new, more subtle, but no-less-pernicious form of ageism' than stereotypically negative attitudes about old age.[29] While the old ageism continues to write people off prematurely, as dependent, inactive and irrelevant, the 'new ageism' fails to engage with the problems and inequalities that older people experience, implying that these are the result of individuals' failure to think themselves young.

But for all its flaws as a description of the reality of retirement, Laslett's vision has been significant in reframing the way present society has come to *think about* middle and old age. What Laslett regarded as the most radical aspect of the Third Age was that it de-coupled the idea of chronological or biological ageing from the experience of a distinct life stage, and from the social and cultural norms that had previously surrounded the meaning of adulthood. Shakespeare's 'seven ages of man' had it that man would reach the peak of his authority in public life, as 'the justice . . . Full of wise saws and modern instances', before shifting into 'the lean and slippered pantaloon', frail and childish, in 'a world too wide / For his shrunk shank'.[30] Indeed, up until the mid-twentieth century, it was assumed that individuals' sense of self and achievement was developed during their lives as a working adult. Work and politics were viewed as the domains on which adults made their mark, with retirement as a formal laying-down of arms.

For theorists of the Third Age, the locus of meaning lay outside all that – in a self finally freed from the shackles of social convention to achieve the 'goal of the individual life plan'. Such ideas capture something profound about the trajectory of Western culture over the twentieth century, and a tension that continues to underpin debates about the legacy of the Sixties for our present society. Is our focus on individual, non-material needs and desires a mark of progress, or a distraction from more important goals? And what happens when societies become disenchanted with their capacity to deliver such 'higher-order needs' as 'freedom of expression, participation and emancipation, self-realization and autonomy'?[31]

The culture of narcissism: The sequel

The pursuit of higher-order, self-fulfilment needs was most explicitly pursued by the countercultural movements of the Sixties. With the possible exception of hippie communes, whose inarticulate attempts to eschew any focus on basic needs while trying to live in some level of comfort have long been satirists' bread and butter, most of the counterculture went for an emphasis on having it all: comfort, freedom, equality and personal growth. And even if they didn't exactly manage to live the dream, there was a moment in which they could at least hang on to it. The economy was booming, things were changing, and the spirit of the age was one in which self-realisation was regarded as not only an entitlement, but an imperative.

But the pursuit of higher-order needs, and the focus on culture and intimate life, was also a product of a limited social and political vision. Christopher Lasch's 1979 book *The Culture of Narcissism: American life in an age of diminishing expectations* regarded the therapeutic turn of culture and politics, with its increasing focus on the self, as an outcome of a wider loss of faith in human action to make the world out there a better place.[32] This did not lead, as many have assumed, to an inflation of the individual's sense of purpose and importance, but to the 'beleaguered' selfhood described in Chapter 6.[33]

A culture of narcissism, like its mythical namesake, is one that is self-regarding because it is weak. Western societies' response to the cultural upheavals of the Sixties was to flatter themselves about the ability to pursue individuals' higher-order needs, rather than engaging with the structural and political problems at their core. As Furedi has revealed in his studies of therapy culture and the politics of fear, the trends towards minimal selfhood became more defined from the 1990s onwards, with pronouncements of the 'end of history' and the consolidation of the idea that 'There Is No Alternative' to the market.[34] Politics and policymaking turned inwards, adopting an increasingly managerialist approach to people's intimate and emotional lives. As competing visions of 'the good society' came off the table, political elites focused on strategies that might make individuals feel better about their predicament.

For Furedi, the most significant outcome of this process was the cultivation of a diminished sense of political subjectivity. Whereas many critics of the 'therapeutic turn' see this as a problem of heightened individualism, where self-obsession is prioritised over the common good, Furedi reformulates the problem as one where individuals, as political subjects, are cut adrift from a sense of their capacity to change the world. Individuals are positioned as victims of their circumstances, rather than makers of history. Politics, meanwhile, becomes recast as a technical process to be managed by elites and experts: not mandated by the people, but enacted on their behalf.

The cultivation of this sentiment of diminished subjectivity has some highly destabilising consequences for politics: not least in the gap that has opened up between political elites and the people whom they represent. But it also has some disorienting consequences for the generations socialised into an outlook of victimisation. To the extent that the Sixties generation did embody the pursuit of 'higher-order needs', their mission was to transform the character of adulthood, moving away from what was perceived as a dreary time of conformism and commitment to an open-ended project of experimentation and personal growth. The outcome was a different kind of adult selfhood, which substituted the personal for the political and, as Lasch noted, was formed by diminishing expectations of social change.

Moral confusion

In the Boomer-blaming playlist, the Sixties generation are casti-gated for their selfishness, and accused of being so wrapped up in their pursuit of having it all that they left their children with nothing. The Millennials are presented as either unable to embark on parenthood, due to the economic constraints brought about by their parents' generation, or unwilling to take that step, because of the cultural assumptions inherited from their parents' generation. 'Our parents prospered like no generation before them on the ethic of self-expression,' writes Kamenetz bitterly:

> Then they lovingly passed that wisdom down to us, with a new culture of parenting that emphasized individuality, self-esteem, and 'quality time'. But this intensive attention sometimes had an edge to it. Parents had fewer children than in the past and were far more invested in the success of each one. The message 'Be the best!' sometimes drowned out 'Be who you are' . . .
>
> Now we are smacking into the awareness that not only can't we afford all the stuff we were raised with, we may never be the stars we were told we were, or achieve what our parents had. It would be hard for any American generation to accept, but it's especially hard for this one.[35]

The disenchantment that runs through Millennial angst is informed, in no small part, by young people's sense of a gap between the aspirations of their childhood and the grimmer, more prosaic reality of the world they grow into. They quickly realise that out in the real world, there are no trophies for taking part, and no prizes just for being you. And to an extent, this reflects a real problem with the cultural legacy of the Sixties. Caught up in a fantasy that modern society can satisfy higher-order needs by ignoring, instead of confronting, its demons, cultural narcissism has fostered a gap between expectation and reality that can seem impossible to bridge.

This reality gap is not new, of course, and philosophers, sociologists, historians and psychologists have spent many years pondering the question of how well young people are equipped to bridge it. In

Why Grow Up? Susan Neiman tackles the infantilism of our present society by delving into the question of how philosophers have conceptualised the importance of reaching maturity, and the paths they have taken to reach this destination. But the precondition of growing up, as she sees it, is finding a way to navigate the gap between the world as it is, and the world as we want it to be. As A.O. Scott explains:

> In infancy, we have no choice but to accept the world as it is. In adolescence, we rebel against the discrepancy between the 'is' and the 'ought'. Adulthood, for Kant and for Neiman, 'requires facing squarely the fact that you will never get the world you want, while refusing to talk yourself out of wanting it'. It is a state of neither easy cynicism nor naïve idealism, but of engaged reasonableness.[36]

The Millennial predicament is usually framed as an inability to come to terms with the fact that, at the end of the day, they are not special but ordinary; that life is not glittering with promise, but nasty, brutish, and goes on far too long. In this view, the Boomers are to blame for raising their kids with a bunch of fanciful notions that don't equip them with the skills necessary to work for a living and cope with disappointment and failure. In other words – they have been encouraged to dream about the 'ought' of life, and shielded from having to confront the 'is'.

But this misses the point. The problem confronting younger generations today is not the age-old gap between the 'is' and the 'ought', but a deeper question of what adulthood 'ought' to be anyway. In this, the legacy of the Sixties has certainly played its part. By turning inwards towards the notion of selfhood as a personal project, to be conducted outside society in the belief that more fundamental change is off the agenda, the meaning of adulthood came to be emptied of much of its moral content.

In their study *Lost in Transition: The dark side of emerging adulthood* Christian Smith and colleagues characterise attitudes held by

American adults towards today's youth as falling into two 'unhelpful' camps. The first is described as the '"Chicken Little" approach' – an outlook essentially based on fear, that everything that was good in the past is now 'going down the drain', and that 'something decisive has recently happened that is uniquely corrupting youth today'. The second is the '"nothing new under the sun" approach' – an outlook of complacency, comprising 'a bemused dismissal of any concern about troubles in the lives of youth', and summed up by the 'baby-boomer favorite' phrase, '"It was no different when I was young"'.[37]

Smith and colleagues try to get to the deeper existential questions. *Lost in Transition* is based on an in-depth study with 230 Americans aged 18–23, in which researchers attempted to engage young people in a discussion about the big issues: morality, consumerism, intoxication, sexual behaviour, and civic and political disengagement. Smith is critical of both the 'Chicken Little' reaction and the dismissive idea that the kids are all right, because, he argues, both represent an abdication of adults' responsibilities to the younger generation. Instead, he proposes an approach of 'realistic care' – an approach that is 'informed by the facts of empirical reality, rather than personal memories or simplistic, prefabricated, ideological narratives of either conservative or liberal bents', and recognises that emerging adults need care and guidance from 'responsible adults' of older generations.[38]

The trouble, as Smith sees it, is that such responsible adults either do not exist – or if they do, they are failing to discharge their responsibilities to the younger generation, because of the values in which they themselves have been socialised. He is particularly exercised by the sentiment of 'morality adrift', expressed by the young interviewees, who find themselves perplexed by the very notion of a moral question. Smith sums up the problem as follows:

What we have found, in short, is that moral individualism is widespread among emerging adults and that a sizeable minority profess to believe in moral relativism. We also found that emerging adults resort to a variety of explanations about what makes anything good or bad, wrong or right – many of which reflect weak thinking and provide a fragile basis upon which to build robust moral positions of thought and living. We learned that a substantial minority of emerging adults admitted that, for various reasons, they do violate or would consider violating their own moral standards and those of society if it worked to their advantage and they thought they could get away with it. We found that the majority of emerging adults say that they do not or would not refer to moral traditions or authorities or religious or philosophical ethics to make difficult moral decisions, but would rather decide by what would personally make them happy or would help them to get ahead in life.[49]

What this tells us, argues Smith, is that 'the adult world that has socialized these youth for 18 to 23 years has done an awful job when it comes to moral education and formation'. As a consequence, 'these emerging adults are simply lost. They are morally at sea in boats that leak water badly'.[40] He sees this as reflected in young people's inability to grapple with the issues of our time. For example, the researchers for his study went into the interviews about consumerism 'expecting at least some emerging adults to display a heightened awareness about environmental problems associated with mass consumer economies'. They had also expected 'at least some of them to speak critically about the emptiness or dangers of all-out materialism', 'the political or military complications of such dependence on foreign natural resources like oil', and 'the importance of personal, inward, subjective, or spiritual growth or richness over the material consumptions of products'. But, Smith confesses, 'we heard almost none of that'; and before too long:

[W]e were nearly pushing the emerging adults we interviewed to consider any plausible problematic side to mass consumerism, if they could. They could not . . . For the vast majority, mass consumerism was good, end of story. Some others thought that mass consumerism may have some problems, they admitted, but none that they can understand or that need to affect their own lifestyles and goals.[41]

Smith connects 'emerging adults' captivity to consumerism and materialism' to a wider loss of 'vision and understanding of the most important value of higher education': that is, the production of 'better people, not bigger promotions and paychecks'.[42] Better people 'help over the long run to produce better lives, better politics, better cultures, (genuinely) better economies, better societies' – overall, to develop a sense of the good life that is lacking when people's desires are channelled into credentials, salaries and stuff. 'To live a truly good life,' he suggests, 'entails engaging with some important reality beyond oneself in a way that enhances morality, understanding, or important relationships'.[43]

Lost in Transition is refreshing for its willingness to confront the hole at the heart of what it means to be an adult today. The twin evils of moral individualism and moral relativism reflect a culture in which a wider sense of a good society – and people's responsibility to build that society – has been diminished. The shallowness of a life dominated by consumerism, anything goes, and getting ahead, is hardly something to strive for – and as indicated in the previous chapter, the voices of Millennial angst, in their incoherent way, are articulating this frustration.

But Smith's desire to promote an approach of 'realistic care', which acknowledges adults' responsibilities to the younger generations, also has some problems. Although he sets out an approach informed by 'the facts of empirical reality' which avoids 'ideological narratives', the researchers were clearly happy to prod their interviewees with leading questions, and write up their findings within a narrative of bleak disapproval, as is indicated by the book's focus on the 'dark side' of emerging adulthood. This is as one-sided as the presentation of emerging adulthood as a period of freedom and opportunity. While it is right to emphasise the older generation's responsibility to the younger generation in the wider quest for meaning, this should not mean dismissing young adults' agency and responsibility for creating and shaping the world.

Where does this leave the kids?

The Echo Boomers, it is said, want consumer capitalism to work for them. They want stable careers, houses, disposable income and choices. They feel trapped in 'adultescence' and denied the ability to grow up. They are optimistic, civic-minded and resilient. But, it is also said, they 'have the highest stress levels EVER',[44] and are simply incapable of functioning in a high-stakes, competitive world. They are terrified of leaving the parental home, reluctant to commit to intimate partners, and fearfully pessimistic about the future. So caught up in their own specialness are members of this 'Snowflake Generation' they believe they have the right to behave however they want, without being criticised or offended by anybody else.

This contradictory narrative is partly the result of our obsessive generation-chatter, where discussions of wider cultural, political, economic, and even moral, issues are projected onto the attitudes and behaviours of the younger generations. While generation warriors paint a picture of young people's future that is steeped in social and personal pessimism, more open-minded accounts of young people's hopes and dreams reflect a more nuanced approach. They may indeed be aggrieved about student debt and anxious about being able to afford a place to live, but they are often optimistic about their own abilities to navigate the years ahead.

The 2016 film *Get A Job* draws on familiar Millennial angst themes – the competitive insecurity of the graduate job market, the clash between a childhood spent receiving trophies for everything and a 'real world' in which you have to play to win. The film's male protagonists begin happily slumming it in a shared house dedicated to gaming and soft drugs; the main character, Will, trots proudly off to start his new job only to find himself having been 'downsized' out; his father, who sets himself up as emblematic of the job-for-lifer who rises up the ladder through commitment and hard work, finds himself suddenly made redundant and scrambling to find a position in a world that has moved on. Will's girlfriend throws herself into her career with zeal, only to find that buying into the system doesn't always work out; his dopehead flatmate drifts into middle-school teaching, where he begins by encouraging the kids to build bongs before he finds himself responsible for the basketball team and realises how demoralising it is to receive a trophy just for taking part. In the end, these meandering twenty-somethings come closer to finding their niches – not by regretting the loss of the certainties of the past, but by rolling with the possibilities of the present.

Get A Job was widely panned by critics. But unlike so much of the earnest media discourse about the Millennial plight, it at least brought some nuance and humour to the story. As they navigate the path from graduation to employment, the Millennials in this story are simultaneously creative, cynical, resourceful, lazy, pragmatic, idealistic, self-obsessed and caring. They are not heading anywhere particular, or particularly fast, but they are having a bit of fun and learning some lessons along the way.

One problem with trying to understand the conflicts faced by today's youth as a distinctly *generational* experience is that attitudes expressed by people at a particular stage in their lives tend to be conflated with an outlook that they will hold forever. One 2015 study by the US Pew Research Center demonstrates this tension. The study found that Millennials 'stand out in their willingness to ascribe negative stereotypes to their own generation': 59 per cent of Millennials regarded their generation as 'self-absorbed', while 30 per cent of Generation Xers, and 20 per cent of Baby Boomers, said the same of their own generations. Over three-quarters of Boomers regarded their generation as hard-working, but only 36 per cent of Millennials used the phrase to describe themselves.[45] The study was widely reported as an example of generational self-loathing, with headlines such as 'The Wasted Generation: Even millennials think they are self-absorbed and lazy'[46] and

'Millennials Most Likely Generation to Criticise Themselves'.[47] For Eleanor Robertson, writing under the headline 'Why Are the Baby Boomers Desperate to Make Millennials Hate Ourselves?', it was further proof of the generational conspiracy:

> [W]estern millennials believe that we're failures – immoral and irresponsible. We believe we're not proper adults. We believe we're lazy and self-absorbed. Basically, we believe what the baby boomers have told us. We've drunk their Kool-Aid.[48]

But as the study's authors noted, some of the differences in ideas about responsibility 'may be related more to age and life stage than to the unique characteristics of today's generations'. As responsibilities tend to increase with age, they argue, 'it is possible that, in any era, older people would be more likely than younger people to view their generation as "responsible"'. Indeed, the study also found that a sense of generational identity was relatively weak among young adults: only 40 per cent of adults aged 18 to 34 consider themselves part of the 'Millennial generation'.[49]

Artificial attempts to impose a set of generational characteristics on a diverse cohort of people who are still finding their way in life leads to a one-sided, and usually overly bleak, narrative, both about young people themselves and the circumstances in which they find themselves. In this respect, twenty-first-century generationalism not only attacks the value attached to the old: it is also narrowing our sense of what it means to be young. The dreams, idealism and experimentation associated with the teenager of the late twentieth century are sneered away as self-indulgent hedonism, both by those who complain about 'entitled Millennials' who need to stop whining and start working, and by those who celebrate 'emerging adulthood' as a period of life-training in which young people should be shepherded through a series of allegedly improving but purposeless activities.

The biggest problem confronting 'emerging adults' is that their excitement about growing up has to contend with a powerful negativity about what it means to take responsibility for the world. The cult of Boomer-blaming peddles the conceit that older people have wrecked the world at the expense of the young. The values and conventions of the past are held in question, and the people who embody them despised for standing in the way of the juggernaut of 'the future'. These sentiments give little incentive for the Echo Boomers to embrace an adult identity, in which they become part of the problem simply by being older. No wonder young people find themselves hovering in an uncertain transition, aware that they should be growing up but unsure how to do it – or why they even should.

CHAPTER 10

Social insecurities and grown-up policymaking

Generation warriors start from the assumption that there is a conflict of interest between young and old, which is reflected in and exacerbated by the distribution of social resources. They take upon themselves a mission to expose this conflict wherever they see it – a mission made more urgent by a sceptical public who, it is believed, need to be trained in the art of 'generational thinking'. Only when people are aware of the scale of intergenerational conflict, argue the warriors, can political elites pursue the hard task of resolving it, by lowering expectations of the kind of life we can hope for in retirement, and being 'realistic' about the grim prospects for the young people just starting out in the world of work.

In these fantasy generation wars, there are projected to be no winners. Older people are demonised for draining the public purse with their needs and entitlements, and infecting our modern society with their outdated behaviour and attitudes. Younger people have their optimism and resourcefulness beaten out of them by the truncheons of pessimism, grievance and hopelessness. And to what end? Politicians banging the war drums might save a bit of cash on pensions and create a useful distraction from the bigger issues at stake, but at the heavy cost of increasing political dissatisfaction and instability, and attacking the bonds that hold us together.

So what can be done? In terms of the generation wars, the answer is simple: just stop fighting them. There is no conflict between the generations, and there is nothing to be gained from inciting one. This is a symbolic conflict, driven by an elite in thrall to two fashionable prejudices: **doomography** and **gerontophobia**. By exposing these prejudices and the pessimistic outlook on which they are based, we can look for more positive ways of addressing the problems that are evaded by the distorted focus on so-called generational inequalities.

The dead weight of doomography

In the Boomer-blaming playlist, the austerity ballads warble about generational inequity because they see a future getting inexorably poorer. We have seen how this assumption is presented, not as a viewpoint, but as a natural fact. Endless charts show the rise in public spending and the proportions of elderly people as though one explains the other, and these are set against data evidencing the misery of young people: low wages, limited career progression, rising house prices, mounting personal debt. A causal relationship is assumed between the comparative good fortune of today's older people, the uniquely straitened circumstances of younger people, and the increasingly heavy burden that will be shouldered by the generations to come. The message is clear: 'Look upon our graphs, ye benighted, and despair'.

Demography is one thing: doomography is something else. Demographic analysis done properly is far more than the relentless extension of present-day trends. By capturing cultural dynamics as well as social and economic changes, the study of population shows human societies to be remarkably resilient and resourceful. Aside from the general bonus of cheating death and prolonging life – surely good things, even by the most miserabilist standards – the developments that have led to our ageing society have also resulted in improved living standards and a host of opportunities that simply did not exist for generations past. Doomography refuses to engage with this bigger picture, choosing instead to isolate and obsess on particular trends (increased longevity, population growth, low birth rates, increased migration) and speculate about the problems these will cause in the future. Rather than an attempt to understand demographic changes and consider how they might shape the future, it is a fatalistic effort to batten down the hatches, born out of the pessimism of the present.

Right from the start, concerns about intergenerational equity have rested on doomographic perceptions. Its emergence within academic circles is widely attributed to the publication of Samuel H. Preston's 1984 Presidential Address to the Population Association of America, in which Preston theorised that demographic change had set children and the elderly on 'divergent paths'.[1] 'Conditions have deteriorated for children and improved dramatically for the elderly and demographic change has been intimately involved in these developments,' wrote Preston.[2] This led him to frame policymaking as a zero-sum game, where provision for older people came at the expense of the young. Preston stressed that it was not his intention 'to paint the elderly as the villains of the piece' – not least because by 'prevailing standards, their motives and behavior are certainly no less pure than those of other groups'. But, he continued:

[O]ne can't simply stand on grounds of scientism and wish away the possibility that there is direct competition between the two groups. Indeed, the self-evident public resistance to higher levels of taxation and public expenditure suggests that, in the public sphere at least, gains for one group come partly at the expense of another.[3]

Deciding which group should reap the 'gains' of policymaking at the expense of which other group requires a value judgement about who is the more deserving. And since the 1980s, that judgement has moved steadily in the direction of promoting the value of the young over the value of the old. Headline arguments pose the cause of the generation wars as the problem of greedy older people having more than they need, at the expense of the younger generation. But as we have seen, these headline arguments are deliberately framed to mislead. Policies couched in the language of 'intergenerational equity' do not seek to redistribute resources from old to young; rather, they aim to curtail the entitlements of older people in order to cut public spending overall. Pensioners, meanwhile, find themselves treated with hostility and contempt – for holding the wrong values, using too many resources, and burdening the wage-earning, tax-generating population with the weight of their care.

We need to stop this generation blame game, and begin a more constructive discussion about what our societies can do to develop policies that work for everybody. This is neither as simple, nor as complicated, as it sounds. It is not simple because we are making policy in circumstances that are not of our choosing, against a backdrop of economic stagnation, cultural fragmentation and political instability. But it is not that hard either. If our societies could build welfare states from the rubble of the Second World War, it is surely not beyond the wit of twenty-first-century man and woman to tackle, head on, some of the economic and cultural conflicts that are masked by the shrill rhetoric of the generation warriors.

Pensions for living on

The most prominent generation wars issue, where the twin prejudices of doomography and gerontophobia are clearly intertwined, is that of pensions. Throughout the developed world, societies are struggling to maintain their commitment to providing people with an income once they have retired from work, and are scrambling to find ways of justifying a reduction in entitlements. The Boomers have found themselves to be a particular target, because of the size of their cohort, the relative generosity of their pension entitlements, and their expectations of retirement.

Alarmist media reports reached fever pitch around 2007, as the oldest Baby Boomers came of pensionable age at the point where the global economic crisis was beginning to bite. Michael Astrue, then commissioner of the US Social Security Administration, warned of 'a "silver tsunami" that could swamp the system'.[4] This entirely predictable event was framed by media reports as the coming of 'Boomergeddon':[5] a crisis, wrote the journalist Catherine Philp, provoked by 'a tidal wave of retiring baby boomers', few of whom had 'saved adequately for a retirement that may last as long as their working lives', but who were recklessly determined to carry on enjoying 'lavish lifestyles their parents could only dream of'. Some, 'refusing to let go of their old ways of sex, drugs and rock 'n' roll', would infect their senior years with 'new health problems'; others had spent their earlier years 'dutifully eating their granola and practising their yoga' – but their longevity is likely to be an equal burden on society'.[6] Not only were there too many Baby Boomer pensioners – they were the wrong kind of pensioners.

By viewing the pensions crisis through the prism of doomography, reductions in pension entitlements are presented as a necessary response to a natural crisis – there are too many old people claiming pensions, not enough young people working to pay for them, and therefore we need to scale back how much retired people can expect to live on in the future. This is nothing more than misanthropic buck-passing, which obscures the real drivers of both the pensions crisis and the response to it. The image of an enormous pensioner population propped up by a tiny trunk of workers is a Generation X-era fantasy: it simply does not hold in a context where populations are growing, and the size of the Millennial cohort is exceeding that of the Boomers. We have known about increases in life expectancy for a long time, and the net result has not been a growing number of elderly dependants, but an extension of healthy old age: meaning that a significant proportion of retired people are also engaged in working, not least to top up their meagre pensions, or caring for parents or grandchildren.

What is really driving the pensions crisis are the two problems outlined in Chapter 6: economic stagnation and an overweening outlook of risk avoidance. In claiming their pensions, the Baby Boomers are not seeking some kind of free handout from their children: they paid into the schemes, and it is hardly unreasonable to expect the schemes to pay out. But in an economic context of low productivity and wages, more is being squeezed from less. Grasping attempts to mitigate the effects of the pensions crisis have led to companies transferring the risks of retirement onto individuals, through favouring souped-up savings schemes that guarantee people nothing in the way of income – making retirement precarious and, in many cases, simply unaffordable.[7]

In all this, a relentlessly gerontophobic rhetoric has cast pensioners as the undeserving rich. Society has now apparently solved the problem of 'pensioner poverty' to the point where we have a 'retirement aristocracy'[8] that is far more affluent than everybody else. Therefore, goes the claim, we need to make these rich wrinklies pay for their privilege, for the sake of younger and future generations. Yet research consistently highlights the diversity of fortunes within the Baby Boomer generation, and the extent to which people's experience in later life is shaped by factors of social class, income inequality, employment, (ill) health, gender, ethnicity and family support networks.[9] Plunging the old folk back into pensioner poverty will not result in any extra resources for younger people in the here and now. What it will do is to drive down expectations, ensuring that their own retirement is a pennypinching affair.

Some reforms to pension provision, such as raising the state pension age, make sense in terms of bringing retirement in line with increased longevity, healthier ageing and the kind of jobs that people do. We no longer expect a 65-year-old to shuffle off in slippers following years of hard manual labour in the factories or mines. There is something insulting about expecting that senior figures should hang up their boots just because they have been there a long time: and in an era of generalised cost-cutting, retirement is often a convenient excuse for employers to save on higher salaries. But we should also recognise that most jobs in the so-called 'post-material economy' are not cushy white-collar positions; that people of pension age often have other commitments to attend to, such as care of grandchildren and elderly relatives; and that working to supplement one's pension is only attractive if there are decent and flexible jobs around. People should not be compelled to retire from paid work, but they should be able to do so. A civilised society should not make people work until they drop.

When it comes to pensions, we should strip away the self-serving myth that a pension is some kind of nice-to-have benefit. A pension is part of a salary – it is something we earn through our years of work, not a gift kindly bestowed by employers at their discretion. Above all, we should be clear that projections of an endless, unmanageable pensions crisis brought about by people having the audacity to retire and live for a few years longer are merely a cover for the deeper problem of economic stagnation, which will only be exacerbated by demanding that working people save more to receive less. And it only takes a basic grasp of mathematics to recognise that those hardest hit by the downgraded pension entitlements will not be today's pensioners, but tomorrow's: the younger workers in whose name such reforms are made. Attempts to pit old against young represent a divisive distraction from the goal that, until fairly recently, was seen as well within our grasp – a decent standard of living for working people and pensioners alike.

Houses for living in

Of all the themes running through Millennial angst, the most immediate is the cost of housing. A toxic combination of low wages and spiralling house prices means that the bottom rung of the much-vaunted 'housing ladder' seems to be disappearing into the clouds, further and further out of young people's grasp. As the cost of house prices rises, so does the cost of private renting – particularly in the areas where career opportunities are greatest. The more money people spend on renting, the less they have to save for a deposit – and so the cycle goes on.

The causes of this crisis are not difficult to work out. The 'housing bubble' is a consequence of weak economic growth, and the parasitical reliance on the finance sector to keep things afloat. We know how unstable this situation is: it was the collapse in the 'sub-prime' mortgage market that triggered the global financial crisis of 2007–8, from which developed countries are still barely recovering; and a society in which people struggle to house themselves is clearly getting something wrong. Yet rather than bringing the housing market back to Earth, the crisis just added ammunition to the battle against those greedy Baby Boomers.

The Boomers are presented as the source of a number of housing evils. First, they are blamed for their comparative good fortune and financial irresponsibility. 'We hoovered up housing when it was affordable, then benefited from a massive house-price boom,' wrote Philip Inman bleakly in 2011. 'Rather than saving some of that money for future generations, we borrowed against our assets and spent it all, a big black mark against us when it came to the recent banking crisis and the nation's current ability to invest in its future.'[10] Having gained all that equity just by being alive, it is argued, retired Boomers are widely presented as embarking on a frivolous SKI trip: 'spending the kids' inheritance'.

When they don't fritter it all away on themselves, Boomers who are worried about their children's financial struggles are blamed for increasing social inequalities. 'Prosperous baby boomers have not only done well for themselves out of a ludicrous housing market but they have tied up the future so that their kids will also do well,' wrote Madeleine Bunting in 2010. 'They've bought the buy-to-let properties to provide a nest egg for their offspring; they can support their kids through the volunteering and internships which secure the best jobs.'[11] Reliance on the 'bank of mum and dad' to help with the costs of deposits is routinely sneered at as a cause of growing inequality between Millennial 'haves' and 'have-nots'. Suddenly, being able to draw down some equity from your parents' modest home in a relatively desirable area is seen as a return to the power of inherited wealth.

In the doomographic imagination, the problem of too few houses is redefined as one of too many older people. Gerontophobic prejudices about 'underoccupied' homes imply that old people have no right to expect anything more than a room of their own. But while there is no denying that the housing market in the relatively affluent areas of Britain, Australia and the United States has become frankly bizarre, and that this is exacerbating social inequalities, the Baby Boomers are not the problem here. The problems underlying the housing crisis are structural and political: weak economies leading to housing bubbles; the lack of housing stock in areas where people want to live, leading to inflated prices and overcrowding; and the insecurity brought about by inadequate pension provision, which leads those who can to invest in property to fund their retirement.

Presenting the divide between owners and renters as a problem of inequity between the generations (a 'retirement aristocracy' versus 'Generation Rent') has become a convenient narrative for policymakers to bypass a more fundamental critique of the housing market, to strip retired people of some of their assets, and to encourage younger people to plunder their own futures, in the form of savings and pensions, to keep the bubble from bursting.[12] This fuels the unstable, short-termist approach to housing policy: something that will only make things worse for young people.

The current housing crisis isn't just an economic problem – it is also a political one. The idea that people should have somewhere decent to live seems to come secondary to the idea that having a mortgage is the only way in which people can be expected to get started on their lives, and feel as though they have a stake in society. This is why the concerns about the generational 'democratic deficit' are underpinned by an obsession with low home ownership rates among young people, and why generation warriors make so much of the argument that young people are delaying starting families of their own because they cannot afford to buy houses. Official attempts to engage with the housing crisis tend to eschew obvious solutions, such as developing more high-quality social housing, in favour of over-complicated schemes to encourage first-time buyers onto the housing ladder.

No doubt the cost of housing does feature in some young people's decision to stay in the parental home for longer than they (or their parents) might ideally want, and in discussions with their partners about when to have children. But to reduce these complex social trends to one factor is absurdly reductive. The trend for adult children to spend longer living with their parents has been observed for some decades, pre-dating the current housing madness, as has the rising age of mothers at the birth of their first child. These developments could be related to a whole number of things: the expansion of higher education; the availability of more effective contraception; the expectation that women will have careers; the cost of childcare; more comfortable family homes; more open, 'friendly' relationships between parents and their grown-up children; changing norms surrounding commitment in intimate partnerships . . . The list goes on. The cultural and economic landscape in which people are coming of age today is different from the Sixties, Seventies and Eighties on so many counts, it makes little sense to fixate on 'owning a home' as the one decisive change. It also ignores the fact that many people, today and throughout history, have raised families and played a full role in society without having a mortgage. Inciting young people to think that they cannot get started on their lives until they have scraped together a deposit to buy a house adds insult to injury.

Some suggest that the solutions to the housing woes of Britain, the United States and Australia should be to re-think our attachment to home ownership, and 'normalise' the idea that it is fine to rent. Indeed, when there is a shortage both of housing stock and affordable properties to buy or rent, state investment in large-scale social housing programmes could ameliorate some of these problems. But just as having a mortgage does not automatically make you into a citizen, discouraging home ownership is no panacea either. People's aspiration to own a home, a space they can call their own, is perfectly understandable. And there is no reason why this should not be possible – provided we stop treating housing as both the cause and the consequence of much deeper problems and grievances.

The starting point for resolving the so-called generational housing crisis is for policymakers to stop relying on housing to prop up the zombie economy and the pensions deficit. There is nothing all that complicated about building more decent social and private housing where there is demand. All it requires is coming back to the principle that houses should be thought of as homes to be lived in by people now, rather than assets to be plundered by the future.

Universities for educating

One of the accusations that Baby Boomers find most bewildering is that they had 'free higher education'. To an extent, this claim is true – at least in Britain, where university tuition fees for individuals were not introduced until the late 1990s. But a lot has changed since then. For the Boomers, particularly in the UK, going to university was the privilege of a minority – today, it is something that young people are increasingly encouraged, if not expected, to do. Liz Lightfoot, writing in the *Guardian*, sums up the shift:

> Being a student was quite a privilege in the good old days when local authorities and the government footed the bill and there was almost certainly a job at the end of it. In the early 1960s, only 4% of school leavers went to university, rising to around 14% by the end of the 1970s. Nowadays, more than 40% of young people start undergraduate degrees – but it comes at a cost. Today's students leave with debts of £40,000 and upwards to pay back over their working lives.[13]

In the USA, university has never been 'free' to students, although it used to cost them substantially less.[14] Mountainous levels of student debt, particularly in a context of depressed wages and rising house prices, provoke understandable angst both among young people and their parents, who are often required to share the load. But for this, we could point the finger of blame at a number of targets: policies that push increasing numbers of students into higher education, increasing the costs of provision; reductions in state funding of universities, which are compensated for by individual fees; wider processes of marketisation and financialisation that have pushed universities to operate as businesses, with students as consumers of their own degrees.[15] Blaming the Boomers for all this seems more than a little unfair – especially as relatively few of them had the privilege of a university education in their own youth. So what's going on?

It's not (all) about the money. Lurking beneath the hand-wringing and mud-slinging about how much today's students have to pay for their higher education is the more profound dilemma about what they are actually paying *for*. As school-leavers find themselves increasingly under pressure to go to university in order to qualify for a half-decent job, universities are under pressure to do more to promote 'employability' skills amongst their under-graduates, and to show that they are providing 'value for money' in the courses they provide. But if the purpose of higher education were simply to make people employable, we may as well not have it at all – far better for young people just to go and get a job, and to learn their way from there.

The problem is not that higher education fails to equip young people for work, but the role that universities have come to play in sustaining the zombie economy. In demanding that young people obtain an increasing array of credentials in order to qualify for jobs that, two generations ago, would have been seen as well within the capability of school-leavers, policymakers have managed to recast the problem of flabby, unproductive economies as a problem of substandard workers in need of relentless upgrading. This is what the angry Millennial Malcolm Harris is getting at in his critique of the 'pedagogical mask': the sense that 'education' has become a substitute for economic growth, with young people conceptualised as units of 'human capital' rather than potential producers of actual stuff.[16]

But there is far more to education than the 'pedagogical mask'. Education is one of the most important and enduring aspects of the transaction between the generations, grounding young people in a knowledge built up over years of the past, and giving them the intellectual tools to develop that knowledge in the present and into the future.[17] For all that our education systems fall short of their potential, the fact that increasing proportions of young people in the developed world have access to education until their early twenties is an enormous privilege – enabling them, in theory at least, to gain more from the wisdom of generations past than their parents or grandparents ever had the chance to do.

In a recent research project on generational experiences of higher education,[18] my colleagues and I have been struck by the upbeat way in which school students and undergraduates describe their expectations of university, as a time to develop their understanding of their subject, meet new people and engage with the exciting but unnerving challenge of growing up. Yet even while young people are busy studying the intricacies of literature and philosophy, or the complex rigour of mathematics or law, they struggle to set it against a positive narrative about why they should be doing this. In our gerontophobic times, scholarship and the knowledge of wise old academics is often decried as an irrelevant distraction from the kind of things young people need to be learning to equip them for the twenty-first century: information gathering, 'people skills', the latest new idea. In this sense, what Millennials might well envy about the Baby Boomers is not that their higher education cost them less than it does today, but that it gave them something more.

Families for relying on

Over the course of this book, we have seen how the so-called generation wars provide a symbolic cover for other, quite different debates – about the state of the economy, the crisis of politics, the cultural tensions that were revealed by the Sixties and continued unresolved. Perpetuating these phoney wars allows elites to evade these problems, by manipulating public concern for young people into a policy agenda that scapegoats the old. This divisive generationalism has contributed to the people's sense of political fragmentation and social insecurity, whittling away the bonds of history and empathy that give communities a sense of common purpose.

But generations are not only symbolic concepts, and the casualties of the generation wars are not abstract ideas. Generations are also people living in families – grandparents, parents, children, and the intimate web that surrounds them. When generation warriors attack the Baby Boomers for being greedy, sociopathic, selfish and having more than they deserve, they are blaming young people's parents and grandparents for the difficulties that they face. When they claim that young people have no future because of the actions of their elders, that they are the products of 'fiscal child abuse' from which they will never be able to recover, they are inciting young people to look at those whom they love and trust through a lens of suspicion and dislike.

This assault on intimate relations holds in equal contempt the families we live with, and the families we live by. The presumption that old people are a burden who should be forced to pay more for their care simply fails to comprehend that family relationships do not work according to such instrumental logic. Doomographic economists might regard Grandma as unproductive, expensive and expendable – but her family will love and cherish her, even when she is 90 years old and incapable of dressing herself. Gerontophobic crusaders might regard Grandad's values, memories and political views as the toxic legacy of the past, which needs to be silenced and squashed – but his family will recognise that those ideas are an important part of his life history, and their own.

Families, however different or dysfunctional they may be, know that they are bound together by something deeper than a shared opinion, or immediate self-interest. That is what has made the friction and drama of family life such a rich topic of literature, film and music – a set of relationships that goes beyond choice, which has to be lived with rather than resolved. The intimacy of the bond between the generations has meant that, for all of the episodic generational conflicts that have erupted over history, there has never been an outright war. Wars have been fought over politics, economics, religion, resources and any number of other things – but never over something so random as a birthday.

The cult of Boomer-blaming attempts to politicise relations between the generations, turning this intimate bond into a childish sentiment of grievance. Generationalist thinking twists discussions about important social issues into a petty, mean-spirited one-upmanship more suited to the spiteful playground than to the arena of grown-up politics, and incites young people to sacrifice the relationships that they hold dear for the sake of a shallow self-righteousness. This phoney war has already had a powerful impact on public debate. So let's put an end to it now, before it starts to infect the way we think about each other.

Ending the generation wars

In the opening chapters of this book, I argued that the Boomer-blaming playlist provides a fitting mood music for our times. Austerity ballads capture the low expectations of doomography, while punk posturing belts out the gerontophobic politics of division. All tracks are informed by an overwhelming sense of social and cultural pessimism – about the state of the world today, and the prospects for tomorrow. But beyond the elite bubbles of Westminster and Washington, and outside the shrill echo chambers constructed by those seeking to weaponise a particularistic sentiment of generational grievance, most people experience the relations between the generations as something rather more precious and harmonious.

As we raise our children, care for our elderly, educate the younger generation about what has gone before and argue with each other about what should come next, the work of intergenerational collaboration is a symphony that is continually being developed. There are no easy solutions to the problems that besiege our present era; but while being young at the dawn of the twenty-first century may not be exactly blissful, it's a long way from the hell of the elite imagination. Through maintaining a conversation between the generations, we can bring some historical perspective to understanding what is new about the times we are living through, and some collective thinking about the kind of world we want.

In that spirit, I will leave the last word to my grandfather. During his time in the prisoner-of-war camp between 1941 and 1945, young Don penned a long poem, brooding on the purpose of life, the senselessness of war and the monotony of incarceration. Yet even in those dark days, he was able to close with the optimism that comes with being young, alive and confronted with a difficult, yet still open, future:

> This is our life, let us raise
> It to a challenge fit to meet,
> And if Nature's works we praise,
> Praise also man, who, on his feet
> Can stand and sing his song of life.
> Throwing back his head, he should
> Ring out to all the mighty words
> 'Man is yet man and life is good.'

Notes

PREFACE

1. Bristow, J. (2009).
2. Furedi, F. and Bristow, J. (2008).
3. Bristow, J. (2015).

1 THE GENERATION WARS

1. Böcking, D. (2012) 'Euro Crisis Morphs into Generational Conflict', *Der Spiegel*, 9 August 2012. http://www.spiegel.de/international/europe/commentary-why-the-euro-crisis-is-also-a-generational-conflict-a-849165.html
2. Sandbrook, D. (2010) 'How the Baby Boomers Bust Britain', *Daily Mail*, 13 March 2010. https://www.dailymail.co.uk/debate/article-1257631/How-baby-boomers-bust-Britain-Self-indulgence-left-country-financially-socially-morally-crippled.html
3. Hutton, W. (2010) 'We Had It All – Sex, Freedom, Money. Did We Throw It All Away?', *Observer*, 22 August 2010.
4. Oborne, P. (2010) '*The Pinch*, by David Willetts' (Review), *Daily Mail*, 23 February 2010. https://www.dailymail.co.uk/home/books/article-1250596/So-long-losers-How-baby-boomers-took-money-ran-THE-PINCH-BY-DAVID-WILLETTS.html
5. Millar, F. (2010) 'Never Had It So Good: Fiona Millar finds herself agreeing with only one of David Willetts's brains', *Guardian*, 20 February 2010. https://www.theguardian.com/books/2010/feb/20/pinch-baby-boomers-willetts-millar
6. Sandbrook, D. (2011) 'Lucky Generation', *Daily Mail*, 20 February 2011 https://www.dailymail.co.uk/debate/article-1358549/VE-Day-generation-enjoyed-affluent-lives-children-face-different-future.html
7. Phillips, M. (2006) 'Boomergeddon', *Daily Mail*, 1 April 2006.
8. Kaletsky, A. (2010) 'This Is the Age of War between the Generations', *Times* (London), 2 June 2010. https://www.thetimes.co.uk/article/this-is-the-age-of-war-between-the-generations-dqhsblw3qd9

9. Beckett, F. (2010) 'The Grasping Generation: The baby boomers are denying everyone else the freedoms that they once took for granted', *Guardian*, 6 July 2010.

10. Begala, P. (2017) 'The Worst Generation: Or, how I learned to stop worrying and hate the Boomers', *Esquire,* 3 March 2017. http://www.esquire.com/news-politics/a1451/worst-generation-0400/

11. Willetts, D. (2010); Beckett, F. (2010); Howker, E. and Malik, S. (2010); Boorman, N. (2010).

12. Gibney, B.C. (2017); Kamenetz, A. (2006); Southern, L. (2016); Heath, R. (2006).

13. Doherty, M. (2017) 'Q&A: A venture capitalist on how boomers wrecked America', *Maclean's*, 9 March, 2017. http://www.macleans.ca/culture/books/qa-a-gen-x-venture-capitalist-on-how-boomers-wrecked-america/

14. Gibney, B.C. (2017), p. 349.

15. Doherty, M. (2017) 'Q&A: A venture capitalist on how boomers wrecked America', *Maclean's*, 9 March 2017. http://www.macleans.ca/culture/books/qa-a-gen-x-venture-capitalist-on-how-boomers-wrecked-america/

16. Heath, R. (2006), p. 5.

17. Independent Age (2015) 'Ready for Ageing Alliance Challenge the "Myth of the Baby Boomer" ', 8 August 2015. https://www.independentage.org/news-media/press-releases/ready-for-ageing-alliance-challenge-myth-of-baby-boomer

18. Ready for Ageing Alliance (2015).

19. Auer, J. (2013), pp. 152–71 (Kindle edition).

20. Ibid., loc. 265–300 (Kindle edition).

21. Vine, S. (2008) 'Farewell to the Boomers who Busted Us', *Times* (London), 30 August 2008.

22. For a superb critique of present-day generationalism, see White, J. (2013), pp. 216–47.

23. Allen, V. (2017) 'Baby Boomer "Used as Term of Abuse since the Brexit Vote": Charity chiefs say group are facing resentment because they own their own homes and had free university education', *Daily Mail*, 30 November 2017. https://www.dailymail.co.uk/news/article-5130829/Baby-boomer-used-term-abuse-Brexit-vote.html

24. Hiltzik, M. (2013) 'Deficit Hawks' "Generational Theft" Argument is a Sham', *Los Angeles Times,* 27 February 2013.

2 BOOMER-BLAMING: AN ELITE BLOODSPORT

1. Commonwealth of Australia (2015) *2015 Intergenerational Report: Australia in 2055.* https://static.treasury.gov.au/uploads/sites/1/2017/06/2015_IGR.pdf

2. Google search conducted 6 February 2018.

3. Kamenetz, A. (2006), p. ix.

4. Koukoulas, S. (2016) 'Millennials Should Stop Moaning. They've got More Degrees and Low Rates', *Guardian*, 4 April 2016. https://www.theguardian.com/commentisfree/2016/apr/04/millennials-should-stop-moaning-theyve-got-more-degrees-and-low-rates

5. Proud, A. (2015) 'Crybaby Millennials Need to Stop Whinging and Work Hard like the Rest of Us', *Telegraph*, 21 December 2015. https://www.

telegraph.co.uk/men/thinking-man/crybaby-millennials-need-to-stop-whinging-and-work-hard-like-the/

6. Hamblin, K. (2016), p. 433.
7. Walker, A. (ed.) (1996), p. 11.
8. Cook, F.L. (2002).
9. Concord Coalition (2018) 'About Us'. https://www.concordcoalition.org/about-us
10. Concord Coalition (2018) Homepage. https://www.concordcoalition.org/
11. Rix, S.E. (1999), p. 193.
12. Cook, F.L. (2002).
13. Generations United (2018) 'Our Mission'. https://www.gu.org/who-we-are/mission
14. United for All Ages (2018) Homepage. http://unitedforallages.com/
15. Hamblin, K. (2016), pp. 433–4.
16. Cook, F.L. (2002).
17. See discussion in: Best, J. (2017); Best, J. (ed.) (2001).
18. Willetts, D. (2010), p. xv.
19. Resolution Foundation (2018) 'Our Mission'. http://www.resolutionfoundation.org/about-us/mission/
20. Intergenerational Commission (2018) 'About the Commission'. https://www.intergencommission.org/about/
21. Gardiner, L. (2016a), p. 5. https://www.intergencommission.org/wp-content/uploads/2016/07/Intergenerational-commission-launch-report.pdf
22. Gardiner, L. (2016b). https://www.intergencommission.org/wp-content/uploads/2016/09/Generational-voting.pdf
23. Ibid., p. 8.
24. Gardiner, L. and Gregg, P. (2017), p. 4. https://www.intergencommission.org/wp-content/uploads/2017/02/IC-labour-market.pdf
25. Bell, B. and Whittaker, M. (2017). https://www.intergencommission.org/wp-content/uploads/2017/02/IC-labour-market.pdf
26. Corlett, A. and Judge, L. (2017), p. 4. https://www.intergencommission.org/wp-content/uploads/2017/09/Home-Affront.pdf
27. Finch, D. and Gardiner, L. (2017), p. 4. https://www.intergencommission.org/wp-content/uploads/2017/11/Pensions.pdf
28. Gardiner, L. (2017), p. 4. https://www.intergencommission.org/wp-content/uploads/2017/12/Inheritance.pdf
29. Finch, D. (2017), p. 11. https://www.intergencommission.org/wp-content/uploads/2017/01/Live-long-and-prosper.pdf
30. Yates, I. (2015) 'Ageing Boom Not Ageing Bust: It's time to rethink Australia's ageing population in the context of respect, opportunity and productivity', *The Age,* 4 March 2015. https://www.theage.com.au/opinion/ageing-boom-not-ageing-bust-20150304-13uuyd.html
31. Commonwealth of Australia 2015, p. xxiii.
32. Ibid., p. xi.
33. Merrick, R. (2018) 'Baby Boomers to Get Far More Welfare Support than Generation X and Millennials, Warns Report. Wealth taxes are the only way to avoid harsh future welfare cuts, study says – as the post-war generation prepares to drain the public finances.' *Independent,* 5 February 2018. http://www.independent.co.uk/news/uk/politics/baby-boomers-welfare-support-generation-x-millennials-cuts-pensions-new-wealth-tax-a8194726.html

34. Booth, R. (2017) 'Millennials Spend Three Times More of Income on Housing than Grandparents: David Willetts warns of "housing catastrophe" as he launches study that lays bare intergenerational inequality', *Guardian*, 20 September 2017. https://www.theguardian.com/society/2017/sep/20/millennials-spend-three-times-more-of-income-on-housing-than-grandparents

35. Collinson, P. (2017) 'Millennials Set to Reap Huge Rewards of Inheritance Boom. Thinktank: younger generation will profit from high value homes owned by baby boomer parents – but not till they are 60.' *Guardian*, 29 December 2017. https://www.theguardian.com/money/2017/dec/29/millennials-set-to-reap-huge-rewards-of-inheritance-boom

36. For a critical analysis of the flawed assumptions behind the 'age-dependency ratio', see: Mullan, P. (2000); Lodge, E., Carnell, E. and Coleman, M. (2016).

37. Intergenerational Foundation (2018). Homepage. http://www.if.org.uk/the-issue/

38. Howker, E. and Malik, S. (2010), p. 15.

39. Ibid., p. 145.

40. Ibid., p. 223.

41. Howker, E. and Malik, S. (2013).

42. Intergenerational Foundation (2011) '25 Million Unoccupied Bedrooms', press release, 19 October 2011. http://www.if.org.uk/wp-content/uploads/2011/10/IF_housingrel_defin_LE2.pdf

43. Heath, R. (2006), pp. xii–xv.

44. Amazon UK (2018) 'Ryan Heath'. https://www.amazon.co.uk/Ryan-Heath/e/B00MGXKKFE/ref=ntt_dp_epwbk_0; Politico (2018) 'Staff: Ryan Heath'. https://www.politico.eu/staff/ryan-heath/

45. Howker, E. and Malik, S. (2010), p. 221.

46. Heath, R. (2006), pp. 26–7; p. xviii.

47. Gibney, B.C. (2017), p. xxv.

48. Ibid., p. xxvi, emphasis in original.

49. Smiley, J. (2017) '*A Generation of Sociopaths* Review – How Trump and Other Baby Boomers Ruined the World', *Guardian*, 17 May 2017. https://www.theguardian.com/books/2017/may/17/generation-sociopaths-review-trump-baby-boomers-ruined-world

50. Doherty, M. (2017) 'Q&A: A venture capitalist on how boomers wrecked America', *Maclean's*, 9 March 2017. http://www.macleans.ca/culture/books/qa-a-gen-x-venture-capitalist-on-how-boomers-wrecked-america/

51. Gibney, B.C. (2017), p. xiv.

52. Ibid.

3 DRAMATISING THE CRISIS

1. Marwick, A. (1999), p. 3.

2. Ibid.

3. Southern, L. (2016), pp. 215–327.

4. White, M. (2007) 'Gordon the Saint – Meet Brown the Sinner: Michael White has fun reading two rather different biographies of the prime minister', *Guardian*, 14 July 2007. https://www.theguardian.com/books/2007/jul/14/biography.politics

5. Beckett, F. (2010), pp. xii–xiii.

6. Gibney, B.C. (2017), p. xiv.

7. Hutton, W. (2010) 'We Had It All – Sex, Freedom, Money. Did We Throw It All Away?' *Observer*, 22 August 2010.
8. Willetts, D. (2010), p. xv.
9. Sandbrook, D. (2010) 'How the Baby Boomers Bust Britain', *Daily Mail*, 13 March 2010. https://www.dailymail.co.uk/debate/article-1257631/How-baby-boomers-bust-Britain-Self-indulgence-left-country-financially-socially-morally-crippled.html
10. Marwick, A. (1999), p. 806.
11. Semley, J. (2017) 'Bruce Cannon Gibney's *A Generation of Sociopaths*, Reviewed: How boomers mortgaged the future', *The Globe and Mail*, 24 March 2017 (updated 15 April). https://www.theglobeandmail.com/arts/books-and-media/book-reviews/bruce-cannon-gibneys-a-generation-of-sociopaths-reviewed-how-boomers-mortgaged-the-future/article34414304/
12. Howker, E. and Malik, S. (2010), pp. 196–7.
13. Beckett, F. (2010), p. 197.
14. Gibney, B.C. (2017), p. 355.
15. Ibid., pp. 347–8.
16. See Stanford Encyclopedia of Philosophy (2010, revised 2014), 'Carl Schmitt'. https://plato.stanford.edu/entries/schmitt/
17. Gibney, B.C. (2017), pp. 348–9.
18. Ibid., p. 356, emphasis in original.
19. Ibid.
20. Strauss, W. and Howe, N. (1998).
21. Kaiser, D. (2016) 'Donald Trump, Stephen Bannon and the Coming Crisis in American National Life', *Time*, 18 November 2016. http://time.com/4575780/stephen-bannon-fourth-turning/, *Generation Zero Documentary* (2010). https://www.youtube.com/watch?v=bsqu9gh6xhk
22. Howe, N. (2017) 'Where Did Steve Bannon Get His Worldview? From My Book.' *Washington Post*, 24 February 2017. https://www.washingtonpost.com/entertainment/books/where-did-steve-bannon-get-his-worldview-from-my-book/2017/02/24/16937f38-f84a-11e6-9845-576c69081518_story.html?utm_term=.798b526f119e
23. Ibid.
24. Strauss, W. and Howe, N. (1991).
25. Howe, N. (2017) 'Where Did Steve Bannon Get His Worldview? From My Book.' *Washington Post*, 24 February 2017. https://www.washingtonpost.com/entertainment/books/where-did-steve-bannon-get-his-worldview-from-my-book/2017/02/24/16937f38-f84a-11e6-9845-576c69081518_story.html?utm_term=.798b526f119e
26. Ibid.
27. Dobson, A. (1989), p. 176.
28. White, J. (2013), p. 216.
29. Ibid.
30. Ibid., p. 235.
31. Marsh, S. (2017) 'Momentum Video Parodies Older Voters Discussing Corbyn's Policies', *Guardian*, 28 July 2017. https://www.theguardian.com/politics/2017/jul/28/momentum-video-jeremy-corbyn-labour-university-tuition
32. Goodfellow, M. (2017) 'The Dinner Party Video Has Wound Up Momentum's Critics. They Just Don't Get It', *Guardian*, 28 July 2017. https://www.

theguardian.com/commentisfree/2017/jul/28/they-just-dont-get-it-video-upset-corbyn-deniers-labour-momentum

33. Ibid.
34. Orr, D. (2017) 'Momentum's Video Is full of Simplistic Prejudices and Won't Win over Anyone', *Guardian*, 28 July 2017. https://www.theguardian.com/commentisfree/2017/jul/28/momentum-video-simplistic-prejudices
35. Howe, N. (2017) 'Where Did Steve Bannon Get His Worldview? From My Book.' *Washington Post,* 24 February 2017. https://www.washingtonpost.com/entertainment/books/where-did-steve-bannon-get-his-worldview-from-my-book/2017/02/24/16937f38-f84a-11e6-9845-576c69081518_story.html?utm_term=.798b526f119e
36. White, J. (2013), p. 217.
37. See discussion in Furedi, F. (2017).
38. Nagle, A. (2017), p. 7.
39. Thom, M. (2017) 'The Postmodern Roots of the Alt-Right', *spiked,* 15 June 2017. https://www.spiked-online.com/2017/06/15/the-postmodern-roots-of-the-alt-right
40. Nagle, A. (2017), p. 69.
41. Ibid., p. 1.
42. Ibid., p. 7.
43. Willinger, M. (2013).
44. Ibid., pp. 13–14.
45. Thom, M. (2017) 'The Postmodern Roots of the Alt-Right', *spiked,* 15 June 2017. https://www.spiked-online.com/2017/06/15/the-postmodern-roots-of-the-alt-right
46. Kotlikoff, L.J. and Burns, S. (2005).
47. Kotlikoff, L. J. and Burns, S. (2012), p. 69.
48. Malkin, M. (2009) 'The Generational Theft Act of 2009', *CNS News,* 7 January 2009. https://www.cnsnews.com/blog/michelle-malkin/generational-theft-act-2009; Ambinder, M. (2009) 'Generational Theft', *The Atlantic,* 8 February 2009. https://www.theatlantic.com/politics/archive/2009/02/-generational-theft/439/
49. La Roche, J. (2013) 'Hedge Funder Stan Druckenmiller Wants Every Young Person in America to See these Charts about How They're Getting Screwed', *Business Insider*, 20 September 2013. http://www.businessinsider.com/stan-druckenmiller-on-generational-theft-2013-9?IR=T#http://www.businessinsider.com/stan-druckenmiller-on-generational-theft-2013-9?op=1
50. Janda, M. (2017) 'Superannuation for Housing Deposits Would Facilitate Intergenerational Theft', ABC News, 16 March 2017. http://www.abc.net.au/news/2017-03-16/super-for-housing-deposits-intergenerational-theft/8360890
51. Nuccitelli, D. (2016) 'The Inter-generational Theft of Brexit and Climate Change: Youth will bear the brunt of the poor decisions being made by today's older generations', *Guardian,* 27 June 2016. https://www.theguardian.com/environment/climate-consensus-97-per-cent/2016/jun/27/the-inter-generational-theft-of-brexit-and-climate-change
52. Taylor, P. (2014a) *The Next America*. Pew Research Center, 10 April 2014. http://www.pewresearch.org/next-america/#Two-Dramas-in-Slow-Motion; Taylor, P. and the Pew Research Center (2015).

53. Taylor, P. (2014a) *The Next America*. Pew Research Center, 10 April 2014. http://www.pewresearch.org/next-america/#Two-Dramas-in-Slow-Motion.
54. Taylor, P. (2014b) 'Generational Equity and the "Next America"', Pew Research Center: Fact Tank, 18 April 2014. http://www.pewresearch.org/fact-tank/2014/04/18/generational-equity-and-the-next-america/
55. Ibid.
56. Ibid.
57. Conservative Party (2017) *Forward Together: Our plan for a stronger Britain and a prosperous future; The Conservative and Unionist Party Manifesto*, p. 63. https://s3.eu-west-2.amazonaws.com/conservative-party-manifestos/Forward+Together+-+Our+Plan+for+a+Stronger+Britain+and+a+More+Prosperous....pdf
58. Ibid., p. 64.
59. Willetts, D. (2018) 'Why It's Time to Tax Baby Boomers' Wealth', *Times* (London), 5 March 2018.
60. Intergenerational Commission (2018) 'About the Commission'. https://www.intergencommission.org/about/
61. Shrimpton, H., Skinner, G. and Hall, S. (2017). https://www.intergencommission.org/wp-content/uploads/2017/09/The Millennial-Bug.pdf
62. Ibid., p. 4.
63. Ibid., p. 4.
64. Ibid., pp. 5–6.
65. Ibid., p. 6.
66. Gardiner, L. (2017) 'Blog: Votey McVoteface: What's driving the generational turnout gap, and why it matters', Intergenerational Commission, 2 June 2017. http://www.resolutionfoundation.org/media/blog/votey-mcvoteface-whats-driving-the-generational-turnout-gap-and-why-it-matters/

4 WHAT'S SO SPECIAL ABOUT GENERATIONS?

1. Hardyment, C. (2007).
2. Coupland, D. (1991).
3. For an engaging discussion of 'Generation Z', see Combi, C. (2015).
4. Marwick, A. (1999), p. 480.
5. Lusher, A. (2015) 'Move Over, Baby Boomers and Millennials – "Founders" Will Be Shaping the Future: Baby boomers and slackers gave way to millennials. Now we're told that "founders" are the future', *Independent*, 4 December 2015. https://www.independent.co.uk/news/uk/home-news/move-over-baby-boomers-and-millennials-founders-will-be-shaping-the-future-a6759566.html
6. Bristow, J. (2016b), Burnett, J. (2016), Pilcher, J. (1995).
7. Abrams, P. (1970), p. 176.
8. Berger, B.M. (1960), p. 11.
9. Gardiner, L. (2016a), p. 17.
10. Lyons, K. (2016a) 'Generation Y: A guide to a much-maligned demographic', *Guardian*, 7 March 2016. https://www.theguardian.com/world/2016/mar/07/millennials-generation-y-guide-to-much-maligned-demographic
11. Jack, I. (2011) 'We Baby Boomers Blame Ourselves for this Mess, but Is It that Simple?' *Guardian*, 22 January 2011. https://www.theguardian.com/commentisfree/2011/jan/22/ian-jack-baby-boomers-generation
12. Falkingham, J. (1997), pp. 19–21.
13. O'Rourke, P.J. (2014), loc. 78/3510 (Kindle edition).

14. Strauss, W. and Howe, N. (1991), p. 430.
15. Howe, N. (2017) 'Where Did Steve Bannon Get His Worldview? From My Book.' *Washington Post*, 24 February 2017. https://www.washingtonpost. com/entertainment/books/where-did-steve-bannon-get-his-worldview-from-my-book/2017/02/24/16937f38-f84a-11e6-9845-576c69081518_story.html?utm_term=.798b526f119e
16. Nash, L.L. (1978), p. 1.
17. Ibid.
18. Gillis, J.R. (1974), p. 37. See also Eisenstadt, S.N. (1956).
19. Turgenev, I. (1996 [1862]).
20. Raleigh, D.J. (2012), pp. 10–11.
21. Chamberlin, V.A. and Weiner, J. (1971), p. 21.
22. Turgenev (1996 [1862]), pp. 53–4, emphasis in original.
23. Letwin, S.R. (1978), p. 53.
24. Mannheim, K. (1952).
25. Ibid., pp. 300–1.
26. Furedi, F. (2014), p. 41.
27. Wohl, R. (1980), p. 1.
28. Ibid., pp. 1–2.
29. Brittain, V. (1984 [1933]), p. 10.
30. Ibid., p. 13.
31. France, A. and Roberts, S. (2015), pp. 215–30.
32. See for example, Helsper, E.J. and Eynon, R. (2010), pp. 503–20.
33. United for All Ages (2018), p. 3.
34. Wolfe, T. (1976), pp. 26–40.
35. Press Association (1986), *Link* magazine, Spring.
36. Ibid.
37. Gillis, J.R. (1997), p. xv.
38. Ibid., pp. xvi–xvii.
39. Ibid.

5 GENERATION FABLES AND THE 'END OF HISTORY'

1. Wohl, R. (1980), pp. 207–8.
2. Lind, M. (1988) 'The Class of '45', *New York Times*, 27 December 1988. http://www.nytimes.com/1998/12/27/books/the-class-of-45.html
3. Hutton, W. (2010) 'We Had It All – Sex, Freedom, Money. Did We Throw It All Away?', *Observer*, 22 August 2010.
4. Marwick, A. (1999), p. 806.
5. For a magisterial account of these upheavals, see: Judt, T. (2010).
6. Raleigh, D.J. (2012), p. 3.
7. Ibid.
8. Howe, N. and Strauss, W. (2000), p. 3.
9. Booker, C. (1980), p. 6.
10. Fukuyama, F. (1992), p. xi.
11. Jenkins, P. (2006), pp. 1–4.
12. Ibid., p. 11.
13. Pilcher, J. and Wagg, S. (1996), p. 2.
14. Giddens, A. (1994).
15. Savage, J. (1993) 'The Return of Rock', *Times* (London), 20 February 1993.

16. Ibid.
17. *Guardian* (1992) 'Leading Article: The baby boomers come of age', 7 November 1992.
18. Welsh, C., *Spectator*, cited in Edgar, D. (1986) 'It Wasn't so Naff in the 60s After All: The Conservative Party's assault on the legacy of the 1960s', *Guardian*, 7 July 1986.
19. Whalen, J. and Flacks, R. (1989), pp. 9–10.
20. See discussion in Bristow, J. (2015).
21. Macintyre, B. (1992) 'Woodstock in Washington', *Times* (London), 20 November 1992.
22. *Guardian* (1992) 'Leading Article: The baby boomers come of age', 7 November 1992.
23. Palmer, P. (1993) 'The Day-Glo Baby Chair Brigade Hits Town', *Mail on Sunday*, 10 January 1993.
24. Stothard, P. (1992) 'Babyboomers Coming of Age', *Times* (London), 31 March 1992.
25. Gani, A. (2015) 'Clause IV: A Brief History: Jeremy Corbyn has reignited debate over "nationalisation" clause that was a key element of Labour's socialist identity until Tony Blair removed it', *Guardian*, 9 August 2015. https://www.theguardian.com/politics/2015/aug/09/clause-iv-of-labour-party-constitution-what-is-all-the-fuss-about-reinstating-it
26. Kaus, M. (1992) 'Clinton: A cocky con man', *Guardian*, 5 May 1992.
27. Andersen, K. (2015) 'The Best Decade Ever? The 1990s, Obviously', *New York Times*, 6 February 2015. https://www.nytimes.com/2015/02/08/opinion/sunday/the-best-decade-ever-the-1990s-obviously.html
28. Proud, A. (2015) 'Why the Nineties Were Just as Good as the Sixties', *Telegraph*, 21 September 2015. https://www.telegraph.co.uk/men/thinking-man/11877919/Why-the-Nineties-were-just-as-good-as-the-Sixties.html
29. *Guardian* (1992) 'Leading Article: The Baby Boomers come of age', 7 November 1992.
30. Sandbrook, D. (2011) 'Lucky Generation', *Daily Mail*, 20 February 2011. https://www.dailymail.co.uk/debate/article-1358549/VE-Day-generation-enjoyed-affluent-lives-children-face-different-future.html
31. Gibney, B.C. (2017), pp. xv–xvi.
32. Bristow, J. (2015).
33. Edmunds, J. and Turner, B.S. (2005), p. 571.
34. Roberts, Y. (2018) 'Millennials Are Struggling. Is It the Fault of the Baby Boomers?' *Observer*, 29 April 2018. https://www.theguardian.com/society/2018/apr/29/millennials-struggling-is-it-fault-of-baby-boomers-intergenerational-fairness
35. Ibid.
36. Vale, J. (2016) 'Democracy at Risk as Baby Boomers Dominate Voting', *Independent*, 23 September 2016.
37. Lyons, K. (2016b) 'Generation Y, Curling or Maybe: What the World Calls Millennials: Titles – and insults – around the world reflect the reality of life for young adults, from debt and joblessness to housing', *Guardian*, 8 March 2016. https://www.theguardian.com/world/2016/mar/08/generation-y-curling-or-maybe-what-the-world-calls-millennials
38. Ibid.
39. Smith, C. et al. (2011), pp. 10–11, emphasis in original.

6 MILLENNIAL FEARS

1. Howe, N. and Strauss, W. (2000), p. 4.
2. Twenge, J.M. (2014).
3. Kamenetz, A. (2006).
4. Scott, S. (2018), p. 8.
5. Angelini, F. (2013) 'Trapped in Kidulthood: No job security. No pensions. No hope of being better off than our parents. No wonder my generation won't grow up. A daughter's view', *Sunday Times*, 20 October 2013.
6. Ibid.
7. Angelini, F. (2013) 'Trapped in Kidulthood: No job security. No pensions. No hope of being better off than our parents. No wonder my generation won't grow up. Her mother's reply', *Sunday Times*, 20 October 2013.
8. Ibid.
9. Kamenetz, A. (2006), pp. 92–3.
10. Eads, L. (2014) 'Top 10: Where Are they Now?' TheDrinksBusiness.com, 31 March 2014. https://www.thedrinksbusiness.com/2014/03/top-10-demised-drinks-brands/7/
11. Parry, H. (2016) 'War on Millennials! Baby Boomers Take to Twitter to Point out the Flaws of the Younger Generation with #HowToConfuseAMillenial Hashtag', *Daily Mail*, 5 September 2016; #howtoconfuseamillenial. https://twitter.com/hashtag/howtoconfuseamillenial?lang=en
12. Harris, M. (2017), p. 5.
13. Ibid., p. 14.
14. Lareau, A. (2011); Lee, E., et al. (2014).
15. Kamenetz, A. (2006), pp. 92–3.
16. Ehrenreich, B. (1990), p. 15.
17. Harris, M. (2017), p. 5.
18. Kamenetz, A. (2006), p. 93.
19. Chartered Institute of Personnel and Development (2015) *Over-Qualification and Skills Mismatch in the Graduate Labour Market*, Policy Report, 18 August 2015. file:///C:/Users/jb1070/Downloads/over-qualification-and-skills-mismatch-graduate-labour-market_tcm18-10231.pdf
20. Ainley, P. and Allen, M. (2013).
21. Jane, T. (2016) 'An Open Letter to My CEO', *Medium*, 19 February 2016, emphasis in original. https://medium.com/@taliajane/an-open-letter-to-my-ceo-fb73df021e7a
22. Truong, A. (2016) 'Yelp Increases Wages after Firing an Employee who Was Critical about Her Low Pay', *Quartz*, 28 April 2016. https://qz.com/672681/yelp-increases-wages-after-firing-an-employee-who-was-critical-about-her-low-pay/
23. Williams, S. (2016) 'The Problem with Millennials and Work Ethic', *HuffPost*, 22 February 2016 (updated 22 February 2017). https://www.huffington-post.com/stefanie-williams/the-problem-millennials-work-ethic-talia-yelp_b_9282244.html
24. Truong, A. (2016) 'The Yelp Employee Who Was Fired After Her Incendiary Open Letter to the CEO Speaks out', *Quartz*, 22 February 2016. https://qz.com/622232/the-yelp-employee-who-was-fired-after-her-incendiary-open-letter-to-the-ceo-speaks-out/

25. Jane, T. (2016) 'An Open Letter to My CEO', *Medium*, 19 February 2016. https://medium.com/@taliajane/an-open-letter-to-my-ceo-fb73df021e7a

26. Shine, J. (2017) 'Won't Get Fooled Again: Malcolm Harris's *Kids These Days: Human capital and the making of millennials*', *Los Angeles Review of Books*, 26 November 2017. https://lareviewofbooks.org/article/wont-get-fooled-again-malcolm-harriss-kids-these-days-human-capital-and-the-making-of-millennials/#

27. Kamenetz, A. (2006), p. xi.

28. Ibid., p. 57.

29. Roberts, S. and Allen, K. (2016) 'Millennials v Baby Boomers: A battle we could have done without', *The Conversation*, 6 April 2016. https://theconversation.com/millennials-v-baby-boomers-a-battle-we-could-have-done-without-57305

30. Lyons, K. (2016b) 'Generation Y, Curling or Maybe: What the World Calls Millennials: Titles and insults – around the world reflect the reality of life for young adults, from debt and joblessness to housing', *Guardian*, 8 March 2016. https://www.theguardian.com/world/2016/mar/08/generation-y-curling-or-maybe-what-the-world-calls-millennials

31. Robertson, E. (2016) 'Why I Am a Communist', *Medium*, 18 November 2016. https://medium.com/@marrowing/why-i-am-a-communist-ca1e3a3efca9

32. Robertson, E. (2015) 'Why Are the Baby Boomers Desperate to Make Millennials Hate Ourselves? New statistics from the Pew Research Centre show the youngest workers have totally internalised the messaging of the luckiest generation in human history', *Guardian*, 4 September 2015.

33. Kamenetz, A. (2006), p. xv.

34. Mullan, P. (2017), pp. 8–9, Figure 0.1.

35. Ibid., pp. 8–10.

36. Ibid., p. 8.

37. Lasch, C. (1984), p. 16.

38. Ibid.

39. See: Giddens, A. (1994); Beck, U. (1992); Furedi, F. (1997).

40. Howe, N. and Strauss, W. (1993), p. 32.

7 'YOUTHQUAKES' AND THE POLITICISATION OF GENERATIONAL IDENTITY

1. MacAskill, E. (2017) 'Jeremy Corbyn Gathers the Faithful for Upbeat Final Rally on Home Turf', *Guardian*, 8 June 2017. https://www.theguardian.com/politics/2017/jun/08/jeremy-corbyn-gathers-the-faithful-for-upbeat-final-rally-on-home-turf; Khomami, N. and Ellis-Petersen, H. (2017) 'Jeremy Corbyn Calls for Unity in Glastonbury Speech', *Guardian*, 24 June 2017. https://www.theguardian.com/music/2017/jun/24/jeremy-corbyn-calls-for-unity-in-glastonbury-speech

2. Oxford Dictionaries (2017) 'Word of the Year 2017 is . . .' https://en.oxforddictionaries.com/word-of-the-year/word-of-the-year-2017

3. Bulman, M. (2017) '"I Was Clearly Wrong": What MPs who opposed Jeremy Corbyn said then and what they're saying now', *Independent*, 9 June 2017. http://www.independent.co.uk/news/uk/politics/jeremy-corbyn-labour-

mps-what-they-said-then-now-owen-smith-chuka-ummuna-tom-watson-yvette-cooper-a7781411.html

4. Ipsos MORI (2017) 'How Britain Voted in the 2017 Election', 20 June 2017. https://www.ipsos.com/ipsos-mori/en-uk/how-britain-voted-2017-election

5. Curtis, C. (2017) 'How Britain Voted at the 2017 General Election', YouGov, 13 June 2017. https://yougov.co.uk/news/2017/06/13/how-britain-voted-2017-general-election/

6. BBC News (2017) 'Reality Check: Has there been a surge in youth turnout?', 9 June 2017. http://www.bbc.co.uk/news/election-2017-40220032

7. The British Election Study Team (2018a) 'The Myth of the 2017 Youthquake Election', British Election Study, 29 January 2018. http://www.british electionstudy.com/bes-impact/the-myth-of-the-2017-youthquake-election/#.WzOOuPZFzD5; Prosser, C., Fieldhouse, E., Green, J., Mellon, J., Evans, G. (2018) 'Tremors But No Youthquake: Measuring changes in the age and turnout gradients at the 2015 and 2017 British General Elections', *SSRN*, 28 January 2018. https://papers.ssrn.com/sol3/papers.cfm?abstract_id=3111839

8. The British Election Study Team (2018b) 'Youthquake – A Reply to Our Critics', 12 February 2018. http://www.britishelectionstudy.com/bes-impact/youthquake-a-reply-to-our-critics/#.Wp69S-jFLIU

9. The British Election Study Team (2018a) 'The Myth of the 2017 Youthquake Election', British Election Study, 29 January 2018. Emphasis in original. http://www.britishelectionstudy.com/bes-impact/the-myth-of-the-2017-youthquake-election/#.WzOOuPZFzD5

10. Milton, J. (2017) 'Young People Will Decide this Year's Election – Here's Why Every Vote Matters', *NME*, 6 June 2017. http://www.nme.com/blogs/young-people-election-2017-every-vote-matters-2084836; Perry, K. (2017) 'You're Going to Vote, but Are Your Mates?' *NME*, 7 June 2017. http://www.nme.com/blogs/nme-blogs/take-plus-one-vote-2075989#3YfBi1eQXJvEXC 8d.99

11. Oxford Dictionaries (2017) 'Word of the Year 2017 Is . . .' https://en.oxforddictionaries.com/word-of-the-year/word-of-the-year-2017

12. Sparrow, A. and Phipps, C. (2017) 'Election 2017: Corbyn ends final day of campaigning with London rally – as it happened', *Guardian*, 7 June 2017. https://www.theguardian.com/politics/live/2017/jun/07/general-election-2017-campaign-final-day-human-rights-politics-live

13. Wattenberg, M.P. (2018). http://onlinelibrary.wiley.com/doi/10.1111/psq.12452/full

14. Ibid.

15. McCarthy, N. (2016a) 'Young Voted Clinton, Old Voted Trump', *Statista*, 9 November 2016. https://www.statista.com/chart/6651/young-voted-clinton-old-voted-trump/

16. Grathwohl, C. (2017) 'Youthquake: Behind the scenes on selecting the Word of the Year', Oxford Dictionaries, 14 December 2017, emphasis in original. https://blog.oxforddictionaries.com/2017/12/14/youthquake-word-of-the-year-2017-commentary/

17. See Bristow, J. (2001) 'Wake up! The Truth about Youth Apathy', *spiked*, 9 May 2001. https://www.spiked-online.com/2001/05/09/wake-up-the-truth-about-youth-apathy/ For a discussion of the tensions involved in official mechanisms for increasing 'youth participation', see Bessant, J. (2004), pp. 387–404.

18. Walsh, L. and Black, R. (2013) 'Finding the Missing Youth Vote', *The Conversation*, 13 August 2013. https://theconversation.com/finding-the-missing-youth-vote-16958; Collin, P. and Walsh, L. (2016) 'Many Young People Aren't Enrolled to Vote – but Are We Asking them the Wrong Question?' 15 May 2016. https://theconversation.com/many-young-people-arent-enrolled-to-vote-but-are-we-asking-them-the-wrong-question-59248

19. Bamat, J. (2017) 'Mélenchon and Le Pen Win over Youth in French Vote', France24, 24 April 2017. https://www.france24.com/en/20170424-france-presidential-election-youth-vote-melenchon-le-pen

20. Schultheis, E. (2018) 'How Italy's Five-Star Movement is Winning the Youth Vote: They can't find jobs, and the centrist parties have failed them, opening space for the populists', *The Atlantic*, 2 March 2018. https://www.theatlantic.com/international/archive/2018/03/italys-populist-youth/554408/

21. Witte, G. and Birnbaum, M. (2018) 'Italy's Election Results Highlight Struggle to Govern in Europe as Populist Forces Rise', *Washington Post*, 5 March 2018. https://www.washingtonpost.com/world/europe/italian-vote-highlights-growing-struggle-to-govern-in-europe-as-populist-forces-rise/2018/03/05/73cc6820-1bd2-11e8-98f5-ceecfa8741b6_story.html?utm_term=.cafaf6ef4e87

22. Grathwohl, C. (2017) 'Youthquake: Behind the scenes on selecting the Word of the Year', Oxford Dictionaries, 14 December 2017. https://blog.oxforddictionaries.com/2017/12/14/youthquake-word-of-the-year-2017-commentary/

23. R.J.E. (2017) 'The Biggest Political Divide in Britain is Age: Forget Brexit, class and education. This election has pitted the young against the old', *Economist*, 8 June 2017. https://www.economist.com/blogs/speakerscorner/2017/06/youth-booth

24. Wattenberg, M.P. (2018), p. 2. http://onlinelibrary.wiley.com/doi/10.1111/psq.12452/full

25. Ibid., p. 4.

26. Galston, W.A. and Hendrickson, C. (2016) 'How Millennials Voted this Election', Brookings Institution, 21 November 2016. https://www.brookings.edu/blog/fixgov/2016/11/21/how-millennials-voted/

27. Stanley-Becker, I. and Noack, R. (2017) 'Young and to the Left? Not in Germany, Where the Merkel Generation Prefers an Old Hand', *Washington Post*, 22 September 2017. https://www.washingtonpost.com/world/europe/young-and-to-the-left-not-in-germany-where-the-merkel-generation-prefers-an-old-hand/2017/09/22/ace6eef4-9e1a-11e7-b2a7-bc70b6f98089_story.html?utm_term=.3608a80e2133

28. Farand, C. (2017) 'German Election 2017: How Angela Merkel became the "cool" option for young voters', *Independent*, 18 September 2017. http://www.independent.co.uk/news/world/europe/angela-merkel-germany-election-2017-cdu-cool-vote-when-is-sunday-berlin-young-a7954191.html

29. *FT* Reporters (2017) 'Germany's Election Results in Charts and Maps', *Financial Times*, 25 September 2017. https://www.ft.com/content/e7c7d918-a17e-11e7-b797-b61809486fe2

30. Electoral Commission (2018) 'EU Referendum Results'. https://www.electoralcommission.org.uk/find-information-by-subject/elections-and-referendums/past-elections-and-referendums/eu-referendum/electorate-and-count-information; House of Commons Library (2017), 'Turnout at elections', 27

July 2017. https://researchbriefings.parliament.uk/ResearchBriefing/Summary/CBP-8060%23fullreport

31. FullFact (2016) 'Young Voters and the EU Referendum', 22 July 2016. https://fullfact.org/europe/young-voters-and-eu-referendum/

32. Birch, S. (2016), p. 110.

33. Curtice, J. (2017), pp. 5–6. http://www.bsa.natcen.ac.uk/media/39149/bsa34_brexit_final.pdf#page=7

34. Wallace, G. (2016) 'Voter Turnout at 20-year Low in 2016', *CNN*, 30 November 2016. https://edition.cnn.com/2016/11/11/politics/popular-vote-turnout-2016/index.html

35. McCarthy, N. (2016a) 'Young Voted Clinton, Old Voted Trump', *Statista*, 9 November 2016. https://www.statista.com/chart/6651/young-voted-clinton-old-voted-trump/

36. *Independent* (2016) 'Letters: The over-fifties have gambled away my generation's future. This cannot be allowed to stand', 26 June 2016. https://www.independent.co.uk/voices/letters/the-baby-boomers-have-a7104461.html

37. Moore, J. (2016) 'Baby Boomers, You Have Already Robbed Your Children of Their Future. Don't Make It Worse by Voting for Brexit', *Independent*, 22 June 2016; Matthews, A. (2016) ' "This Vote Doesn't Represent the Younger Generation Who Will Have to Live with the Consequences": Millennials vent fury at baby boomers for voting Britain OUT of the EU', *Mailonline*, 24 June 2016. https://www.dailymail.co.uk/news/article-3658671/This-vote-doesn-t-represent-younger-generation-live-consequences-Millennials-fury-baby-boomers-voting-Britain-EU.html

38. Milbank, D. (2016) 'Baby Boomers Have Been a Disaster for America, and Trump is Their Biggest Mistake Yet', *Washington Post*, 25 October 2016.

39. McCarthy, N. (2016a) 'Young Voted Clinton, Old Voted Trump', *Statista*, 9 November 2016. https://www.statista.com/chart/6651/young-voted-clinton-old-voted-trump/; McCarthy, N. (2016b) 'The 2016 Election's Generation Gap', *Forbes*, 9 November 2016. https://www.forbes.com/sites/niallmccarthy/2016/11/09/the-2016-elections-generation-gap-infographic/#300d07fe497b

40. Moore, P. (2016) 'How Britain Voted', YouGov, 27 June 2016. https://yougov.co.uk/topics/politics/articles-reports/2016/06/27/how-britain-voted

41. Kingman, D. (2017) p. 12–13. http://www.if.org.uk/wp-content/uploads/2017/10/Generation-Remain_final_October_2017.compressed.pdf

42. Ibid., p. 7.

43. Ibid., pp. 26–7.

44. Hochschild, A. (2016), p. 9.

45. Ibid., p. 15, emphasis in original.

46. Ibid., p. 144.

47. Goodhart, D. (2017); Freedland, J. (2017) '*The Road to Somewhere* by David Goodhart – A Liberal's Rightwing Turn on Immigration', *Guardian*, 22 March 2017. https://www.theguardian.com/books/2017/mar/22/the-road-to-somewhere-david-goodhart-populist-revolt-future-politics

48. Watt, N. (2016) 'EU Referendum Remain Campaign Tells Supporters: Talk to Gran', *Guardian*, 13 April 2016. https://www.theguardian.com/politics/2016/apr/13/eu-referendum-remain-campaign-tells-supporters-talk-to-gran

49. Kingman, D. (2017), p. 7. http://www.if.org.uk/wp-content/uploads/2017/10/Generation-Remain_final_October_2017.compressed.pdf

8 'DEMOCRATIC DEFICITS' AND THE TYRANNY OF 'FUTURE GENERATIONS'

1. Roberts, D. (2017) 'Death of "1.5m Oldsters" Could Swing Second Brexit Vote, Says Ian McEwan', *Guardian*, 12 May 2017. https://www.theguardian.com/politics/2017/may/12/15m-oldsters-in-their-graves-could-swing-second-eu-vote-says-ian-mcewan

2. Elgot, J. (2016) 'Young Remain Voters Came out in Force, but Were Outgunned', *Guardian*, 24 June 2016. https://www.theguardian.com/politics/2016/jun/24/young-remain-voters-came-out-in-force-but-were-outgunned

3. Coren, G. (2016) 'The Wrinklies Have Well and Truly Stitched Us Up', *Times* (London), 25 June 2016.

4. Graham-Harrison, E. (2016) 'Young People on the EU Referendum: "It is the end of one world, of the world as we know it"', *Observer*, 26 June 2016. https://www.theguardian.com/politics/2016/jun/26/young-people-vote-anger

5. Schroeder, S. (2017) 'German Election: Free and fair for young voters?', *Deutsche Welle*, 7 September 2017. http://www.dw.com/en/german-election-free-and-fair-for-young-voters/a-40387045

6. Ibid.

7. Milton, J. (2017) 'Young People Will Decide this Year's Election – Here's Why Every Vote Matters', *NME*, 6 June 2017. http://www.nme.com/blogs/young-people-election-2017-every-vote-matters 2084836

8. Fry, R. (2018) 'Millennials Projected to Overtake Baby Boomers as America's Largest Generation', Fact Tank, Pew Research Center, 1 March 2018. http://www.pewresearch.org/fact-tank/2018/03/01/millennials-overtake-baby-boomers/

9. Intergenerational Foundation (2012) 'Press Release: 65 year olds have seven times more voting power than 18 year olds', 1 May 2012. http://www.if.org.uk/wp-content/uploads/2012/04/gerontocracy_release_defin3.pdf; Berry, C. (2012). http://www.if.org.uk/wp-content/uploads/2012/04/IF_Democratic_Deficit_final.pdf

10. Berry, C. and Hunt, T. (2016), p. 7. http://www.if.org.uk/wp-content/uploads/2016/02/The-Rising-Tide-of-Gerontocracy_Report_approved.pdf

11. Ibid.

12. Ibid.

13. Travis, A. and Barr, C. (2017) ' "Youthquake" Behind Labour Election Surge Divides Generations', *Guardian*, 20 June 2017. https://www.theguardian.com/politics/2017/jun/20/youthquake-behind-labour-election-surge-divides-generations

14. Greer, B. (2017) 'Is Generation X to Blame for Brexit?' *The New European*, 5 April 2017. http://www.theneweuropean.co.uk/top-stories/is-generation-x-to-blame-for-brexit-1-4962891

15. Vale, J. (2016) 'Democracy at Risk as Baby Boomers Dominate Voting', *i-Independent*, 23 September 2016; Gardiner, L. (2016b). https://www.intergencommission.org/wp-content/uploads/2016/09/Generational-voting.pdf

16. Gardiner, L. (2016b), p. 2. https://www.intergencommission.org/wp-content/uploads/2016/09/Generational-voting.pdf

17. 'Baby Boomers Bother to Vote'. Letter from W. St Clare, Great Missenden, Buckinghamshire, to the *i*, 24 September 2016.

18. Fry, R. (2017) 'Millennials and Gen Xers Outvoted Boomers and Older Generations in 2016 election', Fact Tank, Pew Research Center, 31 July 2017. http://www.pewresearch.org/fact-tank/2017/07/31/millennials-and-gen-xers-outvoted-boomers-and-older-generations-in-2016-election/

19. Gardiner, L. (2016b), p. 8. https://www.intergencommission.org/wp-content/uploads/2016/09/Generational-voting.pdf

20. Gardiner, L. (2017) 'Blog: Votey McVoteface: What's driving the generational turnout gap, and why it matters', Intergenerational Commission, 2 June 2017. https://www.resolutionfoundation.org/media/blog/votey-mcvoteface-whats-driving-the-generational-turnout-gap-and-why-it-matters/

21. Ibid.

22. Bell, T. (2017) 'Blog: The Millennials and Politics: Are they getting into the swing of it?' Intergenerational Commission, 9 June 2017. https://www.resolution foundation.org/media/blog/the-millennials-and-politics-are-they-getting-into-the-swing-of-it/

23. Gardiner, L. (2016b), p. 2. https://www.intergencommission.org/wp-content/uploads/2016/09/Generational-voting.pdf

24. Sherriff, L. (2015) 'This Election Was all about Young People Voting. So What Do They Have to Say about the Result?' *Huff Post UK*, 8 May 2015. https://www.huffingtonpost.co.uk/2015/05/08/election-young-people-voting-what-they-think-result_n_7240564.html

25. Marwick, A. (1970), p. 51.

26. Intergenerational Commission (2018). https://www.intergencommission.org/wp-content/uploads/2018/05/A-New-Generational-Contract-Full-PDF.pdf

27. *Guardian* (2018) 'Editorial: The Guardian View on Generational Inequality: It's time for a new deal', 8 May 2018. https://www.theguardian.com/commentisfree/2018/may/08/the-guardian-view-on-generational-inequality-its-time-for-a-new-deal

28. Frey, W.H. (2018), p. 4. https://www.brookings.edu/wp-content/uploads/2018/01/2018-jan_brookings-metro_millennials-a-demographic-bridge-to-americas-diverse-future.pdf

29. Edmunds, J. and Turner, B.S. (2005), p. 559, p. 571.

30. Frey, W.H. (2018), p. 4. https://www.brookings.edu/wp-content/uploads/2018/01/2018-jan_brookings-metro_millennials-a-demographic-bridge-to-americas-diverse-future.pdf

31. BBC News (2018) 'Brexit: Too many older Leave voters nostalgic for "white" Britain, says Cable', 11 March 2018. http://www.bbc.co.uk/news/uk-politics-43364331?SThisFB

32. Frey, W.H. (2018), p. 4. https://www.brookings.edu/wp-content/uploads/2018/01/2018-jan_brookings-metro_millennials-a-demographic-bridge-to-americas-diverse-future.pdf

33. Kingman, D. (2017), p. 6. http://www.if.org.uk/wp-content/uploads/2017/10/Generation-Remain_final_October_2017.compressed.pdf

34. The 'democratic imbalance' between old and young is only one way in which the principle of equal votes has been represented as a problem for democracy, in the wake of the Brexit vote and the Trump election. See: Hume, M. (2017).

35. Berry, C. and Hunt, T. (2016), pp. 5–6. http://www.if.org.uk/wp-content/uploads/2016/02/The-Rising-Tide-of-Gerontocracy_Report_approved.pdf

36. Ibid.
37. Založnik, M. (2016) 'Here's What Would Have Happened if Brexit Vote Was Weighted by Age', *The Conversation,* 4 July 2016. https://theconversation.com/heres-what-would-have-happened-if-brexit-vote-was-weighted-by-age-61877
38. Ibid.
39. Gov.uk (2018) 'School Leaving Age'. https://www.gov.uk/know-when-you-can-leave-school
40. Wood, B.E. and Munn, N. (2018) 'How Lowering the Voting Age to 16 Could Save Democracy', *The Conversation,* 22 March 2018. https://theconversation.com/how-lowering-the-voting-age-to-16-could-save-democracy-93567
41. Kingman, D. (2013) 'Why British Citizens Should be Allowed to Vote at 16', Intergenerational Foundation. http://www.if.org.uk/wp-content/uploads/2014/02/Lowering-the-Voting-Age-to-16-IF-Response.pdf
42. Schroeder, S. (2017) 'German Election: Free and fair for young voters?', *Deutsche Welle,* 7 September 2017. http://www.dw.com/en/german-election-free-and-fair-for-young-voters/a-40387045
43. Hanton, A. (2011) 'Voting Age – An Intergenerational Issue', Intergenerational Foundation, 10 July 2011. http://www.if.org.uk/2011/07/10/voting-age-an-intergenerational-issue/
44. Burke, E. (2014 [1790]) (Kindle edition).
45. Willetts, D. (2010), pp. 260–3.

9 AMBIVALENT ADULTHOOD

1. Cosslett, R.L. (2015) 'Does the Government Hate Young People? It Certainly Feels that Way: We'd love to grow up, we really would. But policies on everything from student loans to housing seem designed to ensure we can never achieve adulthood', *Guardian,* 16 October 2015. https://www.theguardian.com/commentisfree/2015/oct/16/government-young-people-student-loans-housing
2. Kamenetz, A. (2006), pp. xi–xii.
3. Angelini, F. (2013) 'Trapped in Kidulthood: No job security. No pensions. No hope of being better off than our parents. No wonder my generation won't grow up. A daughter's view', *Sunday Times,* 20 October 2013.
4. Arnett, J.J. (2000), pp. 469–80.
5. Arnett, J.J. (2015), p. 2, p. viii.
6. See for example: Bellah, R.N., Madsen, R., Sullivan, W.M., Swidler, A. and Tipton, S.M. (1996); Giddens, A. (1991); Putnam, R. (2001); Bauman, Z. (2000).
7. The first edition of Arnett's book, *Emerging Adulthood: The winding road from the late teens through the twenties,* was published in 2004. The journal *Emerging Adulthood (EA),* published by Sage, 'is an interdisciplinary and international journal for advancements in theory, methodology, and empirical research on development and adaptation during the late teens and twenties. It covers clinical, developmental and social psychology, and other social sciences'. https://journals.sagepub.com/home/eax
8. Arnett, J.J. (2015), p. 7.
9. Ibid.
10. Haverig, A. and Roberts, S. (2011), p. 601.

11. Mintz, S. (2015), p. ix.
12. Ibid., pp. 68–9.
13. Ibid., p. 69.
14. Arnett, J.J. (2015), pp. 15–16.
15. Ibid., p. 322.
16. Ibid., pp. 322–3, citing Arnett, J.J. and Schwab, J. (2012) *The Clark University Poll of Emerging Adults: Thriving, struggling, and hopeful*, Worcester, MA: Clark University.
17. Ibid., p. 15.
18. Oxford Dictionaries 2018. https://en.oxforddictionaries.com/definition/adulting
19. Steinmetz, K. (2016) 'This Is What "Adulting" Means', *Time*, 8 June 2016. http://time.com/4361866/adulting-definition-meaning/
20. Booker, C. (1992 [1969]).
21. For a thoughtful collection of essays on this question, see Erikson, E.H. (1963).
22. Lesthaeghe, R. (2014), p. 1. https://www.researchgate.net/publication/269181773_The_second_demographic_transition_A_concise_overview_of_its_development_Table_1
23. Ariès, P. (1996 [1962]); Lesthaeghe, R. (2010), p. 213.
24. Lesthaeghe, R. (2010).
25. Mintz, S. (2015), p. 1.
26. Laslett, P. (1987), p. 135.
27. Ibid.
28. For example, see: Scherger, S., Nazroo, J. and Higgs, P. (2011), pp. 146–72.
29. Jacoby, S. (2011), pp. 7–8.
30. Shakespeare, W. *As You Like It*, Act II, scene VII.
31. Lesthaeghe, R. (2010), pp. 213–14.
32. Lasch, C. (1979).
33. Lasch, C. (1984), p. 16.
34. Furedi, F. (1997); Furedi, F. (2003); Furedi, F. (2005).
35. Kamenetz, A. (2006), pp. 117–18.
36. Neiman, S. (2014); Scott, A.O. (2015) 'Review: "Why Grow Up?" by Susan Neiman', *New York Times*, 15 June 2015. https://www.nytimes.com/2015/06/21/books/review/why-grow-up-by-susan-neiman.html
37. Smith, C. et al. (2011), pp. 5–6.
38. Ibid., p. 7.
39. Ibid., pp. 59–60.
40. Ibid., p. 60.
41. Ibid., pp. 70–1.
42. Ibid., pp. 99–100.
43. Ibid., p. 103.
44. *Daily Mail* (2013) 'America's Stressed Generation: "Millennials" between 18 and 34 have the highest stress levels EVER', 8 February 2013. https://www.dailymail.co.uk/news/article-2275736/Daunting-college-loans-joblessness-making-youngest-generation-American-adults-stressed-out.html
45. Pew Research Center (2015) *Most Millennials Resist the 'Millennial' Label – Generations in a mirror: how they see themselves.* http://assets.pewresearch.org/wp-content/uploads/sites/5/2015/09/09-03-2015-Generations-release.pdf; *Guardian* (2015) 'Millennials See Themselves as Greedy, Self-absorbed and

Wasteful, Study Finds', 7 September 2015. https://www.theguardian.com/society/2015/sep/04/millennials-see-themselves-as-greedy-self-absorbed-and-wasteful-study-finds

46. Zolfagharifard, E. (2015) 'The Wasted Generation: Even millennials think they are self-absorbed and lazy, claims study', *Daily Mail*, 4 September 2015. https://www.dailymail.co.uk/sciencetech/article-3221560/Millennials-self-absorbed-wasteful.html

47. Harrold, A. (2015) 'Millenials Most Likely Generation to Criticise Themselves, Says Study', *Independent*, 4 September 2015. https://www.independent.co.uk/news/world/americas/millenials-most-likely-generation-to-criticise-themselves-says-study-10486959.html

48. Robertson, E. (2015) 'Why Are the Baby Boomers Desperate to Make Millennials Hate Ourselves? New statistics from the Pew research centre show the youngest workers have totally internalised the messaging of the luckiest generation in human history', *Guardian*, 4 September 2015. https://www.theguardian.com/commentisfree/2015/sep/04/why-are-the-baby-boomers-desperate-to-make-us-millennials-hate-ourselves

49. Pew Research Center (2015) *Most Millennials Resist the 'Millennial' Label – Generations in a mirror: how they see themselves.* http://assets.pewresearch.org/wp-content/uploads/sites/5/2015/09/09-03-2015-Generations-release.pdf

10 SOCIAL INSECURITIES AND GROWN-UP POLICYMAKING

1. Cook, F.L. (2002); Marshall, V.W., Cook, F.L. and Marshall, J.G. (1993), pp. 119–140.

2. Preston, S.H. (1984), p. 436.

3. Ibid., p. 450.

4. Bone, J. (2007) 'From Boom to Bust: The silver generation that could leave Uncle Sam broke', *Times* (London), 17 October 2007; Goldenberg, S. (2007) 'Demographics: The "silver tsunami" that threatens to overwhelm US social security system', *Guardian*, 18 October 2007.

5. See: Bristow, J. (2016a), pp. 575–591.

6. Philp, C. (2006) 'Golden State Faces Boomergeddon as "Me Generation" Turns It Grey', *Times* (London), 6 October 2006.

7. See: Salt, H. (2017) 'Risk Is Not a Four-Letter Word', *Contingencies*, May/June 2017. http://www.contingenciesonline.com/contingenciesonline/may_june2017?pg=34#pg34

8. Koster, O. (2009) 'Pensions Aristocracy', *Daily Mail*, 5 June 2009. https://www.dailymail.co.uk/news/article-1190862/Pensions-aristocracy-How-baby-boomer-generation-retire-lucrative-deals.html

9. Scherger, S., Nazroo, J. and Higgs, P. (2011).

10. Inman, P. (2011) 'Baby Boomers Aren't Evil – Just Selfish', *Guardian*, 3 January 2011.

11. Bunting, M. (2010) 'Generational Warriors Have a Point. But Go Easy on the Old', *Guardian*, 23 August 2010. https://www.theguardian.com/commentisfree/2010/aug/22/generational-warriors-should-go-easy-on-the-old

12. Schemes such as the UK government's Help to Buy have tended to benefit people with relatively high incomes in the first place – although couched in the language of 'fairness' and 'equality', their primary aim seems to be to keep

the bubble afloat. See: Maunder, S. (2018) 'Who Benefits Most from Help to Buy? More than 6,000 buyers have household income of more than £100,000', *Which*, 2 June 2018. https://www.which.co.uk/news/2018/06/who-benefits-most-from-help-to-buy/ See also: BBC News (2018) 'Theresa May: Young are "right to be angry" about lack of homes', 5 March 2018. http://www.bbc.co.uk/news/uk-politics-43279177; Janda, M. (2017) 'Superannuation for Housing Deposits Would Facilitate Intergenerational Theft', ABC News, 16 March 2017. http://www.abc.net.au/news/2017-03-16/super-for-housing-deposits-intergenerational-theft/8360890///

13. Lightfoot, L. (2016) 'The Student Experience – Then and Now', *Guardian*, 24 June 2016. https://www.theguardian.com/education/2016/jun/24/has-university-life-changed-student-experience-past-present-parents-vox-pops

14. Selingo, J.J. (2015) 'Baby Boomers and the End of Higher Education', *Washington Post*, 12 November 2015. https://www.washingtonpost.com/news/grade-point/wp/2015/11/12/baby-boomers-and-the-end-of-higher-education/?utm_term=.a1679c8ea3bd

15. See critique in Williams, J. (2012).

16. Harris, M. (2017).

17. For a more in-depth discussion of education and the generational transaction, see Bristow, J. (2016b).

18. 'Generational Encounters in Higher Education: The academic–student relationship and the meaning of the university experience', a qualitative study led by Jennie Bristow, Sarah Cant and Anwesa Chatterjee, 2017–2019, funded by a British Academy Small Research Grant.

Bibliography

Abrams, P. (1970) 'Rites de Passage: The conflict of generations in industrial society', *Journal of Contemporary History* 5(1), pp. 175–190.

Ainley, P. and Allen, M. (2013) 'Running up a Down-Escalator in the Middle of a Class Structure Gone Pear-Shaped', *Sociological Research Online,* 18(1), para. 2.6.

Alcock, P., Haux, T., May, M. and Wright, S. (eds) (2016) *The Student's Companion to Social Policy,* 5th ed. London: Wiley Blackwell.

Ariès, P. (1996 [1962]) *Centuries of Childhood.* London: Pimlico.

Arnett, J.J. (2015) *Emerging Adulthood: The winding road from the late teens through the twenties,* 2nd ed. Oxford: Oxford University Press.

Arnett, J.J. (2000) 'Emerging Adulthood: A theory of development from the late teens through the twenties', *American Psychologist* 55(5), pp. 469–480.

Auer, J. (2013) *Baby Boomers: Busting the myths.* Prospect Hill: Pink Gum Publishing.

Bauman, Z. (2000) *Liquid Modernity.* Cambridge: Polity.

Beck, U. (1992) *Risk Society: Towards a new modernity.* Thousand Oaks: Sage Publications.

Beckett, F. (2010) *What Did the Baby Boomers Ever Do for Us? Why the children of the sixties lived the dream and failed the future.* London: Biteback.

Bell, B. and Whittaker, M. (2017) *The Pay Deficit: Measuring the effect of pension deficit payments on workers' wages.* London: Resolution Foundation.

Bellah, R.N., Madsen, R., Sullivan, W.M., Swidler, A. and Tipton, S.M. (1996) *Habits of the Heart: Individualism and commitment in American life.* Updated ed. Berkeley, Los Angeles and London: University of California Press.

Berger, B.M. (1960) 'How Long is a Generation?', *The British Journal of Sociology* 11(1), pp. 10–23.

Berry, C. (2012) *The Rise of Gerontocracy? Addressing the intergenerational democratic deficit.* London: Intergenerational Foundation.

Berry, C. and Hunt, T. (2016) *The Rising Tide of Gerontocracy: How young people will be increasingly outvoted.* London: Intergenerational Foundation.

Bessant, J. (2004) 'Mixed messages: Youth participation and democratic practice', *Australian Journal of Political Science* 39(2), pp. 387–404.

Best, J. (2017) *Social Problems*, 3rd ed. New York and London: W.W. Norton & Company.

Best, J. (ed.) (2001) *How Claims Spread: Cross-national diffusion of social problems*. New York: Aldine de Gruyter.

Birch, S. (2016) 'Our New Voters: Brexit, political mobilisation and the emerging electoral cleavage', *Juncture* 23(2), pp. 107–110.

Booker, C. (1992 [1969]) *The Neophiliacs: A study in the revolution in English life in the fifties and sixties*. London: Collins.

Booker, C. (1980) *The Seventies: Portrait of a decade*. Harmondsworth: Penguin.

Boorman, N. (2010) *It's All Their Fault: A manifesto*. London: The Friday Project Limited.

Bristow, J. (2016a) 'The Making of "Boomergeddon": The construction of the baby boomer generation as a social problem in Britain', *British Journal of Sociology* 67(4), pp. 575–591.

Bristow, J. (2016b) *The Sociology of Generations: New directions and challenges*. Basingstoke: Palgrave Macmillan.

Bristow, J. (2015) *Baby Boomers and Generational Conflict*. Basingstoke: Palgrave Macmillan.

Bristow, J. (2009) *Standing Up to Supernanny*. Exeter: Imprint Academic.

Brittain, V. (1984 [1933]) *Testament of Youth*. London: Virago.

Burke, E. (2014 [1790]) *Reflections on the Revolution in France*. SMK Books.

Burnett, J. (2016) *Generations: The time machine in theory and practice*. London and New York: Routledge.

Chamberlin, V.A. and Weiner, J. (1971) 'Galdós' *Doña Perfecta* and Turgenev's *Fathers and Sons*: Two interpretations of the conflict between generations', *PMLA* 86(1), pp. 19–24.

Combi, C. (2015) *Generation Z: Their voices, their lives*. London: Windmill.

Commonwealth of Australia (2015) *2015 Intergenerational Report: Australia in 2055*. Canberra: The Commonwealth of Australia.

Cook, F.L. (2002) 'Generational Equity', *Encyclopedia of Ageing*. Macmillan Reference USA.

Corlett, A. and Judge, L. (2017) *Home Affront: Housing across the generations*. London: Resolution Foundation.

Coupland, D. (1991) *Generation X: Tales for an accelerated culture*. London: Abacus Books.

Curtice, J. (2017) 'The Vote to Leave the EU: Litmus test or lightning rod?', *British Social Attitudes: The 34th report*. London: National Centre for Social Research.

Dobson, A. (1989) *An Introduction to the Politics and Philosophy of José Ortega y Gasset*. Cambridge: Cambridge University Press.

Edmunds, J. and Turner, B.S. (2005) 'Global Generations: Social change in the twentieth century', *British Journal of Sociology* 56(4), pp. 559–577.

Ehrenreich, B. (1990) *Fear of Falling: The inner life of the middle class*. New York: Harper Perennial.

Eisenstadt, S.N. (1956) *From Generation to Generation: Age groups and social structure*. New York and London: The Free Press.

Erikson, E.H. (ed.) (1963) *Youth: Change and challenge*. New York and London: Basic Books.

Falkingham, J. (1997) 'Who Are the Baby Boomers? A demographic profile', in: M. Evandrou (ed.) *Baby Boomers: Ageing in the 21st century*, pp. 15–40. London: Age Concern England.

Finch, D. (2017) *Live Long and Prosper? Demographic trends and their implications for living standards.* London: Resolution Foundation.

Finch, D. and Gardiner, L. (2017) *As Good As It Gets? The adequacy of retirement income for current and future generations of pensioners.* London: Resolution Foundation.

France, A. and Roberts, S. (2015) 'The Problem of Social Generations: A critique of the new emerging orthodoxy in youth studies', *Journal of Youth Studies* 18(2), 215–230.

Frey, W.H. (2018) *The Millennial Generation: A demographic bridge to America's diverse future.* Washington, DC: Brookings Institution.

Fukuyama, F. (1992) *The End of History and the Last Man.* London: Penguin.

Furedi, F. (2017) *What's Happened to the University? A sociological exploration of its infantilisation.* London: Routledge.

Furedi, F. (2014) *First World War: Still no end in sight.* London: Bloomsbury Continuum.

Furedi, F. (2005) *Politics of Fear: Beyond left and right.* London and New York: Continuum.

Furedi, F. (2003) *Therapy Culture: Cultivating vulnerability in an uncertain age.* London: Routledge.

Furedi, F. (1997) *Culture of Fear: Risk taking and the morality of low expectation.* London: Continuum.

Furedi, F. and Bristow, J. (2008) *Licensed to Hug: How child protection policies are poisoning the relationship between the generations and damaging the voluntary sector.* London: Civitas.

Gardiner, L. (2017) *The Million Dollar Be-question: Inheritances, gifts, and their implications for generational living standards.* London: Resolution Foundation.

Gardiner, L. (2016a) *Stagnation Generation? The case for renewing the intergenerational contract.* London: Resolution Foundation.

Gardiner, L. (2016b) *Votey McVoteface: Understanding the growing turnout gap between the generations.* London: Resolution Foundation.

Gardiner, L. and Gregg, P. (2017) *Study, Work, Progress, Repeat? How and why pay and progression outcomes have differed across cohorts.* London: Resolution Foundation.

Gibney, B.C. (2017) *A Generation of Sociopaths: How the baby boomers betrayed America.* New York: Hachette Books.

Giddens, A. (1994) *Beyond Left and Right: The future of radical politics.* Palo Alto: Stanford University Press.

Giddens, A. (1991) *Modernity and Self-identity: Self and society in the late modern age.* Cambridge: Polity.

Gillis, J.R. (1997) *A World of Their Own Making: A history of myth and ritual in family life.* Oxford: Oxford University Press.

Gillis, J.R. (1974) *Youth and History: Tradition and change in European age relations 1770–present.* New York and London: Academic Press.

Goodhart, D. (2017) *The Road to Somewhere: The new tribes shaping British politics.* London: Penguin.

Hamblin, K. (2016) 'Older People', in: P. Alcock, T. Haux, M. May and S. Wright (eds) *The Student's Companion to Social Policy*, 5th ed. London: Wiley Blackwell, pp. 432–438.

Hardyment, C. (2007) *Dream Babies: Childcare advice from John Locke to Gina Ford.* London: Francis Lincoln.

Harris, M. (2017) *Kids These Days: Human capital and the making of millennials.* New York: Little, Brown and Company.

Haverig, A. and Roberts, S. (2011) 'The New Zealand OE as Governance through Freedom: Rethinking "the apex of freedom"', *Journal of Youth Studies* 14(5), pp. 587–603.

Heath, R. (2006) *Please Just F* Off It's Our Turn Now: Holding baby boomers to account.* Melbourne: Pluto Press Australia.

Helsper, E.J. and Eynon, R. (2010) 'Digital Natives: Where is the evidence?', *British Educational Research Journal* 36(3), pp. 503–520.

Hochschild, A. (2016) *Strangers in Their Own Land: Anger and mourning on the American right.* New York: The New Press.

Howe, N. and Strauss, W. (2000) *Millennials Rising: The next great generation.* New York: Vintage Books.

Howe, N. and Strauss, W. (1993) *13th Gen: Abort, retry, ignore, fail?* New York: Vintage Books.

Howker, E. and Malik, S. (2013). *Jilted Generation: How Britain has bankrupted its youth.* 2nd ed. London: Icon Books.

Howker, E. and Malik, S. (2010) *Jilted Generation: How Britain has bankrupted its youth.* London: Icon Books.

Hume, M. (2017) *Revolting! How the Establishment are undermining democracy and what they're afraid of.* London: Harper Collins.

Intergenerational Commission (2018) *A New Generational Contract: The final report of the Intergenerational Commission.* London: Resolution Foundation.

Jacoby, S. (2011) *Never Say Die: The myth and marketing of the new old age.* New York: Pantheon Books.

Jenkins, P. (2006) *Decade of Nightmares: The end of the sixties and the making of eighties America.* Oxford: Oxford University Press.

Judt, T. (2010) *Postwar: A history of Europe since 1945.* London: Vintage Books.

Kamenetz, A. (2006) *Generation Debt: Why now is a terrible time to be young.* New York: Riverhead Books.

Kingman, D. (2017) *Generation Remain: Understanding the Millennial vote.* London: Intergenerational Foundation.

Kotlikoff, L.J. and Burns, S. (2012) *The Clash of Generations: Saving ourselves, our kids, and our economy.* Cambridge, MA and London: The MIT Press.

Kotlikoff, L.J. and Burns, S. (2005) *The Coming Generational Storm: What you need to know about America's economic future.* Cambridge, MA and London: The MIT Press.

Lareau, A. (2011) *Unequal Childhoods: Class, race, and family life.* 2nd ed. Berkeley and Los Angeles: University of California Press.

Lasch, C. (1984) *The Minimal Self: Psychic survival in troubled times.* New York: W.W. Norton & Company.

Lasch, C. (1979) *The Culture of Narcissism: American life in an age of diminishing expectations.* New York: Warner Books.

Laslett, P. (1987) 'The Emergence of the Third Age', *Ageing and Society* 7(2), pp. 133–160.

Lee, E., Bristow, J., Faircloth, C. and Macvarish, J. (2014) *Parenting Culture Studies.* Basingstoke: Palgrave Macmillan.

Lesthaeghe, R. (2014) 'The Second Demographic Transition: A concise overview of its development', *Proceedings of the National Academy of Sciences* 111(51), December, early edition, pp. 1–4.

Lesthaeghe, R. (2010) 'The Unfolding Story of the Second Demographic Transition', *Population and Development Review*, 36(2), pp. 211–251.

Letwin, S.R. (1978) 'Trollope on Generations without Gaps', *Daedalus* 107(4), pp. 53–70.

Lodge, E., Carnell, E. and Coleman, M. (2016) *The New Age of Ageing: How society needs to change*. Bristol: The Policy Press.

Mannheim, K. (1952) 'The Problem of Generations', in: P. Kecskemeti (ed.) *Essays on the Sociology of Knowledge*. London: Routledge & Kegan Paul Ltd.

Marshall, V.W., Cook, F.L. and Marshall, J.G. (1993) 'Conflict over Intergenerational Equity: Rhetoric and reality in a comparative context', in: V.L. Bengtson and W.A. Achenbaum (eds) *The Changing Contract across Generations*. New York: Aldine Transaction.

Marwick, A. (1999) *The Sixties: Cultural revolution in Britain, France, Italy and the United States, c.1958–c.1974*. Oxford: Oxford University Press.

Marwick, A. (1970) 'Youth in Britain, 1920–1960: Detachment and commitment', *Journal of Contemporary History* 5(1), pp. 37–51.

Mintz, S. (2015) *The Prime of Life: A history of modern adulthood*. Cambridge, MA and London: The Belknap Press of Harvard University Press.

Mullan, P. (2017) *Creative Destruction: How to start an economic renaissance*. Bristol: The Policy Press.

Mullan, P. (2000) *The Imaginary Time Bomb: Why an ageing society is not a problem*. London and New York: I.B. Tauris.

Nagle, A. (2017) *Kill All Normies: Online culture wars from 4chan and Tumblr to Trump and the alt-right*. Alresford: Zero Books.

Nash, L.L. (1978) 'Concepts of Existence: Greek origins of generational thought', *Daedalus* 107(4), pp. 1–21.

National Centre for Social Research (2017) *British Social Attitudes: The 34th report*. London: National Centre for Social Research.

Neiman, S. (2014) *Why Grow Up? Subversive thoughts for an infantile age*. London: Penguin.

O'Rourke, P.J. (2014) *The Baby Boom: How it got that way, and it wasn't my fault, and I'll never do it again*. London: Grove Press UK (Atlantic Books).

Oxford Dictionaries (2018) Online: English Oxford Living Dictionaries. Oxford: Oxford University Press.

Pilcher, J. (1995) *Age and Generation in Modern Britain*. Oxford: Oxford University Press.

Pilcher, J. and Wagg, S. (1996) *Thatcher's Children?: Politics, childhood and society in the 1980s and 1990s*. London and New York: Routledge.

Preston, S.H. (1984) 'Children and the Elderly: Divergent paths for America's dependents', *Demography* 21(4), pp. 435–457.

Putnam, R. (2001) *Bowling Alone: The collapse and revival of American community*. New York: Simon & Schuster Ltd.

Raleigh, D.J. (2012) *Soviet Baby Boomers: An oral history of Russia's cold war generation*. Oxford: Oxford University Press.

Ready for Ageing Alliance (2015) *The Myth of the Baby Boomer*. London: Ready for Ageing Alliance.

Riesman, D. with Glazer, N. and Denney, R. (1966 [1950]) *The Lonely Crowd: A study of the changing American character*. New Haven and London: Yale University Press.

Rix, S.E. (1999) 'The politics of old age in the United States', in: A. Walker and G. Naegele (eds) *The Politics of Old Age in Europe*. Buckingham and Philadelphia: Open University Press, pp. 178–196.

Scherger, S., Nazroo, J. and Higgs, P. (2011) 'Leisure Activities and Retirement: Do structures of inequality change in old age?', *Ageing and Society* 31(1), pp. 146–72.

Scott, S. (2018) *Millennials and the Moments that Made Us: A cultural history of the U.S. from 1982–present*. Winchester and Washington: Zero Books.

Shrimpton, H., Skinner, G. and Hall, S. (2017) *The Millennial Bug: Public attitudes on the living standards of different generations*. London: Resolution Foundation.

Smith, C. with Christoffersen, K., Davidson, H. and Herzog, P.S. (2011) *Lost in Transition: The dark side of emerging adulthood*. Oxford: Oxford University Press.

Southern, L. (2016) *Barbarians: How baby boomers, immigration, and Islam screwed my generation*. Toronto: Rebel News Network.

Strauss, W. and Howe, N. (1998) *The Fourth Turning: What the cycles of history tell us about America's next rendezvous with destiny*. New York: Broadway Books.

Strauss, W. and Howe, N. (1991) *Generations: The history of America's future, 1584 to 2069*. New York and London: Harper Perennial.

Taylor, P. and the Pew Research Center (2015) *The Next America: Boomers, millennials, and the looming generational showdown*. New York: Public Affairs.

Turgenev, I. (1996 [1862]) *Fathers and Sons*. Knoxville: Wordsworth Classics.

Twenge, J.M. (2014) *Generation Me: Why today's young Americans are more confident, assertive, entitled – and more miserable than ever before*. New York: Atria Books.

United for All Ages (2018) *Mixing Matters: How shared sites can bring older and younger people together and unite Brexit Britain*. Norfolk: United for All Ages.

Walker, A. (ed.) (1996) *The New Generational Contract: Intergenerational relations, old age and welfare*. London: UCL Press.

Wattenberg, M.P. (2018) 'Polls and Elections: From the Obama Youthquake of '08 to the Trumpquake of '16: How young people's dislike of Hillary Clinton cost her the election', *Presidential Studies Quarterly*, first published 12 February, pp. 1–17.

Whalen, J. and Flacks, R. (1989) *Beyond the Barricades: The sixties generation grows up*. Philadelphia: Temple University Press.

White, J. (2013) 'Thinking Generations', *British Journal of Sociology* 64(2), pp. 216–247.

Willetts, D. (2010) *The Pinch: How the baby boomers took their children's future – and why they should give it back*. London: Atlantic Books.

Williams, J. (2012) *Consuming Higher Education: Why learning can't be bought*. London: Bloomsbury Academic.

Willinger, M. (2013) *Generation Identity: A declaration of war against the '68ers*. London: Arktos Media Ltd.

Wohl, R. (1980) *The Generation of 1914*. London: Weidenfeld & Nicolson.

Wolfe, T. (1976) 'The "Me" Decade and the Third Great Awakening', *New York Magazine*, 23 August, pp. 26–40.

Index